SABOR JUDÍO

SABOR JUDÍO

The Jewish Mexican Cookbook

×××××××××××××××××××××××××× ××××××××××××××××

Ilan Stavans and Margaret E. Boyle

WITH A PREFACE BY LEAH KOENIG
PHOTOGRAPHS BY ILAN RABCHINSKEY

FF

A FERRIS AND FERRIS BOOK

The University of North Carolina Press
Chapel Hill

This book was published under the Marcie Cohen Ferris and William R. Ferris Imprint of the University of North Carolina Press.

Angelina Muñiz-Huberman's poem "Tururú" was originally published in her book *La sal en el rostro* (Mexico City: Universidad Autónoma Metropolitana, 1998). Translation by Ilan Stavans. Used by permission.

Rachel Kaufman's poem "Inquisition Letters" was originally published in her book *May to Remember* (Loveland, OH: Dos Madres Press, 2021). Used by permission.

Designed and typeset by Lindsay Starr.
Cover art by Ilan Rabchinskey.

LIBRARY OF CONGRESS CATALOGING-IN-PUBLICATION DATA

Names: Stavans, Ilan, author. | Boyle, Margaret E., 1983– author. | Rabchinskey, Ilán, photographer (expression) | Koenig, Leah, writer of preface.

Title: Sabor judío : the Jewish Mexican cookbook / Ilan Stavans and Margaret Boyle ; with a preface by Leah Koenig ; photographs by Ilan Rabchinskey.

Description: Chapel Hill : The University of North Carolina Press, [2024] | "A Ferris and Ferris book." | Includes bibliographical references and index.

Identifiers: LCCN 2024020864 | ISBN 9781469682921 (cloth) | ISBN 9781469679099 (epub) | ISBN 9781469682938 (pdf)

Subjects: LCSH: Jews—Food—Mexico. | Jewish cooking. | Cooking, Mexican. | Holiday cooking. | BISAC: COOKING / Regional & Ethnic / Jewish & Kosher | SOCIAL SCIENCE / Ethnic Studies / Caribbean & Latin American Studies | LCGFT: Cookbooks.

Classification: LCC TX724 .S725 2024 | DDC 641.5/6760972—dc23/eng/20240603

LC record available at https://lccn.loc.gov/2024020864

To Miriam and Ofelia Slomianski z'l
and to Alison Sparks
—I. S.

In memory of Malka and Ruben Poplawski
—M. B.

Kaminos de leche i miel.
(Paths of milk and honey)
— Ladino proverb

Af'n lung, *af*'n zung.
(In the heart, in the tongue)
— Yiddish proverb

Barriga llena, corazón contento.
(Full belly, joyful heart)
— Mexican proverb

Contents

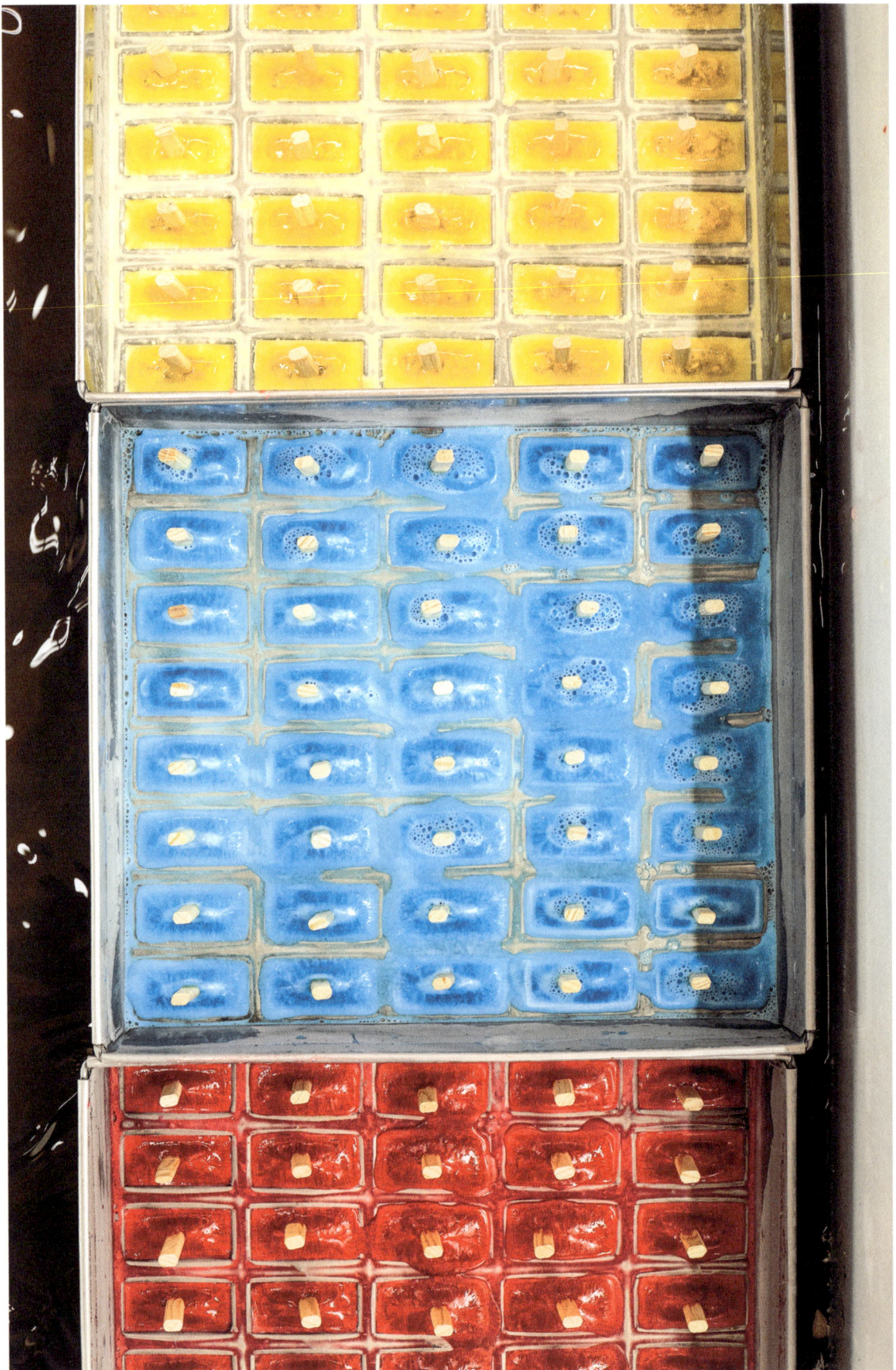

Preface

LEAH KOENIG

As a cookbook author and food writer who has focused on Jewish cuisine for the past fifteen years, I have come to view exploring Jewish food as a chance to discover the world. Jewish communities have lived and cooked just about everywhere across the globe, and along the way they have created a complex mosaic of microcuisines, shaped both by Jewish tradition and by the local ingredients and cooking styles found in homelands ranging from Morocco to Moldova and England to Ethiopia.

So when I was first contacted by Ilan and Margaret to see if I might be interested in helping to test the recipes for a Mexican Jewish cookbook, I jumped at the opportunity. Although I have included a handful of Mexican Jewish–inspired recipes in some of my own cookbooks—for example, the Mexican Chocolate Babka in *The Jewish Cookbook* (Phaidon, 2019)—here was an opportunity to take a deep dive into a largely new-to-me corner of the Jewish world. The experience did not disappoint.

Working with the recipes for *Sabor Judío*—dishes collected from grand-mothers and other beloved home cooks, professional chefs and bakers, and a variety of historical sources—I found myself encountering ingredients I had never before used. I learned the hard way that nopales (cactus pad-dles) should always be handled wearing gloves, lest the prickly spines leave your hands stinging for the rest of the day. I delighted in blitzing rice and cinnamon sticks together until they turned into creamy and endlessly sip-pable horchata. I struggled at first to form tiny boats out of masa de harina while making sopes, eventually finding the pinch-press-pinch rhythm in my hands. I made my first from-scratch mole, gaining huge appreciation for the complexity and nuance of the process along the way. And I tapped into the utter exhilaration of blistering poblanos and tomatillos over a hot griddle to make fresh salsas.

I also encountered so much that felt familiar, like chicken soup with matzo balls—though the chipotle pepper in adobo mixed into the matzo ball batter was a new and welcome addition! There was also a rich noodle kugel that tasted similar to the one I grew up eating in an Ashkenazi-American household, except with chunks of silky mango threaded throughout. As I cooked, I was reminded that the beauty of Jewish food lies in the connections and throughlines that exist in an ultimately disparate cuisine. The dishes on a Shabbat table differ dramatically depending on where someone's family hails from. But the reasons they are at that Shabbat table—to celebrate with family, honor the holiday, and connect to a sense of tradition and heritage—are the same.

Testing recipes can be a monastic process. There is a lot of puttering and pondering that goes along with making 100 recipes, evaluating and tweaking them, and then making them again until everything tastes just right. And much of this work is done in the solitary confines of one's home kitchen. But along the way, Margaret and Ilan kept me from feeling too isolated. They let me bounce questions and ideas off them, peppered me with anecdotes and historical context, and generally cheered me on. (My husband's enthusiastic response to trying many of the dishes helped, too!) They were a joy to work with and learn from.

At its core, *Sabor Judío* accomplishes what every cookbook hopes to accomplish. It shares plenty of tempting recipes, yes. But almost more importantly it captures the story of a group of people and a place that is at once historic and evolving. It puts the dishes into context as part of the global Jewish experience, while honoring the particularities that make this cuisine so uniquely beguiling. I am grateful that I was able to play a small part in bringing these stories and dishes to life, and hope that everyone who encounters them taps into the same sense of joy I felt being invited to the Mexican Jewish table. •

INTRODUCTION

✕✕✕✕✕✕✕✕✕✕✕✕✕✕✕✕✕✕✕✕✕✕✕✕✕✕✕✕✕✕✕✕

This cookbook has a mythical birth.

At age eighty, just before old age robbed her of her memory, Ofelia Slomianski of Mexico City made a copy of a handwritten *recetario*, a recipe book, written in a mix of Yiddish and Spanish, that her own mother had begun after immigrating to Mexico in the 1920s. Bobe Miriam, as she was known to her grandchildren, not only listed all the major dishes she regularly prepared, particularly for the High Holidays, but as the decades went by, perfected her cuisine, inserting new ingredients and revising quantities. The recipes told the stories of life in the kitchen. Bobe Miriam then passed the recipe book to her daughter, who in turn expanded it by refurbishing some dishes, adding others, and in general commenting on what appealed to her own family, adding a new set of stories about the transformation from one generation to another. She debated what worked and what didn't, described how ingredients had changed over time, and detailed prices at the local market. Over time, the family cookbook became a lucid example of kitchen midrash by the most knowledgeable of

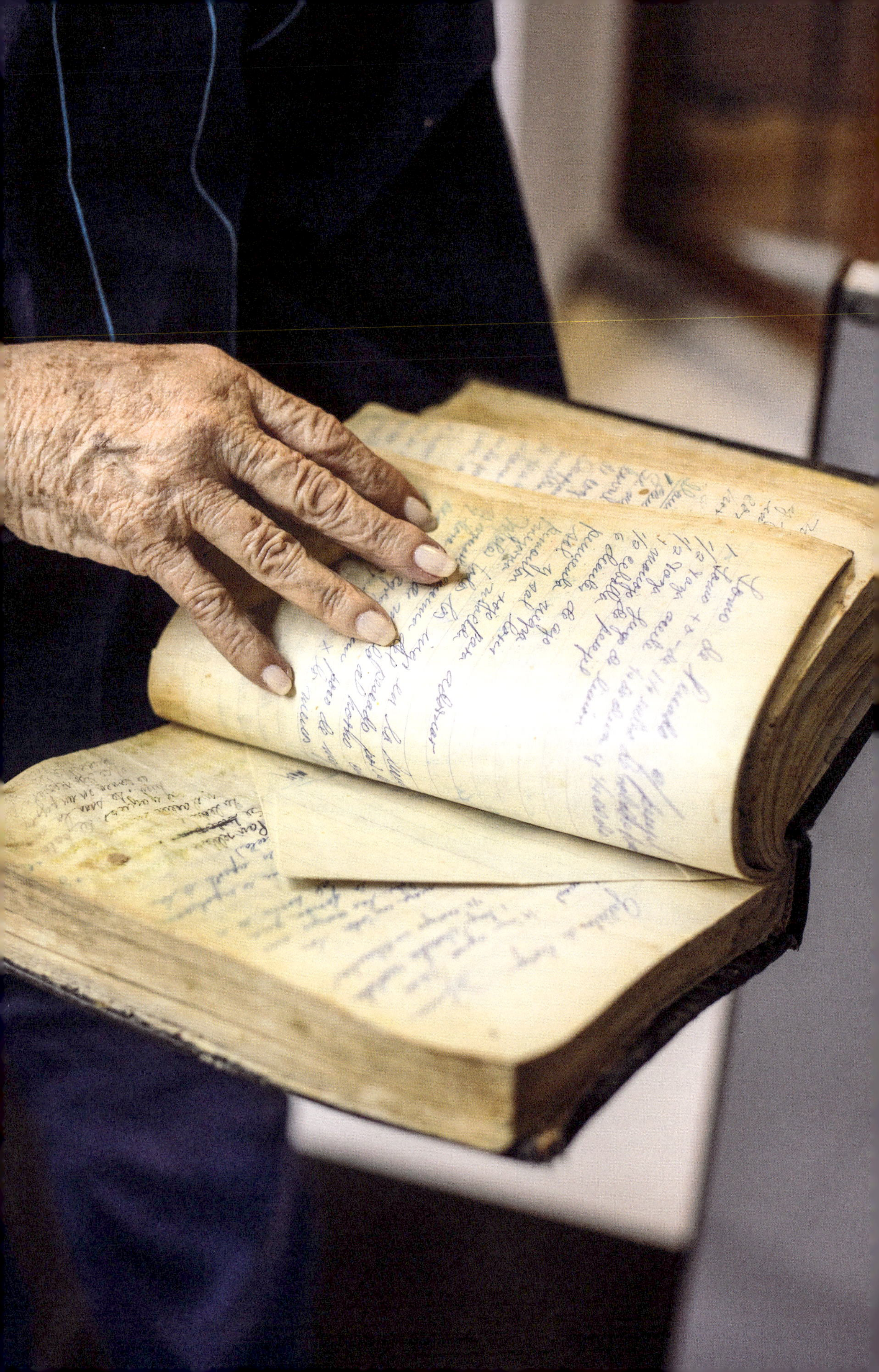

authorities: the women who knew how to cook. Eventually, in the early twenty-first century, as Bobe Miriam's grandson Ilan Stavans began to cook her recipes, he realized that the notebook wasn't just about cooking; it was also a time capsule that chronicled, through dishes, the Jewish family's process of assimilation into Mexico and the way La Comunidad, as the Jewish Mexican community is known, showcases its personality to the world.

Around the same time, a similar recipe notebook by another Jewish immigrant to Mexico in the 1920s, Malka Poplawski, made its way into her great-granddaughter Margaret Boyle's hands. While Baba Malka was still actively cooking, her children, grandchildren, and great-grandchildren took turns observing and documenting her work in the kitchen in Mexico City, filling the notebook's pages with notes and adaptations in Spanish, Hebrew, and English as the family generations expanded across Mexico and into the United States. Baba Malka represented a link to the Old World that Margaret wished to understand and access. At twenty-two, Malka had journeyed alone from Suchowola, Poland, to Córdoba, destined to marry Elías, who had arrived in Mexico a couple of years earlier from the same shtetl across the sea. Elías sold ties on the street, and the couple later opened a general store in Veracruz. Black-and-white photos around their home in Mexico City gave glimpses into the moments of who they had been and what they had become. Margaret tried to imagine leaving siblings and parents behind, what she might carry in a suitcase, the tragedy of so much loss, and the necessity of reinvention and preservation. Like Ilan, she realized that the family notebook was more than itself, a culinary record that traced the evolution of a Jewish Mexican diaspora.

As two Jewish Mexican scholars now living in the United States, we—that is, Ilan and Margaret—discovered quite by accident that our families shared parallel culinary records. As we reflected on our respective family cookbooks, we pondered what, in essence, is Jewish Mexican food? To what extent is it authentic? What does Jewish food borrow from the environment from which it emerges, and in what way does it transform it? Where does its originality lie? As far as anyone knows, Miriam and Malka never met each other, but the similarity of their notebooks is uncanny: some of the same recipes appear in both collections.

These explorations, and our personal passions for cooking, convinced us that it was time to present our family cookbooks and the communities of recipes in contact with them to a broader audience. Both cuisines, Jewish and Mexican, are immensely alluring on the global stage. Yet few people know the stories of the innovative Jewish immigrants to Mexico and their descendants that shaped the foods we eat today.

THE FLAVORS OF Jewish Mexican food reveal layers of extraordinary history. Indigenous civilizations such as the Mexica and Maya, themselves a product of blending cultures, featured beans, corn, chocolates, and chiles as cornerstones of food and drink. Likewise, Afro-mestizo food cultures, derived from enslaved Africans brought to the Americas, were a fixture of Nueva España, as Mexico was known before its independence, and featured menus inflected with foods originating in Africa such as sweet tamarind, salty peanuts, and watermelon, plantains, and yams.

Jewish families with the longest history in the Americas trace their roots to the colonial period, when their ancestors from Spain and Portugal, known as Sephardim, found in Nueva España a safe haven from persecution by the Inquisition. To avoid drawing attention to their religion, they cooked *como todos los demás*, like everyone else, except for observing kosher laws whenever possible. Makeshift cookbooks in Spanish from the period show the degree to which fish, lamb, and a variety of grains and legumes—eggplant, cucumber, garbanzo, and pepitas—formed the diet of secret Jews, also known as crypto-Jews. While these Sephardim kept their culture against all odds, adversity eventually won over. By 1810, when Mexico became an independent nation, almost all Sephardic Jews had assimilated into the environment—but not before leaving behind a rich *acerbo*, a culinary heritage that continues to this day. Soups, fish, meat, and poultry dishes for weekdays, sweet desserts, and a plethora of breads and special diets for Rosh Hashanah and Yom Kippur are still cooked and kept today.

At the end of the nineteenth century, new immigrant waves replenished the nascent country. Yiddish-speaking dwellers known as Ashkenazim, from the so-called Pale of Settlement in eastern Europe, which today comprises Belarus, Moldova, almost all of Ukraine and Lithuania, Latgale within Latvia, parts of eastern Poland, Romania, and western Russia, established new communities. And from the crumbling Ottoman Empire came a new generation of Sephardim: Lebanese, Syrian, and Turkish Jews.

Ashkenazim and Sephardim had not lived together for centuries. Knowing little about each other, these two divergent Jewish traditions connected with suspicion in Mexico City's streets. In fact, in subsequent oral histories, each side often repeated that in the initial years it was easier living with the goyim, non-Jews, than with those Jews whose language and customs they couldn't quite comprehend. This was particularly true when it came to cuisine. The Ashkenazic diet featured gefilte fish, borscht, tzimmes, pan negro, and other shtetl delicacies. Ottoman staples were rice, lamb, bourekas, figs, eggplants, honey, and baklava.

During and following the Second World War, refugees, partisans, and Holocaust survivors emigrated to Mexico. Ilan and Margaret remember growing up with family and friends whose arms displayed tattooed numbers, as well as hearing the chorus of *zakhor*, the command never to forget. These arrivals had been deprived of so much during the war, and it took them time to adapt to the new customs they encountered in Mexico. But their wish to live and the conviction that Jewish culture could find a comfortable place in this new country pushed them forward. In time, many opened restaurants and entered the food business, importing goods from Europe and the Middle East, diversifying products in Mexican supermarkets, and making Mexican food more international.

Yet another wave of Jewish immigrants, this time from Israel, reshaped Jewish Mexican cuisine from the 1970s onward. Sabra flavors—yogurts, cheeses, falafel with tahini, cucumber salad, and other Middle Eastern dishes and spices—were integrated into the menu.

Through marriage and nonstop movement, the ongoing adaptations and fusions of Jewish Mexican cuisine and culture continue to evolve. Ethnic food thrives in Mexico today, especially in its capital, Mexico City, a megalopolis of 18 million where Jewish gastronomy is famously plentiful. Stop by *pastelerías*, or bakeries, in the old neighborhoods of Hipódromo, Condesa, and Del Valle to savor delicious challahs, rugelach, and babkas, all with unique tastes. Or visit Colonia Polanco for Mexican-style delis, where you will find various preparations of gefilte fish and pierogi with assorted salsas. Or Israeli-style falafel bars with salads and dips accented by spicy local ingredients. Or the neighborhoods of Tecamachalco and Las Lomas, with kosher taquerias as well as cantinas catering to Jewish clients. Or the various Hasidic restaurants that have incorporated Mexican flavors to biblical dietary laws.

Jewish Mexican food is certainly not restricted to Mexico City. It thrives in Guadalajara, Monterrey, Cancún, and other Mexican cities. Plus, those who make this cuisine have moved elsewhere. Wander around Los Angeles, Houston, Chicago, and Miami, and chances are you will cross paths with Mexican American Jews who have adapted the piquancy of their *abuela*'s cooking and color palettes and imported and redefined them into modern Mexican delights. They bring curiosity and creativity to family recipes, with a willingness to push against authenticity in favor of new, experimental, and lively cuisine. Jewish Mexican food has a heart, one made of divergent yet stunningly compatible traditions.

As the recipes in the following pages demonstrate, food, taste, language, and homecoming intertwine to invigorate the cuisine. We tell the stories of some of our Mexican ancestors and of other Jewish diasporic peoples to communicate—through food—the conditions of sameness, difference, migration, community building, and national identities.

IN CONCRETE WAYS, our own stories represent the waves of generational ties to Jewish Mexico.

Growing up in Copilco, a neighborhood adjacent to UNAM, Mexico's largest, oldest, and most prominent university, Ilan saw Jewish life from a distance even though he attended Yidishe Shule, a secular Yiddishist school that saw as its mission the continuation of Jewish life in the land of the Aztecs. While his grandparents were Yiddish-speaking Jewish immigrants from Poland and Ukraine, his father, Abraham, a popular telenovela actor, and his mother, Ofelia, a psychologist, considered themselves rebels—at least geographically, since most Mexican Jews lived on the opposite side of Mexico City.

Not until Ilan left Mexico, first for the Middle East and eventually for Europe and then the United States—he settled in New York in 1985—did he realize the richness of his culinary heritage. The daily food at his parents' home had been invariably experimental, combining the recipes of Ilan's grandmothers, including those from Bobe Miriam, with Indigenous dishes his mother learned from neighbors. He had enjoyed huevos divorciados, challah French toast with cajeta, pescado a la veracruzana, rabo de mestiza, and other delicacies, recipes for many of which appear in these pages. The Jewish holidays in Mexico City were similarly celebrated with cuisines that combined Jewish and Mexican flavors. Ilan and his wife, Alison, began cooking Jewish Mexican dishes not only to maintain their cultural identity but to pass that heritage along to their children. Today, Alison's brisket tortas are legendary. Every year for Hanukkah, she and Ilan invite many friends to enjoy her Jewish Mexican dishes; a crowd favorite is her latkes with mole.

Margaret was raised in Los Angeles, a first-generation Mexican Jewish American with the kitchen as the base for connecting with life in Mexico and negotiating hyphenated identities. Her mother and grandparents were born in Mexico City, and her great-grandparents emigrated from Poland and Lithuania to make their homes in Mexico. Margaret's childhood comfort foods were simple and seasonal: squash blossom quesadillas and mango jicama salad. She followed the Jewish observance of her maternal grandparents, who lived a block away in LA, and celebrated family milestones across languages with her large extended family—brisket and rhubarb, gefilte fish en salsa roja, paletas with Manischewitz. The ever-growing kids' table filled to the brim with cousins, later spouses, and then children of their own. Margaret's grandparents taught her about menu planning early in life and orchestrated all varieties of family gatherings through meals. Food was often the way to connect through language gaps, the mix of Spanish, English, Hebrew, and Yiddish. Margaret's years spent following her great-grandmother in the kitchen became the best way of knowing her and telling her stories through food: babka, matzah chilaquiles, and milanesa.

Because many Jews and Mexicans lived in Los Angeles and many of Margaret's friends were children of immigrants, she didn't feel the acuteness of these identities deeply until she left California and couldn't find matzah at her local grocery store. She began to teach herself to cook with other diaspora Jews and Latin Americans, enjoying the hands-on making of hamantaschen, empanadas, and challah. Later, she and her husband, Andrew, joined Community Supported Agriculture initiatives, embracing local food and slow cooking. Now settled in Maine with their two young daughters, the couple cook many recipes selected for this book and linger in their colors and flavors: borscht with crema, poppy seed flan, coffee honey cake. Each recipe tells stories about people we love and the places they have made home.

SINCE STORIES are often best told around a table, we envision this collection as an invitation into a lively family meal, an introduction to language, history, and culture through taste and food. As such, the recipes here are organized by meal, as well as by holiday in the Jewish calendar.

A standard day for Mexican Jews is made of three meals: *desayuno*, *comida*, and *cena*, breakfast, lunch, and dinner. The time, scope, and meaning of these three meals vary in comparison with what Americans are used to. The pace of time feels slower, with meals extending over *sobremesa*—connection and conversation over food—and parties well into the night, evening celebrations often building toward a breakfast meal that follows a long night of dancing.

By American standards, desayuno is a large breakfast. It frequently takes place between 9:00 and 11:00 am. It includes fruit and juice, eggs with meat and cheese along with refried beans and other accoutrements, coffee, and pastries. Desayuno is enjoyed leisurely in the company of family, friends, and business partners. A savory combination of a classic breakfast reinvented is challah French toast with cajeta, featuring queso Yiddish, which Mexican Jews often spread on toast and eat with fresh papaya or mango and lime. Huevos haminados, an egg dish with roots in Greece, Syria, and Lebanon, is another popular item. Other kinds of desayuno include blintzes, frittatas, spiced pickled herring, and a variety of sumptuous juices, including jugo de la fertilidad, which legend has it helps Jewish Mexican women get pregnant.

La comida isn't quite lunch. It takes place around 2:00 p.m. and can last three hours. It is the most complete meal of the day, featuring meat or fish and other dishes. After comida, Mexican Jews may take a break that includes a half-hour siesta. We gather around the table and attend to each other's pace, conversation punctuated by the warm and familiar questions:

Do you have enough food? *¿Quieres más?* Would you like more? *¿Un poquito más?* Just a little more? The conversation often circles around the types of dishes defining different Jewish Mexican families, who prepared them and how, and how a recipe has been improved by others.

A menu might start with grilled corn salad, move to sopa de albóndigas, a meatball soup that dates back to the sixteenth century, and then feature beef tzimmes with panela and pumpkin. The moment a dish arrives at the table, people welcome it with an array of expressions in the language connected to that plate: Yiddish, Ladino, Hebrew, even Polish, Arabic, Hungarian, or Russian. It feels like a fiesta of tastes and sounds. The provenance of any of these dishes, and the words that connect to them, point to the global dimension of Jewish Mexican cuisine.

The cena is served around 9:00 p.m. or even later. This meal is lighter than an American dinner. While it might feature tacos or quesadillas, it lacks the variety and scope of una comida, although it might make one ask out loud, especially the younger set: *"En serio*, are we really eating again?" The menu might start with baba ghanoush con chile, include caldo verde, which is a green broth with corn that could be served with or without matzah balls, and have as its pièce de résistance stuffed poblanos with guacamole and gribenes. These might even be accompanied by a roast eggplant frittata and a cilantro mousse. Cena can be a snack-oriented, light meal, but it still fulfills the promise that no one will be hungry at the end!

Although some of the customs around these meals have undergone changes in recent times, Mexican Jews, like their compatriots, put the culinary accent in the comida. Parties of four to six people commonly spend two or three hours together *luncheando y platicando*, lunching and schmoozing. This is the time to catch up on the ins and outs of community life as well as sports and world affairs. And, of course, food. Discussion during comida often revolves around how one mother's dish is different from those of other women and how the next generation incorporates surprising new ingredients. In short, the comida isn't only a time to eat but an occasion to imagine alternative ways of *comiendo juntos*, eating together.

THE RECIPES WITHIN these pages have been collected through an array of historical sources and from an assortment of family traditions. After posting an ad in *Diario Judío*, the go-to newspaper of La Comunidad, we received hundreds of makeshift cookbooks, letters featuring recipes, and other invaluable information from all sides of the Jewish community, Ashkenazic, Sephardi, and Israeli, cooks young and old, located in Mexico City, Guadalajara, Monterrey, Cancún, and Tijuana, as well as in the United States, Europe, Latin America, and Israel. We contacted the legendary chefs

Irma Appel, Karen Drijanski, and Pati Jinich, who provided us, each in her own way, with astonishing ideas. And we talked at length with writers and historians Alice Backal, Margo Glantz, Claudio Lomnitz, Myriam Moscona, Angelina Muñiz-Huberman, Becky Rubinstein, Esther Schuller, and Mónica Unikel-Fasja, discussing how recipes are expressions of political, social, economic, religious, cultural, and emotional change. Plus, of course, we ourselves, along with our families, in particular Ilan's mother, Ofelia, and Ilan's wife, Alison, for decades have prepared many of these dishes, enhancing their *sabor judío*, their Jewish taste.

Upon receiving the recipes, we quickly found out a secret that travels through generations: everyone measures ingredients in different ways; it all depends on the cook. Angelina Muñiz-Huberman, a prominent Jewish Mexican writer who grew up in a crypto-Jewish household, even has a poem, "Tururú," in her collection *La sal en el rostro*, about this haphazard approach (in Ilan's translation):

> My mother's recipes were based in handfuls:
> A handful of rice. Two handfuls of lentils.
> A bit of oil. A sprinkle of vinegar. A pinch of salt.
> Others were rhythmic: tururú and turururú.
> Of vinegar, tururú. Of oil, turururú.
> I was never able to learn to cook from her.

Consequently, all recipes have been standardized and thoroughly tested to ensure that the home cook can easily join in our storytelling. Many recipes share more about the people who first prepared these dishes, when, and how. Sometimes we talk more about adaptation across generations and places. These written and oral histories have been culled from interviews with the original cooks or their offspring. They showcase the degree to which *mestizaje*, the crossbreeding of cultures, is expressed in Jewish Mexican cuisine.

Assembling these recipes has been a labor of love. Its pillars are the recetarios by Bobe Miriam and Baba Malka. Hundreds of people have contributed to our efforts with variations of recipes wrapped in anecdotes about the pleasure of connecting across generations through the kitchen and around the table. Jewish history isn't only about survival; as these recipes make clear, it is about ingenuity, passion, and tenacity, about family, innovation, and continuity. Mexico has been extraordinarily generous as a host country and home to our families. Jewish and other immigrants have thrived in the country and have in turn enriched the place and culture in substantial ways. The union between these two traditions is best experienced in the cuisine that bridges them.

Together, we have found incalculable joy in preparing these stunning dishes. They come to us from diverse, in appearance incompatible, corners of the globe: the so-called Pale in eastern Europe and the former Ottoman Empire. As they were adapted into Mexico by immigrants in a show of stunning creativity, local recipes were readily reinvented. There is a common Mexican proverb about making do with what we have: *A todo le llaman cena, aunque sea un taco con sal.* Everything could be dinner, even a taco with salt. Indeed, one senses in these dishes the magic of assimilation. Nothing in it is static. Everything in it is vibrant.

¡Buen provecho! Mit a gutn apetit! Kome kon gana! •

Kosherísimo

AT A JEWISH MEXICAN TABLE, you will frequently hear a common expression: *kosherísimo*. It means "very authentic." There's lots of discussion on what passes as kosher and what doesn't. Tacos al pastor? Not really, since al pastor entails spit-grilled slices of pork. But it can be kosher when adapted with chicken. How about caldo verde with corn and matzah balls? Well, yes, kosherísimo.

To fully understand the term, it is important to know that Mexican Jews, just like Jews anywhere else, come in every shape or form: orthodox, Hasidim, conservative, reform, reconstructionist, transdenominational, secular, *acultura-dos* (assimilated), agnostic, Jubu (Jewish Buddhist), Ashkenazi, Sephardic, Mizrahi, crypto-Jews, Israelis, Mestizos, Asian, Black, and anything in between.

It is no surprise, then, that kosher food is such a hot topic of debate. On the surface, there is little margin of confusions: a dish is either kosher, meaning prepared according to strict dietary laws, or not. But there is another subtle option: kosher-style, foods traditionally eaten by Jews, including bagels with lox, bourekas, chicken noodle soup, deli sandwiches, huevos haminados, and so on. These dishes might be the very soul of Jewish Mexican cuisine, but oops, the ingredients aren't always kosher.

It is clear from the recetarios of Bobe Miriam and Baba Malka that upon arriving in Mexico, the two immigrant women, along with their families, kept a strict kosher kitchen. But as time went by, the annotations in their cookbooks by other generations display some questioning of the requirements of Jewish law.

Looking at the many recipes we received in *Diario Judío* and the stories accompanying them, this was the path of many immigrant Jewish households as they arrived in Mexico.

From there onward, the situation changes. Second-generation Jewish Mexicans tend to be more assimilated. Curiously, among some belonging to the third generation (the grandchildren of immigrants) and their offspring, the drive occasionally is to return to the religious devotion of their ancestors. In other words, to reverse assimilation or at least delay it. This explains the resurgence, especially in Mexico City, of kosher butchers, markets, and restaurants.

In their diaries, letters, and other historical documents, secret Jews describe the enormous challenges they faced in secretly committing to the dietary practices of their predecessors. For the most part, the strategy they took had to do with avoiding certain foods at crucial times. For instance, no meat on Shabbat and during the High Holidays, replacing it with different kinds of fish. The recipes we have inherited from them include different kinds of fish (often cod and snapper) and, not surprisingly, the avoidance of pork and of seafood routinely consumed by Christians: shellfish, including all varieties of mollusks and crustaceans.

Nearly all the recipes in *Sabor Judío* can be prepared without any modification either kosher-style or the more strictly kosher way, attending to certified kosher ingredients, distinct utensils separating *milkhik* (dairy) from *fleishink* (meat products), and so on. In other words, the adherence to kosher rules depends on the circumstances of the cook and the preferences and needs of those sitting at the table.

By the way, lately the kosher-related terms have acquired a larger scope in Jewish Mexican lingo, not only relating to food. That vintage dress? Kosher-style. A musical arrangement of Hallelujah with mariachis? *Requete* kosher, meaning "super-kosher." And the *calavera* (sugar skull) with Hebrew letters displayed on its forehead? Kosherísimo. •

DESAYUNO

XXXXXXXXXXXXXXX XXXXXXXXXXXXX

The Spanish word *desayuno*—like "breakfast" in English—means breaking the fast that has lasted all night. Mexican Jews enunciate the word with gusto, announcing a meal not only diverse in its offerings but always enjoyed with other people. The desayuno is an occasion to experiment with dishes and return to classic ones. It is a time to talk about the day's schedule, world affairs, family, and business and, frequently, to imagine altogether new ways of experiencing life.

For starters, there is fruta, lots of it. In their correspondence home, Ashkenazic and Ottoman immigrants often stressed how the palate awakened to new fruits. Mexico is a country of such diverse climates that every season of the year brings another variety. Mexican Jews start the day with a variety of juices: beet, orange, pineapple, pomegranate, papaya, watermelon, melon, strawberry, prickly pear, mamey, mango, zapote (a fruit naturally mixing the flavors of honey and chocolate)—or a combination thereof. At times these become smoothies when mixed with yogurt.

Next comes a plate of sliced fruit, frequently accompanied with lime and a drizzle of honey. Some people also add ajonjolí (sesame seed) or sunflower seeds (semillas de girasol).

One often finds at the Jewish Mexican breakfast table an assortment of oranges, mangos, peaches, papayas, pineapples, bananas, plantains, figs, apples, dates, pomegranates, and guavas.

And there are baskets of bread and pan dulce, sweet wheat-based bread introduced in Mexico by Spanish colonists, settlers, and immigrants, then modified during the French occupation in the mid-1800s. The possibilities of pan dulce are infinite: from *bigote* (moustache) and *concha* (shell) to *oreja* (ear) and *rehilete* (whirligig). Mexican Jews also make original versions of pan dulce in the forms of Torah scrolls, menorahs, dreidels, and hamantaschen.

The main breakfast ingredient is the egg, cooked in different fusion styles alternating between Sephardic and European culinary traditions, always with a local addition: poached in tomato chile sauce or served with machaca (dried, rehydrated beef when kosher or, more commonly in Mexico, pork) and refried beans (frijoles refritos). The humorously named huevos divorciados consists of two fried eggs, each covered with a different-colored salsa, red and green or chipotle and tomatillo. Refried beans might be decorated with tortilla chips known as *totopos*, a term that combines two Nahuatl words, *tlaxcalli* and *totopochtli*, which loosely translates as "noisy-to-chew toasted tortillas."

For those looking for other flavors, there is challah French toast con cajeta, which is kind of dulce de leche, zucchini frittata, avocado tartines topped with tomato and onion slices, queso Yiddish with blintzes, matzah chilaquiles, and spiced pickled herring accompanied with a variety of aged cheeses.

Now you are fortified for the adventurous day ahead. •

Challah French Toast con Cajeta

For Ilan and Margaret, this dish defines childhood. The challah that was left over from Shabbat dinner had hardened over the weekend and could be cut into slices on Monday or Tuesday, soaked in egg and spices, and grilled in an open pan. The magic depends on browning and the enthusiasm of plating, gently drizzling warmed cajeta on top. Cajeta is a caramel sauce made from goat's milk, and it is popular throughout Mexico, sweetening candies, coffee, and ice cream. The history of the caramel's spread coincides with the movement of sugarcane throughout Latin America. From US producers, we recommend a New England favorite, goat caramel from Fat Toad Farm.

You can garnish this dish with fresh fruit: we suggest a variety of seasonal berries, but also experiment with sliced apple or caramelized banana.

SERVES 6
Preparation time: 10 minutes
Cooking time: 35 minutes

1½ cups whole milk

½ cup heavy cream

5 large eggs

¼ cup granulated sugar

2 teaspoons vanilla extract

1 teaspoon ground cinnamon

⅛ teaspoon kosher salt

Unsalted butter, for frying

1 (1-pound) loaf challah, preferably day-old, cut into 1-inch-thick slices

Cajeta, slightly warmed, for topping

Fresh berries, for topping

1. In a large bowl, whisk together the milk, heavy cream, eggs, sugar, vanilla, cinnamon, and salt until well combined.

2. Melt about 1 tablespoon of butter in a large frying pan set over medium heat.

3. Working in batches of 2–3, dip the slices of challah into the egg mixture, soaking them for about 10 seconds per side. Allow the excess egg mixture to drip off, then add the soaked bread pieces to the frying pan. Cook, turning once, until golden brown on both sides, 4–6 minutes per batch. Add more butter to the frying pan as needed.

4. Serve hot, drizzled with the warmed cajeta and topped with fresh berries.

Poached Eggs in Tomato Chile Sauce

Ilan grew up eating these eggs for breakfast. The dish was prepared by Inés López Caballero, the cook who helped in his house in Mexico City for more than twenty years. Originally from Texcoco de la Mora, about 15 miles northeast of the city, she artfully combined Indigenous and Jewish recipes, including this one. Inés had a daughter, Vicky, who grew up in Ilan's household. Many years later, when Ilan's mother, Ofelia, in old age, faced Alzheimer's disease, Vicky generously spent time at her side, cooking dishes Inés had prepared decades before. Those dishes gave Ofelia comfort, anchoring her to the vanishing past.

This recipe is based on the traditional Yucatán dish rabo de mestiza, although it shares many common ingredients with Middle Eastern shakshuka recipes, popular across both Mexico and the United States. While *shakshuka* from the Arabic translates to "all mixed up," *mestiza*, too, references another kind of mixing with Indigenous Mexican identity. Contemporary reclamations of mestizaje, particularly from the Chicano movement, view hybridity in terms of affirmation and liberation. We share this simple dish—enjoyed most frequently at breakfast but appropriate for any meal—in this spirit, a celebration of mixing across the centuries.

. . . .

SERVES 2–4
Preparation time: 15 minutes
Cooking time: 55 minutes

1 poblano chile

2 tablespoons extra-virgin olive oil

1 medium white onion, finely chopped

2 medium garlic cloves, peeled and finely chopped

1 teaspoon dried marjoram

3 large ripe tomatoes (about 1½ pounds), stemmed and finely chopped

1 teaspoon kosher salt, plus more as needed

8 large eggs

8–16 (6-inch) corn tortillas, warmed

Crumbled queso fresco and finely chopped fresh cilantro, for topping

1. Heat the oven to 425°F and place the poblano chile in a small baking pan. Roast, turning the chile every 5 minutes, until soft and blistered all over, 20–25 minutes. Transfer the chile to a small bowl and cover loosely with a clean tea towel. Once cool, remove and discard the skin and seeds, and finely chop the flesh.

2. Heat the oil in a large frying pan set over medium heat. Add the onion and cook, stirring occasionally, until softened and lightly browned, 6–8 minutes. Add the garlic and marjoram and cook, stirring, until fragrant, 1–2 minutes. Stir in the chopped poblano, tomatoes, and salt. Cook, stirring often, until the mixture thickens a bit, 20–25 minutes.

3. Remove from the heat and use an immersion blender to blend the mixture into a textured sauce. (If the mixture is splattering out, you can transfer it to a bowl to blend or use a food processor. Transfer the sauce back to the pan before proceeding.) Taste and add more salt, if needed.

4. Make 8 small wells in the sauce with the back of a spoon and gently crack an egg into each well. Cover the pan and cook, occasionally basting the eggs with the sauce, until the whites are set and the eggs are runny, about 5 minutes. (Cook a little longer if you prefer more set yolks.)

5. Serve the eggs, sprinkled with queso fresco and cilantro to taste, with the tortillas. You may want to use 2 tortillas per egg for a stronger structure.

Queso Yiddish

¿Pero no tienes hambre, Marga? Margaret and her great-grandmother talked to each other through food. Margaret was a name Baba Malka couldn't really pronounce, and so she called her Marga in an accent that sounded like Spanish and Yiddish and Hebrew combined. Margaret always accepted seconds as her way of showing her love, and in her fragmented Spanish she navigated her way through meals with extended family, repeating the phrases "Muchas gracias" y "Qué rico" y "Qué delicioso" like a set of prayers. On her annual visits from Los Angeles to Mexico City, she stayed in her great-grandmother's apartment, and memories of these visits are bound up with food. Before anyone else was awake, Baba Malka would be at work making breakfast, pouring jugos, always plural, chopping herbs, making eggs, preparing and serving new jars she had made and saved over the last year: varieties of pickles, preserves, and cheeses at the ready for her family, a pantry brimming over.

Margaret walked with Baba Malka to the local markets, observing her carefully so that she, too, could prod and smell mangos and papayas with expertise, and she would listen in as Malka would haggle with vendors over the price of live chickens, which would be transported for the very brief end of their lives to the apartment kitchen. Margaret quickly acclimated to long and extended afternoon comidas, surrounded by family: *tíos y tías y primos* and other friends who would kiss them and welcome them home. In the evenings she would sit beside Baba Malka and watch telenovelas that she only half-understood until bedtime, when she would fall asleep listening to Malka whispering another set of prayers in Hebrew. Baba Malka's Queso Yiddish is a beloved recipe, a simple spread that is accented by fresh fruit and local flavors. It is a staple at our breakfast table.

. . . .

MAKES ABOUT 2 CUPS (1 POUND)
Preparation time: 30 minutes
Draining time: 5 hours

½ gallon whole milk

½ teaspoon kosher salt

3 tablespoons fresh lemon juice

1. Pour the milk into a large saucepan set over medium heat. Add the salt and heat the mixture, stirring often, until it reaches a simmer (just shy of a full boil).

2. Remove from the heat, stir in the lemon juice, and let sit for 20 minutes to allow the curds and whey to separate.

3. Place a double layer of cheesecloth into a mesh strainer set over a large bowl. Spoon the curds into the strainer, discarding the liquid (or reserving it for another use).

4. Cover the strainer and refrigerate 3–5 hours, depending on how thick you prefer the cheese to be. Serve chilled.

Suggested serving: Spread the cheese on toast and layer with fresh papaya or mango, drizzle with lime juice, and sprinkle with crushed chile piquín.

Queso Yiddish Blintzes

Ashkenazim have been preparing delicate blintzes with a range of sweet and savory fillings, including cheeses, berries, and spices, since the fourteenth century. These delicious cheese-filled, crepe-like pancakes are an import from the Pale of Settlement, where they were featured in Polish, Ukrainian, and other cuisines. In that sense, they are an example of fusion from Christian menus. In fact, *blintz* in Slavic means "pancake."

Mexican Jewish blintzes aren't made with cottage cheese but often incorporate Queso Yiddish (page 21), a homemade farmer's cheese. The blintzes might be accompanied by cajeta, strawberry and mango marmalade, or fruit with cinnamon, as suggested below. Served in a big pan, they could be seen as the sweet counterpart of enchiladas. Sometimes they are prepared for shivahs, to brighten up the spirit of those in mourning.

But the blintzes aren't always sweet. Depending on the occasion, among Mexican Jews they are served as a main dish, *a la mexicana*, with potatoes, onions, garlic, roast chiles, or other salsas. As an alternate preparation, we include a filling by poet and writer Becky Rubinstein. She is known not only for her literary output but also for her salads and desserts. In her book *Hadas y ensal-Hadas*, she tells fairy tales through recipes. Desserts such as blintzes are her specialty. Rubinstein makes them with huitlacoche, a delicacy sometimes called corn truffles that is easily found fresh in Mexican markets and is sold in US markets in vacuum packs or jars. Rubinstein believes that literature and cuisine go hand in hand. They are ruled by alchemy. Culinary wisdom depends on both knowledge and improvisation: "A good cook knows how to invent!"

· ·

MAKES ABOUT 20 BLINTZES
Preparation time: 30 minutes,
   plus resting
Cooking time: 1 hour

FOR THE FILLING

1 pound Queso Yiddish (page 21)
   or store-bought farmer's cheese

¼ cup granulated sugar

1 egg yolk

1 teaspoon vanilla extract

FOR THE WRAPPERS

2 cups all-purpose flour

2 tablespoons granulated sugar

½ teaspoon kosher salt

1¾ cups water

4 large eggs

3 tablespoons unsalted butter,
   melted and slightly cooled, plus
   more for frying

FOR SERVING

Fresh fruit and ground cinnamon

. . . .

1. Make the filling: Stir together the Queso Yiddish, sugar, egg yolk, and vanilla in a medium-size bowl, cover, and refrigerate until needed.

2. Make the wrappers: Add the flour, sugar, salt, water, eggs, and melted butter to a large, high-powered blender and blend until smooth, scraping down the sides of the blender as necessary. The batter should be the consistency of heavy cream. Let the batter rest for 30 minutes at room temperature.

3. Melt a little butter in the bottom of an 8-inch frying pan set over medium heat. Add a scant ¼ cup of the batter and quickly swirl it around in the pan to cover the bottom evenly. Cook until the top is dry and the underside is golden, about 2 minutes. (Do not flip.) Gently remove the wrapper and transfer it to a plate. Continue with the remaining batter, adding more butter to the pan as needed. Layer small pieces of parchment paper (about the size of the blintz wrappers) in between the finished wrappers to prevent sticking.

4. Assemble the blintzes: Lay one of the wrappers on a flat surface. Place a rounded tablespoon of the filling into the wrapper, about 1 inch from the bottom. Fold the bottom edge up over the filling. Fold both sides in, then gently roll up the blintz all the way. Set the filled blintz, seam-side down, on a large plate while repeating the process with the remaining wrappers and filling. (The filled blintzes can be wrapped well and frozen at this point for up to 3 months.)

5. To fry the blintzes, melt about 1 tablespoon of butter in a large frying pan. Working in batches of 4–5, add the blintzes to the pan, seam-side down, and cook, turning once, until golden brown on both sides, 6–8 minutes. Add more butter as needed to prepare the next batch.

6. Serve the blintzes warm or at room temperature with fresh fruit alongside and sprinkled with a little cinnamon.

Alternate filling: Huitlacoche

FOR THE FILLING

1 medium garlic clove, minced, grated, or pushed through a press

1 medium white onion, finely chopped

1 medium jalapeño chile, seeds removed, if desired, and finely chopped

2 tablespoons extra-virgin olive oil

¼ cup huitlacoche

1 teaspoon kosher salt

1 tablespoon fresh epazote, finely chopped

FOR THE SALSA

4 tablespoons (½ stick) unsalted butter

½ medium white onion, finely chopped

2 poblano chiles, seeds removed, if desired, and chopped

1 teaspoon kosher salt

¼ cup sour cream

FOR SERVING

Shredded Chihuahua cheese

1. Make the filling: Mix the garlic, onion, jalapeño, and oil in a medium-size bowl. Add the huitlacoche, salt, and epazote, stir to combine, and set aside until ready to fill the blintzes.

2. Make the salsa: Melt the butter in a medium frying pan set over medium heat. Add the onion and poblanos and cook, stirring occasionally, until softened and lightly browned, 6–8 minutes. Add the salt and sour cream. Cook, stirring often, for about 2 minutes. Transfer the mixture to a blender and blend until smooth.

3. After filling and frying the blintzes, drizzle them with the salsa and sprinkle them with the shredded Chihuahua cheese before serving.

Matzah Chilaquiles

Chilaquiles, typically freshly sliced and fried tortilla strips bathed with freshly prepared red or green salsa and eggs, are often served for breakfast, but the dish is also enjoyed throughout the day with variations. Margaret's American-born dad couldn't get enough of chilaquiles during their family visits from Los Angeles to Mexico City, and he would eat them as many meals as allowed. Disappearing after a family breakfast at home, he alleged that a second round of chilaquiles needed to be tested at a nearby Sanborns café, a ubiquitous diner found throughout the city, even though inferior to *casero* (homemade) varieties.

During another visit to Mexico over Passover, where adherence to the holiday means for observant Jewish emptying hametz (all leavened bread products, including tortillas) from their home for eight days, Margaret's family was introduced to this matzah-based recipe. With a regular reassurance of "No hay problema, vas a ver," we learned about these unexpectedly delicious workarounds: humble matzah holds the flavors of chilaquiles in unexpectedly delightful ways. The fusion of matzah into chilaquiles brings the Aztec language Nahuatl into our genealogies, referencing the words for chile (*chilli*) and herbs (*aquilli*). We find that the spice of this recipe is a relief for those exhausted by the taste of matzah by day three or four of Passover, as well as enjoyed for its texture and flavor throughout the year.

. . . .

SERVES 2
Preparation time: 5 minutes
Cook time: 20 minutes

Vegetable oil, for frying

4 squares matzah

½ medium red onion, thinly sliced

¼ teaspoon kosher salt, plus more for sprinkling

4 large eggs, lightly beaten

1 cup Tomatillo Salsa (page 143) or store-bought salsa

Queso fresco, Mexican crema, and chopped fresh cilantro, for serving

1. Heat ¼ inch of oil in a large frying pan set over medium heat until shimmering, and line a large plate with paper towels. Working with one piece of matzah at a time, fry the matzah, turning once, until golden and crisp, about 2 minutes per piece. Transfer to the paper towels to drain, then break up into bite-size pieces.

2. Pour out and discard all but 2 tablespoons of the oil from the frying pan. Add the onion and salt and cook, stirring occasionally, until softened and lightly browned, 6–8 minutes. Add the eggs and cook, stirring often, until scrambled, about 2 minutes. Add the fried matzah pieces and salsa, stir, and allow to heat through.

3. Divide between plates and sprinkle with a little more salt. Top as desired with queso fresco, crema, and fresh cilantro.

Huevos con Machaca and Refried Beans

This dish is a true marriage of two cultures. Beans were a feature of the Aztec diet before the arrival of the Spanish conquistadores. (Frijoles refritos are literally "twice-fried beans," and they might be black or red, negros or colorados.) Machaca is a jerkylike spiced beef, with textures ranging from dry and crumbled to resembling stewed beef. Inflected by its regional homes, machaca is usually seasoned with dried chiles, garlic, and oregano, with balances from spicy to smoky. Kosher Mexican Jews typically prepare their machaca at home; here we offer more widely available beef pastrami as a substitution familiar to Romanian Jews across the diaspora who first popularized the ingredient.

. . . .

SERVES 4
Preparation time: 10 minutes
Cooking time: 20 minutes

FOR THE EGGS

2 tablespoons vegetable oil

½ medium white onion, finely chopped

6 ounces machaca (or pastrami), finely chopped

2 medium plum tomatoes, cored, seeds removed, and finely chopped

1 serrano chile, seeds removed, if desired, and finely chopped

6 large eggs, lightly beaten

½ teaspoon kosher salt

¼ teaspoon freshly ground black pepper

FOR THE REFRIED BEANS

2 tablespoons vegetable oil

¼ medium white onion, finely chopped

1 medium garlic clove, chopped

1 (15-ounce) can pinto beans, drained (or 1½ cups cooked pinto beans)

¼ teaspoon kosher salt, plus more as needed

FOR SERVING

8 (6-inch) corn tortillas, warmed

1. Make the eggs: Heat the oil in a large frying pan set over medium heat. Add the onion and cook, stirring occasionally, until translucent, 5–6 minutes. Stir in the machaca, tomatoes, and serrano chile and cook until the tomatoes soften a bit, 6–8 minutes.

2. Add the eggs, salt, and pepper and cook, stirring, until the eggs are just scrambled. Remove from the heat.

3. Meanwhile, make the refried beans: Heat the oil in a separate medium frying pan set over medium heat. Add the onion and garlic and cook, stirring occasionally, until translucent, 5–6 minutes. Add the beans and salt and cook, stirring frequently and gently mashing the beans with the back of a sturdy spoon, until warmed through, 3–5 minutes. Taste and add more salt, if needed.

4. Divide the warmed corn tortillas among plates and top with the egg and bean mixtures. Serve immediately.

Huevos Divorciados con Arroz

Huevos divorciados consist of two sunny-side-up eggs separated on a plate, each topped with a different savory salsa. Sometimes the eggs are further separated with rice (as in this variation) or refried beans, and they can be served over tortillas. The humorous name *divorciados*, which means "divorced," describes the physical separation of the eggs on the plate, as well as the compromise demonstrated by the different toppings associated with each egg.

Divorce in Mexico was legalized in 1917, providing autonomy, economic safety, and the right of everyone to begin and end a marriage. It is part of popular lore that in the mid-twentieth century, Americans would travel to Mexico to get a "Mexican divorce," which was known to be quicker and less expensive than in the United States. Famous figures who made the trip as couples and came back single include Marilyn Monroe and Arthur Miller, Charlie Chaplin and Paulette Goddard, and Elizabeth Taylor and Eddie Fisher. In his childhood, Ilan remembers American cousins who visited the family talking about the allure of Mexican divorces as "the breaking of the chains, as when we were slaves in Egypt."

Mexican Jews are prone to make self-deprecating jokes about their condition. This dish has a recurrent presence in that humor. It signals the capacity to exist with one's enemy by simply allowing each to keep to their own side. The eggs dressed in salsas of different colors always make a colorful plate. The rice offers a neutral element that emphasizes not the rivalry but the encounter between opposites.

....

SERVES 4
Preparation time: 20 minutes
Cooking time: 45 minutes

FOR THE SALSA VERDE

6 small tomatillos (about ½ pound), paper skins removed

1 Anaheim chile, stemmed, halved lengthwise, and seeds removed, if desired

¼ white onion, peeled but not chopped

1 large garlic clove, unpeeled

½ teaspoon kosher salt, plus more as needed

¼ teaspoon freshly ground black pepper

FOR THE SALSA ASADA

3 medium plum tomatoes (about ¾ pound), stems removed but not chopped

¼ white onion, peeled but not chopped

1 serrano chile, stemmed, halved lengthwise, and seeds removed, if desired

¼ cup chicken or vegetable broth

¾ teaspoon kosher salt, plus more as needed

¼ teaspoon freshly ground black pepper

FOR THE RICE

3 medium plum tomatoes (about ¾ pound), stems removed and roughly chopped

1 medium garlic clove, peeled and roughly chopped

2 cups chicken or vegetable broth

2 tablespoons vegetable oil

½ white onion, finely chopped

1 cup long-grain white rice

½ cup frozen diced peas

½ cup frozen diced carrots

1 teaspoon kosher salt, plus more as needed

FOR SERVING

Vegetable oil, for frying

8 (6-inch) corn tortillas

8 large eggs

Kosher salt, for sprinkling

1. Make the salsa verde: Heat a medium frying pan over medium-high heat. Add the tomatillos, Anaheim chile, onion, and garlic and cook, turning occasionally, until blistered and slightly softened, 8–10 minutes. Transfer the ingredients to a blender, along with the salt and pepper, and blend until smooth with some texture. Taste and add more salt, if needed. Set aside. (This salsa can be made up to 1 day in advance and stored, covered, in the refrigerator.)

2. Make the salsa asada: Heat a medium frying pan over medium-high heat. Add the tomatoes, onion, and serrano chile and cook, turning occasionally, until blistered and slightly softened, 8–10 minutes. Transfer the ingredients to a blender along with the broth, salt, and pepper, and process until smooth with some texture. Taste and add more salt, if needed. Return the mixture to the frying pan and cook over medium-high heat, stirring often, until the salsa turns several shades darker red, 5–7 minutes. Set aside. (This salsa can be made up to 1 day in advance and stored, covered, in the refrigerator. Gently warm on the stovetop before serving.)

3. Make the rice: Place the tomatoes, garlic, and broth in a blender and blend until smooth. Heat the oil in a medium pot set over medium heat. Add the onion and cook, stirring occasionally, until softened and lightly golden, 6–8 minutes. Stir in the rice and cook until fragrant and toasted, 1–2 minutes.

4. Stir in the peas, carrots, and corn, followed by the salt, then pour the blended tomato mixture over the top. Stir to combine, raise the heat to medium high, and bring to a boil. Reduce the heat to low, cover the pot, and cook until the rice is tender and the liquid has been absorbed. Turn off the heat and let the rice rest for 10 minutes, then fluff with a fork.

5. To serve: Heat 1 tablespoon of oil in a large nonstick frying pan over medium heat. Add the tortillas, 1–2 at a time (depending on the size of your frying pan), and cook until crisp tender, about 30 seconds per side. Add more oil as necessary.

6. Fry the eggs, 2–4 at a time, setting the fried eggs aside on a plate while continuing with the remainder. Top each tortilla with a fried egg and sprinkle with a little salt. Drizzle a generous amount of the warm salsa asada over half of the eggs and a generous amount of the salsa verde over the other half of the eggs. Plate with the rice and serve hot.

Huevos Haminados

These eggs are a regular presence at the Jewish Mexican table. Huevos haminados (*güevos haminadavos* in Ladino) are Sephardic-style eggs—*haminado*
or *chaminado*, literally meaning "braised"—and a quintessential example of
Shabbat cooking. The eggs are designed to cook over eight to twelve hours,
permitting a hot meal to be ready on a Saturday evening without requiring
anyone to light a flame over Shabbat. Some suggest that the beautiful imprint
left on the hard-boiled eggs by this cooking process predates the tradition of
dyeing Easter eggs.

This dish is known to have been a favorite among conversos. They would
prepare it by boiling the eggs with onion skins, olive oil, and ashes, which
would give the shells a vermilion color. In other places, conversos prepared
the eggs by boiling in water with onion skins in clay pots. Huevos haminados remain a popular dish among Sephardic Jews in Turkey. They are also
popular in Israeli cuisine. In Tunisia, the brown eggs are cooked separately
in a metal pot on an all-night stove with water and tea leaves. For Mexican
Jews with ancestry in Syria, Lebanon, and Turkey, this dish is a reminder of
their Mediterranean roots. As a result of mixed marriages, the breakfast has
jumped out of its original ethnic enclave to become popular among larger
portions of La Comunidad. The Sephardic family recipe for huevos haminados given here is distinctive in featuring whole onions rather than just
onion skins; the variation results in a more richly flavored dish.

MAKES 12 EGGS
Preparation time: 9 hours, mostly
  unattended

12 large eggs, in their shells

2 medium yellow onions, unpeeled
  and halved

4 medium garlic cloves, unpeeled

3 tablespoons coarsely ground coffee

1 teaspoon ground cardamom

1 tablespoon kosher salt

1. Arrange the eggs with the onions,
garlic, coffee, and cardamom in a slow
cooker. Add water to cover by 2 inches.
Set the slow cooker to low and cook for
3 hours.

2. Using tongs, remove the eggs and
lightly crack the shells all over, but do
not peel the eggs. (This step is optional,
but it gives the eggs a beautiful marbling
effect.)

3. Return the eggs to the slow cooker
and cook on low for 6 hours. Remove
the eggs and rinse with cold water.
(Discard the solids and water from the
slow cooker.) Serve the eggs warm,
at room temperature, or cold.

Angelina's Stewed Potatoes and Eggs

Mexican writer Angelina Muñiz-Huberman (b. 1936) is a descendent of crypto-Jews and one of the preeminent scholars on Jewish culture in Spain before and after the expulsion in 1492 and converso life in Mexico during colonial times. A prolific author, she has published more than fifty books in genres ranging from fiction to poetry and from essays to translations to anthologies on kabbalah. Born in France to exiled Spanish parents who had escaped the Spanish Civil War, she was raised Catholic. A decisive moment in her life came when she saw peculiar behavioral patterns in her mother connected with cooking, household affairs, and rituals.

These patterns included lighting candles, sweeping rooms in unique ways, and certain figures of speech. Muñiz-Huberman one day asked her mother, who told her that they were secret Jews. The revelation changed her life. As a child, Angelina tells us, the taste of spiced potatoes with eggs transported her to her grandmother's life in La Mancha before the war. This recipe was passed to Angelina from her grandmother through her mother, each woman inflecting the dish with her own sense of family history.

. . . .

SERVES 4
Preparation time: 15 minutes
Cooking time: 40 minutes

3 medium russet potatoes (about 2 pounds), peeled and sliced ¼-inch thick

4 tablespoons extra-virgin olive oil, divided

1 teaspoon sweet paprika, plus more for sprinkling

3 medium garlic cloves, peeled and finely chopped

1 bay leaf

¾ teaspoon kosher salt, plus more as needed

¼ teaspoon freshly ground black pepper

2 cups chicken or vegetable broth

4 large eggs

1. Heat the oven to 375°F. Place the sliced potatoes in a large baking dish, drizzle with 2 tablespoons of the oil, and toss to coat. Roast, stirring occasionally, until the potatoes are tender but not mushy, about 25 minutes.

2. Heat the remaining 2 tablespoons of oil in a large frying pan set over medium heat. Add the roasted potatoes and fry, stirring occasionally, until golden, about 5 minutes. Stir in the paprika, garlic, bay leaf, salt, and pepper and cook, stirring to coat the potatoes, until fragrant, about 1 minute.

3. Add the broth, raise the heat to medium high, and bring the mixture to a boil. Cook, stirring occasionally, until the liquid reduces by half and the potatoes are very tender, about 5 minutes. (It is okay if some of the potatoes split into pieces.) Taste and add more salt, if needed.

4. Reduce the heat to medium. Crack the eggs into the pan, spacing them apart from one another. Cover the frying pan and let the eggs poach until the whites are set and the yolks are runny, about 5 minutes (or a little longer for fully cooked yolks). Remove from the heat and let rest for a few minutes. Remove and discard the bay leaf. Serve hot, sprinkled with more paprika.

Zucchini Frittata

Frittatas are delicious throughout the day and can be quickly assembled with seasonal vegetables and herbs to showcase the season and served at lunch or dinner. Mexican varieties of the frittata are typically made with onions and varieties of salsas and chorizos. Middle Eastern and Sephardic varieties of the frittata are made primarily with spinach and cheese. This Mexican Jewish variation offered to us by several families through *Diario Judío* incorporates fried zucchini and is accented with fresh parsley.

SERVES 4
Preparation time: 25–30 minutes

6 tablespoons extra-virgin olive oil, divided

6 small zucchini, sliced

Kosher salt and freshly ground black pepper, to taste

¼ cup finely chopped fresh parsley

6 large eggs, beaten

1. Heat 3 tablespoons of the oil in a frying pan over medium-high heat. Place the zucchini slices in the hot oil and brown on both sides. Remove with a slotted spoon and place on a paper-towel-lined plate. Add the remaining 3 tablespoons of oil to the pan.

2. In a medium-size bowl, mix together the salt and pepper, parsley, cooked zucchini, and eggs. Pour the mixture into the frying pan, reduce the heat to low, and cover the pan. Let simmer for 15 minutes, occasionally shaking the pan to prevent the mixture from sticking. This will allow the bottom and center of the frittata to set.

3. Uncover the pan once the bottom is set. Using a spatula, flip the frittata. Slide the frittata onto a flat plate, cut as if it were a pizza, and serve.

Serving suggestion: Accompany with crumbled queso fresco, sliced tomatoes, and a drizzle of garlic-infused olive oil.

Jaco's Tartines de Aguacate con Jalapeño

Jacobo Grinberg Zylberbaum was a mysterious Jewish Mexican neuroscientist turned shaman who believed in altered states of consciousness as a means of engaging with the universe. Some believe that he was a charlatan, whereas others see Grinberg, known to his relatives as Jaco (he was a cousin of Ilan's aunt Hilda), as ahead of his time. To a large extent, the mystique around him spurs from his disappearance in 1994 after a supposed trip to India, which he may never have taken. Grinberg wrote more than fifty books on the human brain and mystical ways of knowledge, among other topics, including the five-volume work *Los chamanes de México* (The shamans of Mexico). This recipe is an homage to him.

Whether the trend of avocado toast was popularized in Los Angeles or New York City is a subject of intense debate, but the adaptation and migration of the recipe continues, here with the distinctly Jewish Mexican flavors of charred jalapeño and rye bread. It is unlikely that tartines, one of today's most popular dishes featuring avocado, was known under such a name (it comes from the French word for a slice of bread spread with butter and jam) while Grinberg was alive. But who knows or, better, who cares? This concoction might push you to understand the universe in unforeseen ways.

SERVES 2
Preparation time: 10 minutes
Cooking time: 10 minutes

1 large jalapeño chile

2 teaspoons extra-virgin olive oil

2 medium garlic cloves, peeled and finely chopped

2 large avocados, peeled and pitted

1½ tablespoons fresh lime juice

½ teaspoon kosher salt, plus more for sprinkling

4 slices sourdough or rye, toasted

1. Place the jalapeño directly over a flame and char, turning as needed, until it is blistered on all sides, 3–5 minutes. Transfer to a paper bag to cool and steam, then peel and chop, discarding the seeds, if desired.

2. Heat the oil in a small frying pan set over medium heat. Add the chopped jalapeño and cook, stirring and mashing with a fork for 2–3 minutes. Add the garlic and cook, stirring, until fragrant, about 1 minute.

3. Transfer the mashed jalapeño mixture to a large bowl along with the avocado, lime juice, and salt and mash until a chunky paste forms.

4. Spread the mixture evenly over the toasted bread. Sprinkle with a little more salt and serve immediately.

Spiced Pickled Herring

It's hard to get more Old World than preserved fish in jars, but this immensely flavorful pickled herring deserves a comeback. These jars pack a punch with earthly aromatics, combining savory, sweet, and heat: pickled beets and raisins with chile de árbol. The bright red chiles have significant spice, measured at five times that of a jalapeño. Many forms of pickling can be found across Jewish Mexican traditions, and this recipe relies on the marriage of eastern European ingredients with local foodstuffs from Mexico. It is delicious served with sliced potatoes and hard-boiled eggs, spread over rye bread, or, even better, placed on Guadalajara's famed birote salado (a sourdough infused with lime juice and beer).

Batch producing jars of herring is a loving tribute to communities of preservation, reinvention, and interdependence. Look for lightly salted herring fillets in the refrigerator case at your supermarket. In an alternate preparation, pickled herring from a jar are diced (reserving the vinegar and spices) and mixed in a small bowl with diced tomato, avocado, and Manila mango.

SERVES 6–8
Preparation time: 20 minutes,
    plus chilling

3 cups water

¼ cup granulated sugar

4 bay leaves

4 whole allspice berries

1⅓ cups white vinegar

1 medium red onion, halved through
    the root and thinly sliced

1 medium red beet, peeled and
    cut into matchsticks

1 chile de árbol, seeds removed, if
    desired, and thinly sliced

¼ cup golden raisins

2 pounds lightly salted herring fillets,
    soaked for 30 minutes in cool water,
    and drained

1. Stir together the water and sugar in a medium saucepan set over high heat. Add the bay leaves and allspice berries, bring to a boil, and boil for 5 minutes.

2. Remove from the heat and stir in the vinegar, red onion, beet, and chile de árbol, and let cool completely.

3. Layer the herring fillets and pickled beets and onion mixture in a glass container with a lid (any size that fits comfortably), then pour the pickling liquid over top. Cover and refrigerate for 5 days before serving. After opening, the herring can be enjoyed from the fridge for up to 1 month.

Pineapple Beet Juice

Margaret's proficiency in juice vocabulary was strong from early childhood: jugos de naranja y alfalfa, jugos de papaya, jugos de apió, de guava, mango, límon, y fresas. She linked each word to the saturated color that her Malka would offer in glass pitchers and cups at the breakfast table each morning. Growing up in Los Angeles permitted easy access to these fruit rainbows from markets and street vendors in most parts of the year, but each visit to Mexico seemed to offer taste of another hue and flavor that would form memories of the people and place. These colorful juices were about health, she was told very early on, and a requirement to a joyful start to the day. This pineapple beet juice is the perfect marriage of tropical endurance.

SERVES 4
Preparation time: 15 minutes

1 large pineapple, peeled and
    roughly chopped

1 medium red beet, peeled and
    roughly chopped

1 large cucumber, peeled and
    roughly chopped

½ cup cold water (if using
    a blender)

1. If using a juicer: Run the pineapple, beet, and cucumber through a juicer, then combine in a pitcher and mix to blend. Serve chilled.

2. If using a blender: Place the pineapple, beet, cucumber, and cold water into a high-powered blender and blend until smooth, adding the ingredients in stages if they do not all fit at once. Line a large bowl with a double layer of cheesecloth. Pour the juice mixture through the cheesecloth, squeezing the cloth to strain, then pour the juice into a pitcher. (Discard the pulp or reserve for another use.) Serve chilled.

Manga Tanga

This popular juice made of mango and lime began as refreshing drink in youth camps in La Comunidad, especially camps for Jewish boy scouts and the Zionist labor organization Hashomer Hatzair. It plays on the fruit snack of sliced jicama or mango, lime, salt, and chile piquín, which, along with cacahuates con chile y limón (peanuts with chile and lime), was ubiquitous during *campamentos* (weekend camps) and other outdoor adventures in the 1970s. It is served cool. The playful moniker "Manga Tanga" calls attention to the etymology of the seventeenth-century Portuguese word *mango*, which comes from the Malay word *mangga* and, supposedly, from the Tamil *man*, "mango tree," and *kay*, "fruit." "Tanga" is a variation of the word *tango*, the Argentine dance. Together, they imply a partner dance of flavors.

SERVES 1–2
Preparation time: 10 minutes, plus optional chilling

2 cups chopped ripe mango flesh (from 2–3 fresh mangos)

2 teaspoons agave nectar, plus more as needed

1½ teaspoons fresh lime juice, plus more as needed

½ cup water, plus more as needed

1. Place the mango, agave, lime juice, and water in a high-powered blender and blend until smooth. Taste and adjust the flavor with more agave, lime juice, or water, if desired.

2. Serve right away or pour the mixture into a carafe or small pitcher, cover, and refrigerate until chilled, at least 2 hours.

Jugo de la Fertilidad

Known as "jugo ABZ" ("celery" in Mexican Spanish is *apio*, "beet" is *betabel*, also known as *remolacha*, and "carrot" is *zanahoria*), this juice requires fresh celery, beets, and carrots in season for a naturally sweet taste. Otherwise, a drizzle of honey perfects the flavor. This mix has become a favorite of athletes. Beets are rich in folate and high in nitrates. In Mexican Jewish cuisine, beets are used in borscht, in salads, and as a garnish. Celery is full of vitamins and minerals, including potassium and calcium. Ilan prepared this juice for Alison, his wife, each morning when they were hoping for her to get pregnant. Two sons later, he learned that rumor had it that Bobe Bela, his maternal grandmother, had done the same on marrying Srulek Stavchansky.

SERVES 4

Preparation time: 15 minutes,
  plus chilling

3 bunches celery, washed well
  and dried

8 medium red beets, peeled

2 medium carrots, peeled

Juice from ¼ large lemon

Honey, to taste

Pass the celery, beets, and carrots through a juicer. Pour the juice into a large pitcher and stir in the lemon juice and honey to taste. Cover and refrigerate until chilled, at least 2 hours.

Aguas Frescas

WATER, LOTS OF WATER. Mexican Jews drink lots of it. Cold and hot, before desayuno, after the cena. From fruits, flowers, and grains, with an array of delicious flavors. The fresher, the better. That is exactly what *agua fresca*, everyone's favorite drink, means: fresh water.

Among La Comunidad, the most famous flavors are agua de horchata (made of rice, cinnamon, and sugar), agua de Jamaica (hibiscus water), and agua de tamarindo (tamarind water). Mexican Jews fashion them in new ways. They might add strawberry to agua de horchata, a twist of lemon to agua de Jamaica, and nuts to agua de tamarindo.

Aside from its organic value, the constant presence of water in Mexican meals is no surprise. To the east and the west, the

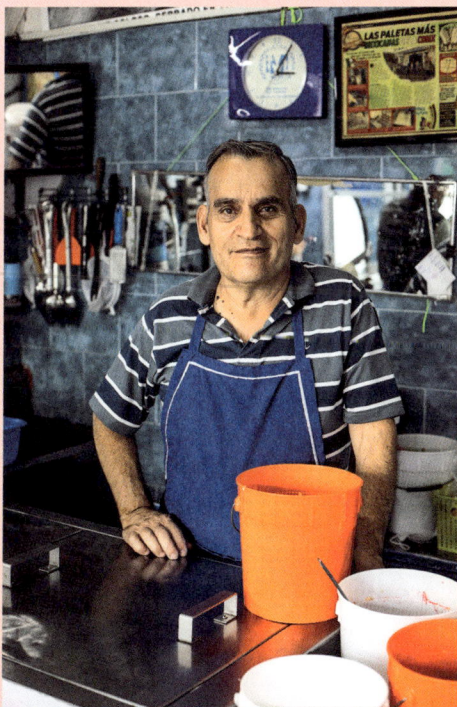

country is circumscribed by large expansions of water, the Gulf of Mexico and the Atlantic Ocean on one side, the Pacific on the other. The beaches are magisterial, as is the food there. And the water people drink.

To the north, there is the Río Bravo, which changes its name if you look at it from the United States, at which point it is called Rio Grande. And to the south, after the Isthmus of Tehuantepec, there is just a narrow land separating the country from Guatemala and Belize.

Also, Tenochtitlán, the original name for Mexico City, was built on five lakes. And the metropolis is visited by torrential rains at specific times of the year. In other words, water is above and below, yesterday and tomorrow.

Until the 1940s, newcomers almost always came by boat. In 1492, Europeans came from the sea. When conquistador Hernán Cortés arrived, some tell the story that Aztecs first believed he was a deity, Quetzalcóatl, whose return one day would take place through the sea. The same medium goes for repeating waves of immigrants roughly up until the 1930s: from France, England, Germany, Russia, Turkey, and other countries, all arrived by boat.

Jews did, too.

The majority of aguas frescas, refreshing fruit flavors of mango, papaya, guava, and watermelon, are nonalcoholic. Of course, tequila, rum, and a select number of liquors are sometimes added for the appropriate occasion. •

Agua de Jamaica con Fresa

Aguas frescas are traditional Mexican beverages of seasonal fruits that are refreshing, nonalcoholic, and thought to pair perfectly with spice. The star of this drink, the hibiscus flower (in Spanish, *flor de Jamaica*), is native to Africa and made its way to Mexico with the transport of enslaved West Africans in the sixteenth century. Food historians teach us about the memories embedded in these native species, familiar domestic foods, and medicinal plants uprooted and carried across oceans, where generations later they are deeply rooted in new soil. Vibrant red hibiscus flowers are the star of this beverage, complemented with fresh strawberries for a deeply refreshing and antioxidant treat that evokes warmth and endurance. Hibiscus flowers are naturally tart, so flavors are balanced for a sweet but not too sweet taste. This beverage is a delicious way to begin a warm summer day but is also enjoyed morning through evening as one of the most requested flavors from neighborhood taqueros, both in Mexico and in the United States.

SERVES 8
Preparation time: 20 minutes,
  plus resting and chilling

8 cups water

1½ cups granulated sugar, divided

½ cup dried hibiscus flowers

1 pound strawberries, stemmed
  and quartered (about 2 cups)

Ice, for serving (optional)

Lime or orange wedges, for serving

Note: Steeping hibiscus flowers to make tea is a common practice for Mexican Jews for an herbal treat that is soothing and heart healthy.

1. Pour the water into a medium saucepan set over high heat and bring to a boil. Add ¾ cup of the sugar, stir to dissolve, then remove from the heat. Add the hibiscus flowers to the hot water and gently stir to combine. Let the mixture sit for 30 minutes.

2. Meanwhile, in a large bowl, combine the strawberries and the remaining ¾ cup of sugar, stir, and let the mixture sit for 30 minutes. Transfer the macerated strawberries (and any juices in the bowl) to a blender and blend until smooth.

3. Strain the hibiscus mixture through a sieve into a large pitcher (discarding the flowers). Pour the blended strawberry mixture into the pitcher and whisk to combine. Cover and refrigerate until chilled, at least 2 hours.

4. Serve in glasses (over ice, if desired), with lime or orange wedges alongside for squeezing.

Agua de Horchata

Yet another example of the versatility of rice in Latin American cuisine, Agua de Horchata accompanies a good Mexican Jewish meal. From a distance, this beverage looks like a regular glass of milk crowned with a dusting of ground cinnamon. On hot days it can be served over ice. The name probably comes from the Latin word for "barley." It is an invaluable companion to a torta or a taco plate.

It is believed that Agua de Horchata originated in North Africa around the eleventh century, from where it traveled to the Iberian Peninsula. It was brought to the Americas during the colonial period, when it became popular among all social classes. There are types of horchatas other than rice. Some are made of sesame seeds or melon seeds, and in Central America it is made of semilla de jícaro, also known as morro seed. In some parts of the Americas, people add ground cocoa, nutmeg, peanuts, or almonds.

SERVES 8–10
Preparation time: 10 minutes,
  plus soaking and chilling

2 cups long-grain white rice,
  rinsed well and drained

1 cinnamon stick

6 cups room-temperature water,
  divided, plus more as needed

¾ cup granulated sugar

2 cups whole milk

2 teaspoons vanilla extract

Ice, for serving (optional)

1. Place the rice and cinnamon stick in a large glass bowl and add 4 cups of the water. Cover the bowl and let the mixture soak overnight at room temperature (at least 8 hours).

2. Pour the soaked rice mixture into a high-powered blender along with the sugar and blend until smooth. (You can tear the cinnamon stick into smaller pieces to facilitate its blending.) Pour the mixture through a fine-mesh sieve into a large wide-mouth pitcher, stirring and pressing the mixture with a spoon, if needed, to help the liquid pass through the sieve. (Discard any remaining solids.)

3. Whisk in the milk, the remaining 2 cups of water, and vanilla. Cover the pitcher and chill the horchata in the refrigerator until cold, at least 4 hours. (The mixture will continue to thicken as it chills.)

4. Just before serving, stir the horchata well and pour into glasses (over ice, if desired). If the horchata gets too thick, you can thin it with a little more water.

Bounties of the Earth

WHAT DISTINGUISHES a table by La Comunidad is its abundant, contrasting color. It comes from what Jewish Mexican poet Gloria Gervitz calls the "generosidad de la tierra," the bounties of the earth, that often have resonant names.

For instance, guanabana, a kind of soursop that tastes like a tart, strawberry-banana hybrid; chayote, a version of savory pear; chiromoya, a variety of sweetsop; huayas, at times called Mexican lychee; jicama, a pure, almost flavorless root vegetable that is a favorite of children; maracuyá, a passion fruit shaped like a brain; and pitaya, spiky on the outside with a white interior dotted with black seeds.

In collecting the recipes for this volume, we were told of immigrants, once they had settled down, poring over historical documents from pre-Hispanic civilizations in search of recipes to incorporate into their new diet.

One of the delicacies of Jewish Mexican cuisine is known as fruta cristalizada, candied fruit, which, at its core, is fruit cooked for long periods of time in sugar or piloncillo. The list of possibilities is endless: pumpkin, fig, mango, peach, and kiwi play a protagonist role. Ilan's favorite are figs, calabaza (candied pumpkin), chabacanos (apricots), pineapple, oranges, other citrus, and tunas verdes y rojas (green and red prickly pears). Margaret enjoys camote (sweet potatoes). From the immigrant generation onward, rather that preparing fruta cristalizada at home, most Mexican Jews buy it in mercados, where the quality is superb.

The Jewish Mexican table abounds in ensaladas, salads that contain several types of lettuces, herbs (cilantro reigning king), corn, tomatoes, cucumbers, onions, squash, artichokes, and several varieties of legumes. Flor de calabaza, jicama, red peppers, verdolaga, and cactus leaves (nopales) also show up in different presentations. No comida or cena is complete without its accoutrement of ensaladas.

There are also the succulent fruit juices, which we showcase in the desayuno section. And, of course, fruit in dessert, including tarts, cakes, compotes, ice cream, gelatinas, paletas, and other sweets.

It is no surprise that in the work by Frida Kahlo and Diego Rivera, both of whom emphasized their Semitic ancestry, the bounties of the earth are depicted glamorously. These ingredients are the protagonists of Jewish Mexican cuisine. •

COMIDA

XXXXXXXXXXXXXXX XXXXXXXXXXXXXXX

After you enjoy una comida with Mexican Jews, you realize the extent to which a meal might become an art. No matter how hectic the day, people approach each course with awe, patience, and anticipation.

On a typical day, everyone starts congregating around 2:00 p.m. Each guest is offered an agua fresca, and people slowly find their place at the table as small bites are served: a bowl of guacamole with totopos, an arrangement of cheese and fruits, or thin slices of jicama with salt and lime.

The first course is soup or salad or both. Soup varieties might include the well-loved sopa de tortilla, a staple of Mexican cuisine adapted by La Comunidad. Other options are Pati Jinich's legendary mushroom jalapeño matzah ball soup or the hearty sopa de albóndiga "Yehuda Halevi." As for salads, we adore Abraham's lentil salad, made with avocado and cherry tomatoes. Or the refreshing cilantro and mint salad, a tradition of our gardens.

The point is not to overwhelm one's appetite and to allow for the crescendo of the main course. People sometimes stand up after soups or salads and take a brief break.

Now comes the most important part of la comida, and often the centerpiece of the day. Depending on the season and the host's ambition, the main dish might be tomato oregano beef kebabs, a Lebanese recipe that has been Mexicanized over decades. Other Sephardic favorites are bourekas con queso blanco and cumin rose kibbe.

Another gem is the brisket tacos in three chiles salsa with rhubarb perfected by Margaret's grandmother Phyllis. Another warming Ashkenazi dish is Raquel's slow-braised beef tzimmes, rich with panela and pumpkin. Ilan's Bobe Miriam was widely known for her pescado a la Veracruzana. It is in her recipe book. When people kindly sent us their recipes for this book, we realized what a fixture it has been for La Comunidad, with each family offering variations in spice. The dish is commonly prepared with haddock or flounder.

During visits with a number of families, we ate Irma Appel's citrus parsley sea bass. Early in life Irma dreamed of cooking Mexican Jewish food professionally, both at home and in restaurant kitchens. And in 1998 she began her catering business, Appel's, which thrives today. Her slogan is "Tradición Gourmet." She has cooked for everybody, from presidents to newlyweds, Jews and non-Jews. Although she isn't religious, she has gone from not engaging in Jewish rituals to being one of the most important kosher-style cooks who caters for La Comunidad. This fish dish is often on the menu at circumcision ceremonies and shivahs.

Other mains include the orange and chipotle–infused pollo Luis de Santángel, the beef milanesa con patatas, and Karen Drijanski's family recipe for Niddo vegetable lasagna, featuring cauliflower, zucchini, butternut squash, and asparagus.

For La Comunidad, la comida is the most important meal of the day. To refresh yourself after the meal's end, you are allowed—even encouraged—to take a short siesta, up to half an hour. When you awaken, you feel like a new person. •

Karen Drijanski at her restaurant,
Niddo, Cuauhtémoc, Mexico City,
January 2023.

Mango Jicama Salad

The two stars of this salad are iconic of Margaret's early food associations in Mexico City and across Los Angeles: peeled and sliced mango and jicama often sold on sticks or in plastic cups and covered in chile and lime. Heaping portions of this salad strike the perfect balance between casual and celebratory, sweet and spicy. Created in the mid-1980s, Tajín is a seasoning blend of chiles, lime, and salt that is now widely used across a variety of sweet and savory dishes and even to rim glasses for spicy cocktails. Jicama is best from late autumn to early spring, although it can be harvested year-round.

SERVES 4
Preparation time: 10 minutes,
    plus 1 hour resting

2 medium yellow mangos, peeled
    and cut into ½-inch cubes

2 medium jicamas, peeled and
    cut into ½-inch cubes

2 small cucumbers, peeled, seeds
    removed, and cut into ½-inch cubes

½ cup finely chopped fresh cilantro

4 tablespoons fresh lime juice

¼ teaspoon chili powder or Tajín

½ teaspoon kosher salt

In a mixing bowl, combine the mangos, jicamas, cucumbers, cilantro, lime juice, chili powder, and salt. Toss well, cover, and refrigerate for at least 1 hour before serving. Adjust salt and chili powder to taste.

Grilled Corn Salad

There is no Mexican cuisine without elote. Maize, corn, particularly grilled corn, has played a central role in people's diet since the Indigenous Toltec, Aztec, and Mayan populations domesticated the grain. You find it everywhere: of course in tortillas, Mexico's manna. Maize is a partner of avocado, tomato, and chile, just to mention those other staples of Mexican cooking.

Mexican Jews, just like everyone else in the country, love grilled elote, corn on the cob. In every city and town, you will find a *marchante* boiling water in a big metal container inside which elotes are being cooked. They are becoming elotes—corn on the cob, rather than esquite, toasted corn kernels in a cup. As soon as you ask for your own, the marchante inserts a wooden stick into the corn cob, then smears the elote with either mayonnaise or Mexican crema, on top of which you can add Tajín, Cotija cheese, and a few drops of lime. *¡Sabrosísimo!*

This grilled corn salad—in Spanish, ensalada de elote asado—pays tribute to the esquites. You might have it by itself for lunch or accompanying a *platillo principal*. Ilan remembers eating it at night while watching his father, who on occasion was in episodes of *Chespirito*, a popular TV show with comedian Roberto Gómez Bolaños, about a working-class boy called El Chavo del Ocho and the clumsy Mexican superhero El Chapulín Colorado. Since the name of every character created by Gómez Bolaños started with a "ch," in Ilan's family the salad was nicknamed "enchachada de chelote achado."

SERVES 4
Preparation time: 25 minutes,
  plus cooling
Cooking time: 15 minutes

6 ears of corn, husks removed

10 scallions, trimmed

1 cup cherry tomatoes, halved

¼ cup roughly chopped fresh mint

½ teaspoon kosher salt, plus more
  as needed

2 tablespoons red wine vinegar

1. Heat a grill or large grill pan to medium heat. Working in batches if necessary, grill the whole corn cobs and scallions, turning as necessary, until softened and charred all around, 4–5 minutes.

2. Transfer the grilled vegetables to a cutting board to cool. Once cooled, cut the kernels off the corn cobs and thinly slice the scallions, transferring both to a large bowl. (Discard the corn cobs or reserve for another use.)

3. Add the cherry tomatoes, mint, salt, and vinegar and mix to combine. Taste and add more salt, if needed. Serve immediately or cover and refrigerate for up to 1 day.

Abraham's Lentil Salad

This dish is named in memory of Ilan's father, Abraham Stavans, who was especially fond of lentil salads, which he would enjoy in commemoration of the premiere of a new play or the conclusion of a popular telenovela in which he starred. Lentils and Abraham have other mythical origin stories: sages tell us that when mourning the loss of his grandfather Abraham, the father of the Jewish people, Jacob prepared soup from lentils—numerous as the stars in the sky, grains of sand, or perhaps the tiny lentils of this salad.

This is a refreshing dish with a distinct Algerian flavor. The cookbook *Sefra dayme*, which chronicles a century of Syrian Jewish cuisine in Mexico, contains recipes for an assortment of salads, including ensalada árabe, made with tomato, cucumber, onion, and olives, beet salad with celery, and eggplant salad with olives, that complement this dish.

SERVES 4–6
Preparation time: 15 minutes
Cooking time: 20 minutes

1 cup dried green lentils

3 tablespoons extra-virgin olive oil

1½ tablespoons fresh lemon juice, plus more as needed

¾ teaspoon kosher salt, plus more as needed

½ teaspoon freshly ground black pepper

½ small red onion, thinly sliced

1 cup cherry tomatoes, halved

1 medium avocado, peeled, pitted, and cut into approximately ½-inch pieces

¼ cup chopped fresh parsley

1. Bring a medium pot of water to a boil over high heat. Stir in the lentils, lower the heat to medium, and cook, stirring occasionally, until the lentils are tender but not mushy, 15–20 minutes. Drain well and let cool. (The lentils can be made a day in advance and stored, covered, in the refrigerator.)

2. In a large bowl, whisk together the oil, lemon juice, salt, and pepper. Add the sliced red onion and let sit for 10 minutes to allow the onion's flavor to mellow. Add the cooked and cooled lentils, cherry tomato, avocado, and parsley and gently toss to combine. Taste and add more lemon juice or salt, if desired. Serve at room temperature or chilled.

Cactus Tomato Salad

The prickly pear cactus, a succulent native to Mexico, can be harvested for its edible fruit. Both the pads of the cactus (nopales or nopalitos) and the cactus fruit (tunas) are popular in Mexican cuisine, and cactus appears in an array of dishes varying from spiced enchiladas to sweet horchata toppings. Many families in La Comunidad prepare this dish ahead of Shabbat so that the flavors can marinate overnight and be enjoyed on the day of rest without labor. Others recommend incorporating cactus into the diet because of its health benefits, studied for regulating blood sugar. This salad is a delicious accompaniment to tacos or tlacoyos or quesadillas and can be used as the filling for any of these dishes.

. . . .

SERVES 4 AS MAIN, 8 AS SIDE
Preparation time: 40 minutes

2 pounds nopales (fresh cactus leaves), spines removed and sliced into ¼-inch strips (see Note)

3 large plum tomatoes (about 1 pound), seeds removed, finely chopped

½ large white onion, finely chopped

½ cup finely chopped fresh cilantro

1 medium jalapeño chile, seeds removed, finely chopped

2 tablespoons fresh lime juice, plus more as needed

½ teaspoon kosher salt, plus more as needed

Crumbled Cotija cheese, for serving

1. Bring a large pot of water to a boil over high heat. Once boiling, add the cactus pieces, turn heat down to medium high, and cook until the cactus is tender but not mushy, 8–10 minutes. Drain and let cool, then transfer to a large bowl.

2. Add the tomatoes, onion, cilantro, and jalapeño to the cooked and cooled cactus. Add the lime juice and salt and toss to combine. Taste and add more salt and lime juice, if desired.

3. Divide into bowls and serve immediately, generously sprinkled with Cotija cheese. Or refrigerate until chilled before serving.

Note: Wear kitchen gloves and use a sharp knife to scrape off and discard the prickly nopales spines. Another way to remove these sharp spines is to burn them off by searing both sides of the cactus.

Cold Pumpkin Salad

This dish is inspired by salata arabie (in Spanish, ensalada árabe), an Arab salad brought to Mexico from Lebanon by Jewish immigrants. The traditional version is made with green tomatoes, known as saladet, along with pickles, white onion, parsley, peppermint, cumin, black pepper, lemons, black olives, and salt. Our variation comes from Ottoman friends. It takes advantage of the delicious calabaza, pumpkin, which, though found in six continents around the world (the orange type ubiquitous in autumn in the United States was cultivated by the Indigenous population before the arrival of European settlers), is original to Mexico. Calabaza is bulbous, with a crooked neck. It has seeds inside called pepitas, which are a favorite snack after they are grilled with salt in the comal.

When Ilan, as a young man, was learning Ladino, his generous teacher would serve an assortment of dishes, including salads and pastries. This was one of them. It was a tense time: in June 1982 the Israeli army invaded Lebanon. Mexican Jews, like those everywhere in the diaspora, found themselves with divided loyalties. Ilan's poem "At Mme. Zeltouni's Dining Room, Colonia Tecamachalco, Thursday, September 16th, 1982," re-creates the experience, as does the fresh flavor of the Cold Pumpkin Salad. Specific dishes are anchored in our minds to the emotions we felt while eating them.

· ·

SERVES 6
Preparation time: 25 minutes
Cooking time: 30 minutes

1 small sugar pumpkin (about 2 pounds), peeled, seeds removed, and cut into 1-inch pieces

¼ cup extra-virgin olive oil

¼ medium white onion, finely chopped

2 tablespoons red wine vinegar

1 tablespoon honey

1 tablespoon dried oregano

¾ teaspoon kosher salt, plus more for topping

¼ teaspoon freshly ground black pepper, plus more for topping

5 ounces fresh baby spinach

2 small plum tomatoes, seeds removed, cut into 1-inch pieces

Toasted pepitas, for topping

1. Heat the oven to 425°F.

2. Place the pumpkin pieces in a large bowl. In a small bowl, whisk together the oil, onion, vinegar, honey, oregano, salt, and pepper until fully combined. Pour about half of the oil and vinegar mixture over the pumpkin and toss well to coat. Spread the pumpkin in a single layer on a large baking sheet and roast, stirring once, until golden and tender, about 30 minutes. Remove from the oven and let cool.

3. Combine the cooked pumpkin, spinach, and tomatoes in a large serving bowl. Drizzle with the remaining oil and vinegar mixture, and sprinkle with a little more salt and pepper, then toss to combine. Serve immediately, topped with toasted pepitas.

Cilantro and Mint Salad

Ilan and Margaret are enthusiasts of cilantro and the other herbs featured in this salad: parsley and mint. This bright salad makes good use of summer harvests, honoring sweet greens and delicate fruit flavors as a perfect complement to almost any meal. In Jewish Mexican households, this salad frequently shows up as part of Shavuot celebrations, a delightful counterpart to dairy-centered meals. To win over the kids at your table, consider retelling *Super Cilantro Girl*, Juan Felipe Herrera's story for young readers about borders, immigration status, and the power of cilantro.

....

SERVES 4
Preparation time: 10 minutes

2 tablespoons extra-virgin olive oil

1 tablespoon fresh lemon juice

¼ teaspoon kosher salt, plus more
   as needed

2 loosely packed cups fresh cilantro
   (from 1–2 small bunches)

2 loosely packed cups fresh mint
   (from 1–2 small bunches)

2 cups roughly chopped fresh spinach

1 loosely packed cup fresh parsley
   (from 1 small bunch)

1 cup roughly chopped arugula

Fresh pomegranate seeds for topping,
   optional

1. Whisk together the oil, lemon juice, and salt in a large serving bowl. Taste and add more salt, if desired.

2. Add the cilantro, mint, spinach, parsley, and arugula and toss to combine and coat with the dressing. Sprinkle with pomegranate seeds, if desired.

Myriam's Tarator

Born in Mexico City to Bulgarian parents León Moscona Benayora and Lydia Yosifova, Myriam Moscona is one of the premier writers of Sephardic narrative, perhaps most celebrated for her books *Tela de sevoya* (Onion-cloth) and *León de lidia* (Fighting lion), as well as her poetry collection *Ansina*, written entirely in Ladino. Her evocative work brings the Sephardic tradition into the Mexican soil. In her autobiography *Tela de sevoya*, she reflects on the colonial Spanish used by crypto-Jews, which underwent a rapid transformation as immigrant waves from the Ottoman Empire and eastern Europe began to arrive. Myriam shares her family's adaptation of this Bulgarian soup, a refreshing cucumber yogurt soup best enjoyed in hot weather. Other versions of tarator are found in Lebanon, where it is served with a tahini-based sauce.

SERVES 6–8
Preparation time: 15 minutes,
  plus chilling

32 ounces plain yogurt

2 large cucumbers, peeled, seeds removed, and cut into ½-inch pieces

1 tablespoon apple cider vinegar

2 small garlic cloves, minced, grated, or pushed through a press

1½ teaspoons kosher salt, plus more as needed

1 teaspoon granulated sugar

Cold water, as needed

Chopped fresh dill, for garnish

1. In a large bowl, stir together the yogurt, cucumbers, vinegar, garlic, salt, and sugar until well combined. Cover and refrigerate for at least 1 hour or up to 1 day before serving.

2. After chilling, if a thinner sauce is desired, stir in cold water 1 tablespoon at a time, until the desired consistency is reached. Serve chilled, generously garnished with chopped dill.

Bread and Tortillas

NO MEAL IS EVER COMPLETE without bread and tortillas. La Comunidad knows this well. A popular saying goes, "Ni mesa sin pan, ni ejército sin capitán" (neither table without bread nor army without captain).

The possibilities are endless. Regardless of the time of day, you will find challah, tortillas of all kinds (corn, wheat, flour), pita, lavash, bolillos and teleras (two kinds of Mexican variations of French baguette), sourdough bread, eight-grain bread, and pan de elote (corn bread), to name but a few.

Tortillas, of course, are the captain. These thin and round flatbreads have a rich history, with roots in the Aztec past. In Nahuatl, a tortilla is called t*laxcalli*, which the Spanish language modified in the colonial period.

There are all types of tortillas: large and small, white and blue, made of corn and flour as well as cactus corn. No matter where you find yourself in Mexico—and, in fact, Mesoamérica—tortillas are a trusted culinary friend. Throughout the Americas, the production of corn tortillas relies on the ancient nixtamalization process of lime-cooking mature corn kernels ahead of preparing masa. There are several varieties of store-bought masa harinas, ranging from heirloom flours in a variety of colors to the readily available Maseca brand. The industrial-scale nixtamalization process is still in its first century; Maseca, for example, started its distribution in Mexico in 1949.

Mexican Jews eat tortillas for breakfast, lunch, and dinner. Eggs, for instance, always come with tortillas, either fried or as a breadlike companion. They are served warm, covered by a tea towel in order to retain their moisture. Totopos—what Americans call "nachos"—are fried, hard tortilla triangles. They are served with guacamole or used to make chilaquiles and tortilla soup. Mexican Jews prefer to fry them themselves rather than buying commercial brands, which taste less authentic. A good, hot tortilla can make or break a Jewish Mexican meal.

Masa is used for other types of Mexican bread, most famously quesadillas, huaraches, sopes, and tlacoyos. Quesadillas are tortillas folded in half-moon shapes with melted cheese. Also served with meat, huitlacoche, and other ingredients, they might be eaten anytime.

Huaraches (the Nahuatl word means "sandals") are oblong shaped. They are usually thicker than a tortilla. They are lightly fried on the comal, then smashed with refried beans, on top of which you might add shredded lettuce, chopped tomato and onion, carne molida (ground meat), and a colorful salsa. Tlacoyos, also of Aztec origin, are smaller than huaraches, while the circular sopes are thicker.

Matzah, which is unleavened bread, takes over in the weeks leading to and during Passover as observant families rid their homes of all chametz—foods with leavening agents, most frequently the five grains (wheat, oats, barley, spelt, and rye). One of the four questions of the Seder asks specifically about why we eat matzah, *haláila hazé kuló matzá*. This annual question and storytelling prompt active reflection on ties among food, rituals, and stories. Even with these dietary shifts, Mexican Jews innovate their menu, preparing matzah brei with salsa and other sumptuous dishes. Matzah is a sweet delicacy. It is eaten with cajeta and fig or peach marmalade. •

Sopa de Tortilla

This dish is thought to represent the fusion of Spanish and Aztec cultures during the colonization of the Americas. The soup traditionally consists of chicken broth, tomatoes, chiles, and onions and is topped with fried tortilla strips, avocado, and queso fresco or Cotija cheese. Given the dish's popularity throughout the Americas, many delicious varieties have emerged, including adding black beans and corn for a southwestern tortilla soup or substituting vegetable broth to make the dish vegetarian. Our Mexican Jewish variety includes meat and omits cheese as a kosher-style adaptation of this popular dish.

SERVES 6
Preparation time:
25 minutes

1 dried pasilla chile

1 (14.5-ounce) can diced fire-roasted tomatoes

2 tablespoons extra-virgin olive oil

1 small white onion, diced

1 cup roughly chopped fresh cilantro, divided

3 medium garlic cloves, peeled and minced

6 cups chicken broth

1 (14.5-ounce) can black beans, drained

2 whole skinless chicken breasts

¾ tablespoon ground cumin

2 whole fresh epazote leaves, or 1 teaspoon dried oregano

½ teaspoon kosher salt

Large tortillas, freshly fried and cut into thin strips, or 10-ounce bag of tortilla chips, for topping

1–2 medium avocados, peeled, pitted, and diced, for topping

2 limes, quartered, for topping

1. Crumble the pasilla chile and place it in a blender with the canned tomatoes. Pulse until smooth.

2. Heat the oil in a large pot set over medium-high heat. Add the onion, ⅓ cup of the cilantro, and the garlic. Sauté until the onion is translucent, about 3 minutes.

3. Add the tomato-chile purée, chicken broth, beans, chicken breasts, cumin, epazote, and salt and stir gently. Bring to a boil, reduce the heat to medium, and cook for 15 minutes.

4. Remove the cooked chicken breasts with tongs and shred the meat with a fork. Return the shredded chicken to the soup, and stir in 1 cup of the tortilla strips.

5. Ladle the soup into bowls and top with the remaining cilantro, fresh avocado, lime juice, and more tortilla chips.

Pati's Mushroom Jalapeño Matzah Ball Soup

James Beard Award–winning chef Pati Jinich is a superstar of the food world, a celebrated Jewish Mexican American chef and writer known for her cookbooks *Pati's Mexican Table*, *Mexican Today*, and *Treasure of the Mexican Table*. Jinich also hosts the enormously successful PBS show *Pati's Mexican Table*, which is as much about culture and community as it is about cooking. Jinich is the resident chef at the Mexican Cultural Institute in Washington, DC, where she resides with her husband and children. In her PBS series *La Frontera*, Pati talks about sights, sounds, and flavor on both sides of the US-Mexico border.

The Jewish Book Council hosted a conversation between Ilan and Pati in 2020 on "pastrami tacos and other Latin American Jewish foods," and research for *Sabor Judío* turned into an extended family reunion when Margaret learned that she and Pati are part of the same family tree, connected through the Drijanski line, where a stunning tradition of food love and expertise is shared among generations.

Pati shared with us her Jewish Mexican matzah ball soup, a recipe she cooks for loved ones throughout the calendar year.

· ·

SERVES 6–8
Preparation time: 25 minutes,
 plus resting
Cooking time: 30 minutes

FOR THE MATZAH BALLS

1 cup store-bought matzah ball mix, from 2 (5-ounce) packages

2 tablespoons finely chopped fresh parsley

¼ teaspoon freshly grated nutmeg

¾ teaspoon kosher salt, plus more for boiling

4 large eggs, lightly beaten

⅓ cup vegetable oil

1 tablespoon seltzer, optional

FOR THE SOUP

2 tablespoons vegetable oil

½ cup white onion, finely chopped

1 large garlic clove, finely chopped

2 medium jalapeño chiles, seeds removed, if desired, and finely chopped

8 ounces fresh white mushrooms, stems removed and thinly sliced

½ teaspoon kosher salt, plus more as needed

½ teaspoon freshly ground black pepper, plus more as needed

8 cups chicken broth

1. Make the matzah balls: In a large mixing bowl, combine the matzah ball mix, parsley, nutmeg, and salt. In a second bowl, lightly beat the eggs with the oil until frothy. Add the beaten egg mixture and the seltzer, if using, to the matzah ball mixture and fold together until combined. Cover the mixture and refrigerate for at least 30 minutes.

2. Meanwhile, bring a large pot of salted water to a boil over high heat, then lower the heat to medium and keep at a steady simmer. With lightly moistened hands, scoop out rounded tablespoons of the matzah ball mixture, roll into balls, and drop into the simmering water. Cover the pot and cook, undisturbed, until puffed and cooked through, 20–30 minutes.

3. Meanwhile, make the soup: Heat the oil in a large soup pot set over medium heat. Add the onion, garlic, and jalapeños and cook, stirring occasionally, until softened and lightly browned, 6–8 minutes. Add the mushrooms, salt, and pepper and cook, stirring often, until the mushrooms are tender, about 8 minutes.

4. Pour in the chicken broth, raise the heat to medium high, and bring to a bubble. Taste and add more salt and pepper, if needed. To serve, divide the matzah balls among bowls and ladle the soup over top. Serve hot.

Cream of Zucchini with Cilantro Soup

This bright green soup can be dressed up with a variety of garnishes: a swirl of crema fresca (Mexican crema) to complement the gorgeous color, fried and diced zucchini or corn tortillas for extra texture, or freshly chopped cilantro and slices of lime for additional brightness. The first ancestors of the zucchini were likely domesticated in Mexico more than 7,000 years ago, and familiar side dishes inspired by the flavors and star ingredients of this soup include Margaret's great-aunt Estela's household favorite calabacitas.

SERVES 4
Preparation time: 30 minutes

3 tablespoons unsalted butter

½ large white onion, finely chopped

4 medium zucchini (about 1½ pounds), unpeeled and sliced into ½-inch-thick circles

¼ cup roughly chopped fresh cilantro

3 cups water

1 cup whole milk

1½ teaspoons kosher salt, plus more as needed

½ teaspoon freshly ground black pepper

Vegetable oil, for frying

Small (6-inch) corn tortillas, for serving

¼ cup crema fresca, for garnish

1. Melt the butter in a medium frying pan set over medium heat. Add the onion and cook, stirring occasionally, until golden and soft, about 15 minutes, and set aside.

2. Meanwhile, add the zucchini and cilantro to a medium saucepan and pour the water over top. Raise the heat to high and bring to a boil, then cook, stirring occasionally, until the zucchini pieces are tender, about 5 minutes.

3. Remove from the heat and scrape the onion and any butter from the frying pan into the zucchini mixture. Add the milk, salt, and pepper and blend until smooth with an immersion blender. (Or transfer in batches to a standard blender, being careful not to overfill, and blend until smooth.) Taste and add more salt, if needed.

4. Heat ¼ inch of oil in a medium frying pan until shimmering (you can use the same pan you fried the onion in), and line a large plate with paper towels. Working with one tortilla at a time, fry the desired amount of tortillas, flipping once with tongs, until lightly golden, about 1 minute per batch. Transfer the fried tortillas to the plate to briefly drain.

5. Serve the soup warm, with the fried tortillas (either whole or broken into pieces) for dunking and swirled with crema. Or cover and refrigerate the soup and serve chilled.

Wish on a Star Soup

Packets of sopa de estrellitas are a staple of Mexican family kitchens and considered by some to be a cure-all—an antidote to cool weather, colds, difficult news. This dish takes inspiration from this quick comfort food and incorporates fresh ingredients for an extra-soothing and simple dish that is wildly popular with children (and adults nostalgic for their childhood!). Although star-shaped pasta is traditional, other small pasta varieties can be substituted, if desired, making the dish a close cousin to varieties of sopa de fideo (noodle soups) found throughout the region. This recipe is a favorite of Margaret's mother, Gina, and her brother Eddie, who had this soup at the ready throughout childhood and still put this dish at the top of their favorite Jewish Mexican dishes.

SERVES 4
Preparation time: 25 minutes

4 medium plum tomatoes (about 1½ pounds), roughly chopped

½ medium white onion, roughly chopped

3 cups vegetable broth

2 tablespoons extra-virgin olive oil

1 large garlic clove, finely chopped

8 ounces small, star-shaped pasta (about 1¼ cups)

¾ teaspoon kosher salt, plus more as needed

¼ teaspoon freshly ground black pepper, plus more as needed

Mexican crema and crumbled queso fresco, for topping

1. Combine the tomatoes and onion in a large blender and blend on high speed until smooth. Add the vegetable broth and blend on low speed until combined. Set aside.

2. Heat the oil in a large soup pot set over medium heat. Add the garlic and dry pasta and cook, stirring occasionally, until the garlic is fragrant and the pasta is coated with the oil and lightly toasted, 3–5 minutes.

3. Pour the tomato and broth mixture over the pasta, add the salt and pepper, then raise the heat to medium high and cook, stirring often to keep the pasta from sticking, until the pasta is softened, about 10 minutes.

4. Divide into serving bowls and serve hot, dolloped with crema and sprinkled with queso fresco to taste. The pasta continues to absorb liquid as the soup sits. When reheating, thin it out with extra broth, as desired.

Sopa de Albóndiga "Yehuda Halevi"

This recipe is in honor of the philosopher, poet, physician, and polemicist Yehuda Halevi, born in either Toledo or Tudela, in 1075 or 1086, and died, we believe, as he arrived, in 1141, in the Land of Israel during the Crusades and while Spain underwent the period sometimes referred to as La Convivencia.

The cuisine of conversos has miraculously survived in a variety of sources, including cookbooks, correspondence, references in autobiographical accounts, and even snippets of information in dictionaries such as Sebastián de Covarrubias's *Tesoro de la lengua española o castellana*. Halevi left us memorable chantable poems, *piyyutim*, which have been integrated into Jewish liturgy, as well as the apologetic book *Sefer Ha-Kuzari*, completed in 1139–40 CE, in which the king of the Khazars entertains the conversion of his people to one of the three Abrahamic religions: Judaism, Christianity, and Islam, ultimately opting for the first one. Halevi wrote poems such as this one (in Ilan's translation), which conveys the dilemma of living a diasporic life:

> My heart is in the East, and I am in the faraway West.
> How can I savor food? How might it be sweet to me?
> How might I render my vows and bonds, while
> Zion is under the might of Edom and I am in Arab bondage?
> It would be good for me to leave behind all goods from Spain
> while I behold in my eyes the precious dust of the forsaken
> > sanctuary.

This traditional soup of rice with meatballs incorporates Jewish, Arabic, and Christian influences into a comforting homecoming that can be enjoyed as a meal in itself.

. . . .

SERVES 6
Preparation time: 35 minutes
Cooking time: 35 minutes

FOR THE SOUP

2 tablespoons extra-virgin olive oil

½ medium white onion, finely chopped

1 medium jalapeño chile, seeds removed, if desired, and finely chopped

4 medium garlic cloves, peeled and finely chopped

½ teaspoon ground cumin

½ teaspoon smoked paprika

2 medium carrots, peeled, halved lengthwise, and sliced

2 small zucchini, halved lengthwise and sliced

2 small Yukon Gold potatoes, peeled and cut into 1-inch cubes

2 tablespoons finely chopped fresh parsley

1 teaspoon kosher salt, plus more as needed

½ teaspoon freshly ground black pepper

8 cups chicken broth

FOR THE MEATBALLS

⅓ cup long-grain white rice, soaked for 30 minutes and drained well

1 pound lean ground beef

¼ medium white onion, grated on the large holes of a box grater and squeezed of excess liquid

1 large egg, lightly beaten

2 medium garlic cloves, minced, grated, or pushed through a press

3 tablespoons finely chopped fresh cilantro

2 tablespoons finely chopped fresh parsley

1 teaspoon chili powder

½ teaspoon kosher salt

¼ teaspoon freshly ground black pepper

FOR SERVING

Thinly sliced avocado

Chopped fresh cilantro

Lime wedges

1. Heat the oil in a large soup pot set over medium heat. Add the onion and jalapeño and cook, stirring occasionally, until softened and lightly browned, 6–8 minutes. Add the garlic, cumin, and smoked paprika and cook, stirring, until fragrant, 1–2 minutes.

2. Add the carrots, zucchini, potatoes, parsley, salt, pepper, and chicken broth. Raise the heat to high and bring to a boil, then lower the heat to medium, partially cover the pot, and simmer until the vegetables are tender, 15–20 minutes. Remove from the heat and set aside while making the meatballs.

3. Add the soaked and drained rice to a large bowl along with the ground beef, grated and squeezed onion, egg, garlic, cilantro, parsley, chili powder, salt, and pepper. Scoop rounded tablespoons of the meat mixture, roll into balls, and place on a large plate while continuing with the remaining mixture.

4. Bring the soup back to a simmer over medium heat. Add the meatballs to the soup, lower the heat to medium low, partially cover the pot, and simmer until the meatballs are cooked through and the rice is tender, 15–20 minutes. (Do not stir for the first 5 minutes, or the meatballs will fall apart.) Taste and add more salt, if needed. (If you used a low-salt or salt-free broth, you might need to add a good bit more salt.)

5. Serve hot, ladled into bowls and topped with avocado and cilantro, with lime wedges on the side for squeezing.

Tomato Oregano Beef Kebabs

Grilling kebabs over charcoal or gas grills instantly transports us to out-door gatherings, with fragrant vegetable and meat kebabs served alongside a bounty of rice, spreads, and salsas for a casual meal to be enjoyed with friends, family, and long exhales. This kebab of La Comunidad is made with beef but relies on the Sephardic kafta (more commonly made from lamb), and the flavor intensifies as the meat marinates, at least two hours but pref-erably overnight for the most concentrated flavor. We suggest serving these kebabs with a pico de gallo, but other salsas from this book can be substi-tuted depending on time and heat preferences. A note on spices: Mexican oregano is not the same as (Mediterranean) oregano. It's easy to find in most US markets, but if you need a substitute from your pantry, marjoram, with its citrus notes, works well.

SERVES 4–6
Preparation time: 15 minutes,
   plus marinating
Cooking time: 10 minutes

⅓ cup extra-virgin olive oil

2 tablespoons fresh lemon juice

1 small white onion, peeled and
   roughly chopped

2 teaspoons dried Mexican oregano

½ cup canned tomato sauce
   (not marinara)

¼ packed cup fresh parsley

2 small garlic cloves, peeled and
   roughly chopped

½ teaspoon kosher salt, plus more
   as needed

¼ teaspoon freshly ground black
   pepper, plus more as needed

2 bay leaves

1½ pounds beef shoulder, cut into
   1½-inch pieces

Vegetable oil, for grilling

Cooked long-grain white rice,
   for serving

Pico de Gallo (page 159) or store-
   bought, for serving

1. Combine the olive oil, lemon juice, onion, oregano, tomato sauce, parsley, garlic, salt, and pepper in a blender and blend until smooth.

2. Pour the marinade into a glass container with a lid. Add the bay leaves and beef pieces and mix to fully coat the beef with marinade. Cover and refrigerate for at least 2 hours or up to overnight.

3. Heat an electric or charcoal grill to medium and brush the grates with a little oil. Thread the marinated meat onto 6 metal or wooden skewers, dividing the meat evenly among the skewers and leaving about ¼ inch of space between each piece of meat. (If using wooden skewers, soak them in water for at least 30 minutes before threading the meat to prevent burning.) Grill the meat, turning occasionally, until well charred and cooked medium-rare, about 10 minutes. Serve hot, over a bed of rice and topped with pico de gallo.

Bourekas con Queso Blanco

We think of bourekas as first cousins to empanadas. They show up for Shabbat dinner, at High Holidays, or just at a daily breakfast, lunch, or dinner. Spanish-language Sephardic writers have integrated them into their narratives. They appear in Myriam Moscona's poetry and Rosa Nissán's novels as well as in popular films such as Guita Shyfter's *Like a Bride*.

Puff pastry is a staple of Sephardic cooking. Its infinite shapes in bourekas depend on the creativity of the baker: crescents, triangles, squares, rectangles, stars. The pastries might be topped with sesame, poppy, and other seeds. Connoisseurs swear that different boureka traditions can be pinpointed, with astonishing precision, to particular regions of Spain, Italy, Turkey, Syria, Lebanon, North Africa, Greece, the Balkans, and Israel.

Mexican Jews of Sephardic descent have turned bourekas into protagonists in their dietary adventures. The use of prepared puff pastry makes this recipe relatively straightforward, but the process of filling and baking will still be rewarding, producing lightly golden bourkeas bursting with cheese and dill.

· ·

MAKES 12 PASTRIES
Preparation time: 30 minutes
Baking time: 25 minutes

FOR THE QUESO BLANCO FILLING

4 ounces crumbled feta cheese
  (about ¾ cup)

¾ cup shredded kashkaval cheese
  (or low-moisture mozzarella)

1 large egg, lightly beaten

2 tablespoons finely chopped fresh dill

⅛ teaspoon kosher salt

¼ teaspoon freshly ground black
  pepper

FOR THE PASTRY

All-purpose flour, for dusting

1 (1-pound) package frozen
  puff pastry, thawed

1 large egg, beaten

Sesame seeds, for sprinkling

1. Make the queso blanco filling: Mix the feta, kashkaval, egg, dill, salt, and pepper in a medium-size bowl and set aside.

2. Heat the oven to 350°F. Lightly dust a flat work surface with flour and lay the thawed puff pastry over top. Using a lightly floured rolling pin, roll the pastry into a 12 × 12-inch square, trimming off any ragged edges. Using a sharp knife, cut the pastry into 12 equal 3 × 3-inch squares.

3. Spoon 1 rounded tablespoon of the filling into the center of each square, then fold the squares corner to corner diagonally to make a triangle. Use the flat tines of a fork to press the edges to seal. Arrange the bourekas on the baking sheet, leaving ½ inch of space in between each pastry.

4. Brush the top of each boureka with a little egg wash (you will not use all of it), and sprinkle the tops with sesame seeds. Bake until puffed and golden brown, 20–25 minutes. Remove from the oven and transfer to wire racks to cool.

Raquel's Slow-Braised Beef Tzimmes with Panela and Pumpkin

Margaret's great-grandmother Baba Raquel left Lithuania for Mexico City as a girl; her family sent her by steamship by herself during an intense period of pogroms, anti-Jewish massacres. In the later years of Raquel's life, Margaret remembers her slipping into memories about the voyage, as well as family members living and dead, and asking for cigarettes. When compiling recipes for this collection, we relied on handwritten letters she wrote to her newly married daughters, including Margaret's grandmother, one living in Mexico, another in Brazil, and the third in the United States. Writing in Spanish and Yiddish, Raquel shared advice about marriage and new homes and family recipes. In one letter to her daughter Estela, she reminded her of when she had cooked the dishes and of the people who had taught her the original recipes, and she expressed hopes of her grandchildren enjoying the flavors.

This tzimmes recipe—a celebratory Rosh Hashanah holiday staple for its embrace of joyful sweetness—is inflected by the warmth from panela, an unrefined whole cane sugar sold in blocks or tablets. More commonly known as piloncillo in Mexico, panela has had a culinary presence throughout Latin America since the fifteenth century and can be sourced in the Latin American section of most US grocery stores. The recipe below allows for deep infusion of the panela flavor, but you can reduce the amount according to preference to bring out the pumpkin and beef flavors.

. . . .

SERVES 6
Preparation time: 20 minutes
Cooking time: 2½ hours

3 pounds boneless beef chuck, cut into 1-inch pieces

1½ teaspoons kosher salt, plus more as needed

½ teaspoon freshly ground black pepper

3 tablespoons extra-virgin olive oil, plus more as needed

2 medium white onions, finely chopped

2½ cups water

1½ cups fresh orange juice

8 ounces panela

2 cinnamon sticks

3 whole cloves

1 star anise pod

2 medium carrots, peeled and sliced into ½-inch moons (about 1 cup)

1½ pounds Mexican pumpkin or sugar pumpkin, peeled, seeds removed, and cut into 1-inch pieces (about 4 cups)

2 tablespoons all-purpose flour

1. Sprinkle the beef evenly with the salt and pepper. Heat the oil in a large Dutch oven set over medium-high heat. Working in batches, add the beef and sear, stirring occasionally, until browned all over, 6–8 minutes per batch. Transfer the browned beef to a plate while continuing with the rest, adding a little more oil if the pan starts to look dry.

2. Add the onions to the Dutch oven and cook, stirring occasionally, until golden and soft, 8–10 minutes. Stir in the water, orange juice, panela, cinnamon sticks, cloves, and star anise, raise the heat to high, and bring to a boil, breaking up the panela with a sturdy spoon. (It might not fully dissolve during this step.)

3. Add the browned beef and any juices that accumulated on the plate back to the Dutch oven. Cover, turn the heat to low, and cook for 1 hour.

4. Stir in the carrots and pumpkin, cover the Dutch oven again, and cook until the vegetables and meat are very tender, about 1 hour. Spoon the flour into a small bowl and whisk in about ¼ cup of hot liquid from the Dutch oven until the flour dissolves into a paste. Stir the paste back into the meat mixture, raise the heat to high, and cook until the liquid thickens into a stew, about 5 minutes.

5. Remove the cinnamon sticks, cloves, and star anise. Taste and add more salt, if needed. Serve hot.

Stuffed Artichoke Hearts

Jewish-style artichokes are often deep-fried and served with lemon. In many Sephardic Jewish households, artichokes are an essential component of the Passover Seder dinner, symbolizing both the pride of Roman Jewish culture and the coming of spring. Irma Appel's artichoke dishes are some of the most popular offerings requested by her clientele, and the artichoke is the favorite vegetable of the chef herself. She tells us she'll eat artichokes prepared in all possible ways: whole artichokes freshly boiled or grilled with dips, in omelets, quiches, soups, spreads, or salads.

SERVES 6
Preparation time: 20 minutes
Cooking time: 25 minutes

¾ pound lean ground beef

2 tablespoons plain bread crumbs

1 large egg

2 tablespoons finely chopped fresh parsley, plus more for serving

¾ teaspoon ground cardamom

½ teaspoon kosher salt

¼ teaspoon freshly ground black pepper

10 large frozen artichoke bottoms, defrosted

3 tablespoons extra-virgin olive oil

1 tablespoon fresh lemon juice

½ cup chicken or vegetable broth

Sliced green olives and sliced hard-boiled eggs, for serving

1. Combine the ground beef, bread crumbs, egg, parsley, cardamom, salt, and pepper in a medium-size bowl and mix with your hands to fully combine.

2. Divide the meat mixture evenly among the artichoke hearts, gently pressing and mounding the meat into each artichoke's bowl-shaped base.

3. Heat the oil in a large frying pan over medium heat. Add the stuffed artichokes to the pan, filling side up, then add the lemon juice and broth. Cover the pan and cook, gently basting the stuffed artichokes with the broth once or twice, until the artichokes are tender and the filling is cooked through, about 25 minutes.

4. Transfer the stuffed artichokes to a serving plate and top with more chopped parsley and the sliced olives and hard-boiled eggs.

Cumin Rose Kibbe

Enjoyed as a national dish across the Middle East, these richly spiced kibbe pair wonderfully with rice, and we suggest serving them with a selection of condiments to match the preferences of your table, including tahini, guacamole, and salsa roja or verde, as is customary throughout Mexico. This rose-inflected variety reminds us of a poem by Rosario Castellanos, "Charla," about the abundance of language, in which she suggests that each petal of various flowers—bougainvilleas, dahlias, geraniums, jasmine, and roses—is a syllable and that a garden is as vast and inexhaustible as language itself, much like the multilingual dinner table of Mexican Jews in Spanish, Hebrew, Yiddish, Arabic, Persian, and English.

MAKES ABOUT 40 KIBBE
Preparation time: 45 minutes
Cooking time: 40 minutes

FOR THE FILLING

2 tablespoons extra-virgin olive oil

1 large white onion, finely chopped

1 tablespoon dried rose petals

2 teaspoons cumin seeds

1 tablespoon ground sumac

1 teaspoon dried mint

½ teaspoon ground cinnamon

½ teaspoon kosher salt, plus more
   as needed

½ teaspoon freshly ground black
   pepper

1 pound lean ground beef (or a
   mixture of ground lamb
   and beef)

FOR THE DOUGH

3 cups fine bulgur

1 cup all-purpose flour

1 teaspoon ground cumin

1 teaspoon kosher salt

¼ cup vegetable oil, plus more
   for frying

½–¾ cup warm water

1. Make the filling: Heat the oil in a large frying pan set over medium heat. Add the onion and cook, stirring occasionally, until softened and lightly browned, 6–8 minutes.

2. Meanwhile, grind the rose petals and cumin seeds in a mortar and pestle or a spice grinder. Add the rose, cumin, sumac, mint, cinnamon, salt, and pepper to the onion and cook, stirring, until fragrant, 1–2 minutes. Add the beef and cook, breaking up the meat into smaller pieces as necessary, until browned and cooked through, 5–6 minutes. Set filling aside.

3. Make the dough: In a large bowl, whisk together the bulgur, flour, cumin, and salt. Stir in the oil and ½ cup warm water until the dough begins to come together. Knead the dough in the bowl with your hands, gradually incorporating up to ¼ cup more water until you have a moist dough. Pinch off rounded tablespoons of the dough, then roll and squeeze them into balls. Set the dough balls aside while continuing with the remaining dough.

4. Form the kibbe: Use your index finger to make a deep indentation into a dough ball, then use your index finger and thumb together to pinch around the indentation to make a bowl shape. Place 1 rounded teaspoon of the beef mixture into the bowl, then close the dough and roll it back into an oblong ball shape. (Moisten your hands to keep the dough from sticking.) Set filled kibbe aside while continuing with the remaining dough and filling.

5. Heat 2 inches of oil in a medium saucepan set over medium heat until it reaches 350°F on a deep-fry thermometer. Working in batches of 5–6, gently transfer the stuffed kibbe into the oil and cook, flipping once halfway through, until golden and crisp, 4–5 minutes total. Remove with a slotted spoon and transfer to a paper-towel-lined plate to drain. Serve hot.

Saucy Cheese Stuffed Eggplant

Another recipe from La Comunidad relying on homemade queso Yiddish, this cheese sauce stuffed eggplant is a comforting dish that makes excellent use of summer eggplants and tomatoes. Whereas in the Ladino song "Si savesh la buena djente" the tomato and eggplant engage in a battle for supremacy, here the two coexist in perfect harmony, mediated by blankets of cheese. For a variation that uses less oil, the eggplant slices can be roasted in the oven rather than fried on the stovetop.

SERVES 6
Preparation time: 30 minutes,
    plus resting
Cooking time: 1 hour

4 medium eggplants (about 4½ pounds), unpeeled and sliced into ½-inch thick rounds

2 tablespoons extra-virgin olive oil, plus more for frying

½ small white onion, finely chopped

4 medium plum tomatoes (about 1 pound), peeled and finely chopped

1 (28-ounce) can puréed tomatoes

1¼ teaspoons kosher salt, divided, plus more as needed

½ teaspoon freshly ground black pepper, divided

1 cup Queso Yiddish (page 21)

½ cup finely chopped Oaxaca cheese

1 medium garlic clove, minced, grated, or pushed through a press

1 tablespoon finely chopped fresh basil

1 teaspoon dried oregano

¼ teaspoon ground nutmeg

½ cup grated Parmesan cheese

1. Lay the eggplant slices in a single layer across 2 paper-towel-lined baking sheets. Sprinkle with a little salt and let sit for 30–60 minutes to sweat out some moisture, then blot dry with more paper towels.

2. Meanwhile, make the tomato sauce: Heat 2 tablespoons of oil in a large frying pan set over medium heat. Add the onion and cook, stirring occasionally, until softened and lightly browned, 6–8 minutes. Add the fresh tomatoes and cook, stirring occasionally, until softened, 3–5 minutes. Stir in the puréed tomatoes, ¾ teaspoon salt, and ¼ teaspoon pepper. Bring the mixture to a simmer, then lower the heat to medium low and cook, stirring often, until slightly thickened, 8–10 minutes. Taste and add more salt, if needed. Set aside.

3. Heat approximately ¼ inch of oil in a second large frying pan. Working in batches, fry the eggplant slices, flipping once halfway through, until softened and lightly browned on both sides, 6–8 minutes per batch. Add more oil to the pan when it starts to look dry. Set the browned eggplant rounds on a large plate while continuing to fry the rest.

4. Heat the oven to 350°F and lightly grease a 9 × 13-inch baking dish. In a large bowl, mix together the queso Yiddish, Oaxaca cheese, garlic, basil, oregano, nutmeg, ½ teaspoon salt, and ¼ teaspoon pepper.

5. Spoon a rounded teaspoon of the filling along one side of a fried eggplant slice and roll up the eggplant around the filling like a taquito. (It is okay if the eggplant breaks a bit while rolling.) Set the filled eggplant into the baking dish, seam-side down, and continue with the remaining eggplant and filling until the bottom of the dish is covered. Pour the tomato sauce over top, and sprinkle evenly with the Parmesan. Sprinkle with salt and pepper to taste.

6. Bake until bubbly and the cheese on the top is melted and slightly browned, about 20 minutes. Remove from the oven and let cool slightly before serving.

Brisket Tacos in Three-Chile Salsa with Phyllis's Rhubarb

This recipe fuses dishes prepared by two matriarchs in Ilan's and Margaret's families, Anat Nurko and Phyllis Poplawski. Anat prepares the three-chile marinade as learned from other women in her family, while Phyllis shares the rhubarb sauce joyfully passed down the generations and enjoyed as an accompaniment to all the varieties of brisket she prepares. Both women describe the kitchen as a place that brings them peace and connects them to earlier generations while emphasizing the joy they have in sharing and watching their children and grandchild prepare these dishes for their own families. When Margaret celebrated her first High Holidays away from home during college, Phyllis, her grandmother, shipped her rhubarb and brisket in the mail.

Brisket became popular in Jewish cultures due to its affordability and is now a staple dish of most holiday meals. When preparing this recipe, consider wrapping the brisket and salsa in foil to simplify the cleaning process and enrich the flavor profile, as Margaret's grandmother Phyllis recommends. The combination of tart rhubarb topping savory brisket is extraordinary, and the rhubarb sauce can be used as a complement to other preparations of brisket for festive meals.

. . . .

SERVES 8–10
Preparation time: 45 minutes,
    plus marinating
Cooking time: 4 hours

FOR THE BRISKET

3 cups water, plus more for covering
    the chiles

3 dried pasilla chiles

3 dried ancho chilcs

3 dried guajillo chiles

4 medium plum tomatoes (about
    1 pound), cored, seeds removed,
    and roughly chopped

½ medium white onion, peeled
    and roughly chopped

2 medium garlic cloves, peeled and
    roughly chopped

2½ teaspoons kosher salt, plus more
    as needed

1 brisket (4–5 pounds)

FOR THE RHUBARB SAUCE

2 large rhubarb stalks, cut into ½-inch
    pieces (about 2 cups)

⅓ cup granulated sugar

¼ cup water

FOR SERVING

Small (6-inch) corn tortillas, warmed

Chopped fresh cilantro

1. Place the pasilla, ancho, and guajillo chiles in a medium saucepan and cover with water by a couple of inches. (The chiles will float to the top.) Set the saucepan over high heat, bring to a boil, and continue boiling until the chiles are soft, about 15 minutes. Drain and let cool to the touch.

2. Wearing gloves, open each chile and remove the veins and seeds. Place the chile flesh and skin in a blender along with the tomatoes, onion, garlic, salt, and the 3 cups of water. Blend until smooth, then taste and add more salt, if needed.

3. Place the brisket in a large baking dish or roasting pan, cover with the chile salsa, then cover tightly with aluminum foil. Refrigerate for at least 2 hours or up to overnight.

4. Heat the oven to 325°F. Place the brisket in the oven and cook for 2 hours. Remove the baking dish, carefully flip the brisket over, and continue cooking until fork tender, about 2 hours. Remove from the oven and let rest for at least 30 minutes before slicing or shredding.

5. Meanwhile, make the rhubarb sauce: Combine the rhubarb, sugar, and water in a small saucepan set over medium heat. Bring to a boil, stirring often, and cook until the liquid thickens and the rhubarb is tender, 5–10 minutes. Remove from the heat and let cool slightly, then use an immersion blender to purée until smooth. Allow the sauce to cool completely.

6. To serve: Arrange the brisket in corn tortillas and top each taco with a little of the rhubarb sauce and chopped cilantro.

Feelin' Taco

~~~~~~

"AND ON THE EIGHTH DAY, exhausted and in a spell of hunger, God created tacos de brisket." This is a common joke in La Comunidad.

Among Mexican Jews in the United States, hilarious taco puns abound. For instance, "Kosher tacos have Jewish fillings." Or "And Moses pronounced the eleventh commandment: You shall feed your family with tacos."

Essentially a working-class dish because of its adaptability and affordability, the taco has become ubiquitous to every segment of society. It is believed that the taco arrived in the United States in 1905. It spread its influence during the Mexican Revolution and, most emphatically, through the Bracero Program, starting in 1942, as Mexico and the United States signed the Mexican Farm Labor Agreement, allowing waves of Mexicans to help the labor force north of the Rio Grande while millions of Americans were recruited in the army to fight during the Second World War.

Just as there is no Mexico without tacos, so there is no Jewish Mexican diet without a devout taco. There are tacos with brisket, tacos with pescado a la veracruzana, zucchini tacos, tacos of beans and mushrooms, chicken tacos with mango chutney, beet tacos, and kebab tacos with cherry, known as kebab garaz among Syrian Jews. Or the Chelmelquitengo Lamb Tacos with Raisins and Pomegranate (page 132).

Toppings are crucial: cilantro, parsley, chopped onion, all kinds of salsa, and maybe grilled pineapple or mango in slices.

A fine taco displays not only the personality of its maker but that of its eater. The best tacos are jazzy: creative, fusion driven, alternating traditions, improvisational, and—always!—full of filling. Or should we say "feeling"?

What makes a fine taco is the quality of the tortilla: its flavor, texture, and size. Ingredients should almost spill over but not quite. The joy is to bite into a taco and have the sensation that flavors compete with, but never overwhelm, one another.

You can eat one taco, two, three . . . Among Mexican Jews, there are tournaments to see who can create the most delicious tacos—and who can eat the most.

The trophy comes in the form of a taco-looking Torah.

Whenever someone is hungry, you hear the expression "Siento un taco," roughly translated as "feelin' taco," as if the speaker magically saw a taco floating around, ready to be devoured. The expression showcases the degree to which Mexican Jews see tacos as their lifelong companions no matter what: in happiness and pain, no matter what adversity life might throw at you.

In fact, the joke goes among members of La Comunidad that, when tacos were created, the Almighty bestowed a vow: "Behold, thou, the taco, art consecrated unto me according to the law of Moses and of Israel, Amen." •

Enchiladas de Pollo con Mole "Frida Kahlo"

Mole—considered by some the national dish of Mexico—appears in several recipes across our collection, and while many rely on ready-to-serve mole, this one starts at the beginning for a more elaborate preparation that is worth the reward. This particular variety is a Oaxacan-style mole negro, with inspiration taken from artist Frida Kahlo. An icon of the art world, Kahlo was of mixed Indigenous and Spanish descent on her mother's side while her father came from Germany—sometimes referred to as Lutheran, other times Jewish. But the Jewishness of Frida Kahlo wasn't why she was a central figure in Margaret's childhood home. it was the collision between her innovation and physical suffering that positioned her as a guide to both Margaret's mom, a type 1 diabetic, and Margaret, who had back surgery for scoliosis as a child. To a soundtrack by the Doors, posters of Frida's self-portraits hung in their Los Angeles home—*Me and My Parrots*, *Self-Portrait as a Tehuana*—with tiny *alebrijes* (small, brightly colored folk art carvings of surreal animals) scattered around the house doubling down on the Oaxacan magic.

Many of the dishes served at Frida Kahlo's family home, the Casa Azul, were published in *Frida's Fiestas*, by Frida's stepdaughter, Guadalupe Rivera. The recipe here is not original to the collection but takes inspiration from the original's slow cooking and attention to spice. You will end up with more mole than needed for the enchiladas; we suggest drizzling leftovers on pierogi, latkes, or other savory foods.

. . . .

SERVES 6
Preparation time: 2 hours
Baking time: 10 minutes

FOR THE FILLING

1½ pounds boneless, skinless chicken thighs

1 small white onion, halved

1 celery stalk, halved

2 teaspoons kosher salt

FOR THE MOLE

4 dried ancho chiles, stemmed and seeds removed

4 dried pasilla chiles, stemmed and seeds removed

4 dried chilhuacle negro chiles, stemmed and seeds removed

5 tablespoons vegetable oil, divided

½ medium white onion

2 large tomatoes, seeds removed, finely chopped

3 medium garlic cloves, peeled

1 medium ripe plantain, peeled and sliced

1 (1-inch) slice stale challah, torn into large pieces and toasted

¼ cup sliced almonds

2 cinnamon sticks

3 whole cloves

1 tablespoon golden raisins

2 tablespoons pumpkin seeds

1 teaspoon sesame seeds

1 teaspoon dried oregano

½ teaspoon cumin seeds

½ teaspoon ground allspice

4 ounces Oaxacan dark chocolate, broken into pieces

3 tablespoons granulated sugar

2½ teaspoons kosher salt, plus more as needed

FOR ASSEMBLY

¼ cup vegetable oil

14 (6-inch) corn tortillas

Roughly chopped fresh cilantro and toasted sesame seeds, for topping

1. Make the filling: Place the chicken thighs, onion, celery, and salt in a stock pot and cover with 5 cups of water. Bring the mixture to a boil over high heat, then lower the heat to medium low and simmer until the chicken is tender, about 30 minutes.

2. Transfer the chicken to a cutting board, let cool, shred, and set aside. Strain the broth and set aside, discarding the vegetables.

3. Make the mole: Working in batches as necessary, place the ancho, pasilla, and chilhuacle negro chiles in a large, dry frying pan over medium heat and toast, turning once, until fragrant, about 1 minute per side. Transfer the toasted chiles to a bowl and cover with boiling water. Let soak for 20 minutes, then drain, reserving the soaking liquid.

4. Heat 2 tablespoons of oil in the same frying pan set over medium heat. Add the onion and cook, stirring occasionally, until softened, 6–8 minutes. Add the tomatoes and garlic and cook, stirring often, until softened, 5–7 minutes. Transfer the mixture to a blender along with ½ cup of the reserved chicken broth and blend until smooth. Transfer to a bowl and set aside.

5. Heat 1 tablespoon of oil in the frying pan. Add the plantain and cook, stirring occasionally, until golden, about 5 minutes. Transfer half of the cooked plantain to the blender, reserving the rest for garnish. Add the toasted challah to the blender.

6. Heat 1 tablespoon of oil in the frying pan. Add the almonds, cinnamon sticks, cloves, raisins, pumpkin seeds, sesame seeds, oregano, cumin, and allspice to the frying pan and toast, stirring often, until fragrant, 2–3 minutes. Add the spice mixture to the blender along with 3 cups of the reserved chicken broth and blend until very smooth. Transfer to a bowl and set aside.

7. Add the soaked and drained chiles, along with 1½ cups of the soaking liquid, to the blender and blend until smooth. Heat the remaining tablespoon of oil in a large Dutch oven. Add the blended chiles and cook, stirring often, until the mixture thickens, 5–10 minutes. Add the tomato mixture and cook, stirring often, until thickened, 8–10 minutes. Add the plantain mixture and simmer, stirring often, until thickened, 8–10 minutes.

8. Stir in the chocolate, sugar, and salt and cook until the mole is very thick, making large, slow bubbles, about 15 minutes. Taste and add more salt, if needed.

9. Heat the oil in a small skillet set over medium heat. Submerge each tortilla in the oil just long enough to soften, 10–20 seconds each, then transfer to paper towels to drain.

10. Heat the oven to 400°F. Spread about 1 cup of the mole in a 9 × 13-inch baking dish. Dip a tortilla in mole, fill with ¼ cup of the chicken mixture, roll up tightly, and place seam-side down in the baking dish. Repeat with the remaining tortillas and filling. Pour a generous amount of the remaining mole over top, reserving the rest for another use. Bake until the filling is warmed through, about 10 minutes.

11. Remove from the oven and serve hot, topped with cilantro, sesame seeds, and the remaining plantain.

Pescado a la Veracruzana

Surrounded by water from the Sea of Cortez, the Pacific, and the Gulf of Mexico to its Caribbean shores, Mexico has an enviable variety of fish. The selection ranges from abulón to bacalao, huachinango to mojarra. Perhaps unsurprisingly, each region in Mexico famously prepares its favorite fish types in unique, often competing ways. At the same time, it is sometimes said that the best fish one can get in Mexico comes from the coast of Veracruz. In Mexico City, before supermarkets made fish available citywide, fresh fish was often purchased from the Mercado La Merced. A generation later, from the marketplace of Coyoacán. But no matter where you procure the fish for this recipe, the flavor of Pescado a la Veracruzana, with garlic, onions, capers, olives, and chiles, will magically transport you to the moment of arrival of immigrants to the port of Veracruz, where many of Ilan's and Margaret's ancestors first set foot in Mexico in the 1920s.

SERVES 12
Preparation time: 20 minutes
Cooking time: 30 minutes

8–10 medium tomatoes, roughly chopped

6 medium garlic cloves, peeled

1 teaspoon oregano

2 medium white onions, thinly sliced, divided

½ teaspoon kosher salt

1 cup water

2–3 tablespoons canola oil

2 cups green olives

2 tablespoons capers

1 cup banana peppers (chiles güeros), seeds removed, chopped

2 pounds halibut or other white fish fillets

1. Make the Salsa Veracruzana: Combine the tomatoes, garlic, oregano, salt, ¼ of the onions, and 1 cup of water in a blender and process until smooth.

2. Heat the oil in a medium-size sauté pan set over medium heat. Sauté the remaining onions over medium heat until soft but not brown, 6–8 minutes, then turn the heat down to medium low.

3. Add the blended tomato mixture to the pan. Gently add the olives, capers, and banana pepper and bring to a simmer.

4. Turn the heat to low and add the fish, one fillet at a time.

5. Cover and let simmer for about 20 minutes, until the fish is just cooked through. Plate the fish with salsa drizzled over top.

Citrus Parsley Sea Bass

Before her catering business took off, Irma Appel ran a restaurant, La Condesa del Mar, devoted exclusively to seafood, starting in the late 1990s. It wasn't a Jewish restaurant per se, but there were Jewish dishes, including matzah ball soup and chopped liver. Every morning she would wake up early to buy fish and produce at the enormous market Central de Abastos.

This recipe was prepared at the restaurant and first created by Silvia Weil, a Sephardic Jew and dear friend to Irma. As Silvia explained, the dish thrives from the freshness of the fish and the intensity of the parsley and citrus, and she cautions not to skimp on time for marination. Irma reminds us that the magic of cooking depends on the loving relationship one establishes with each and every ingredient. One of Irma's frequent sayings is that if you want people to visit you, offer them food. But that isn't enough; you must channel your affections through the meal you create.

SERVES 4–6

Preparation time: 15 minutes, plus marinating

Cooking time: 15 minutes

¼ cup extra-virgin olive oil

¼ cup vegetable oil

¼ cup fresh lemon juice

1 cup fresh orange juice

1 lightly packed cup roughly chopped parsley

½ small white onion, roughly chopped

4 small garlic cloves, peeled and roughly chopped

1 teaspoon ground marjoram

1 teaspoon kosher salt

½ teaspoon freshly ground black pepper

2 pounds sea bass fillets, bones removed

1. Combine the olive oil, vegetable oil, lemon juice, orange juice, parsley, onion, garlic, marjoram, salt, and pepper in a blender and purée until smooth.

2. Arrange the fish in a large glass baking dish and pour the marinade over top. Cover the baking dish and refrigerate for at least 1 hour (or up to overnight).

3. Heat the oven to 350°F. Transfer the fish to the oven and cook, uncovered, until cooked through and the fish flakes easily with a fork, about 15 minutes. Serve hot.

Flounder Paella with Mango

Rice appears in multiple types of Mexican Jewish cuisine, at times next to beans, at others in paellas, and often as an accompaniment to *platillos principales*. Paella is a rice-based dish that emigrated from the Iberian Peninsula to Mexico. It is believed to originate in Valencia. The Muslim population of Spain cooked paella from the tenth century onward, so by the time of the expulsion of the Jews in 1492, it was a fixture of the national cuisine.

A good paella requires its own paella pan. This two-handled pan is called a *paellera*, which is how the dish got its name. Although there are ways to prepare a quick paella, in general the dish requires time and dedication. Ingredients are incorporated sequentially, ensuring that flavors deepen in the process. The recipe presented here is relatively fast to make.

Mexican Jews have embraced many types of paella for different occasions. The dish is a combination of fish and fruit that stresses the encounter between the cultures of Spain and the Americas. This recipe is inspired by a version Ilan savored with playwright, director, and novelist Hugo Hiriart, in conversation about his film about Mexican Jewish life, *Novia que te vea*.

SERVES 6–8
Preparation time: 20 minutes
Cooking time: 1 hour

5 tablespoons extra-virgin olive oil, divided, plus more for serving

2 medium sweet onions, finely chopped

2 large garlic cloves, peeled and finely chopped

2½ cups short-grain white rice (such as bomba or arborio)

3 medium plum tomatoes (about 1 pound), stems removed and cut into ½-inch pieces

2 teaspoons saffron threads, crushed

2 teaspoons smoked paprika

Kosher salt and freshly ground black pepper

8 cups fish broth, vegetable broth, or water

1½ pounds flounder fillets, skin removed and cut into approximately 2-inch pieces

Sliced Manila mangos, for serving

Lime wedges, for serving

1. Heat 3 tablespoons of the oil in a paella pan or other large (at least 12-inch), deep-sided frying pan over medium heat. Add the onions and cook, stirring occasionally, until softened and golden, 8–10 minutes. Add the garlic and cook, stirring, until fragrant, about 1 minute.

2. Stir in the rice and let cook until lightly toasted, about 2 minutes. Then add the tomatoes, saffron, smoked paprika, 1¼ teaspoons salt, and broth. (If the liquid doesn't all fit at once, add it in stages.) Raise the heat to medium high and bring the mixture to a bubble, then lower the heat to medium and let cook, without covering or stirring, until the rice has almost completely absorbed the liquid, 35–40 minutes.

3. Meanwhile, heat the remaining 2 tablespoons of oil in a large grill pan or frying pan over medium heat. Season the flounder pieces with salt and pepper and cook, turning once, until browned on both sides, about 6 minutes total. Nestle the fish into the pan with the rice to finish cooking through.

4. Serve the paella from the pan, drizzled with a little more olive oil, topped with sliced mangos, and with lime wedges on the side for squeezing.

Spinach Herb Empanadas

The history of empanadas can be traced to early Muslim civilizations in the sixteenth century, and these stuffed pockets of dough have since become a popular dish throughout Europe and Latin America. Although empanadas are linked in the popular imagination to Latin American countries such as Argentina, Venezuela, and El Salvador, Mexico offers a superb cornucopia of possibilities. Jewish Mexican households have adapted them for various occasions, from a casual dish served on a weekday to Shabbat breakfast.

This recipe for Spinach Herb Empanadas is a favorite of Tammy Buchwald's family in Guadalajara, though it is a close contender with the many other varieties they typically prepare, including potato leek, roast poblano chiles with corn (rajas con elote), and assorted mushrooms.

. . . .

SERVES 8
Preparation time: 30 minutes,
    plus chilling
Baking time: 12–14 minutes

FOR THE EMPANADA DOUGH

3 cups all-purpose flour

¾ cup (1½ sticks) unsalted butter

¼ teaspoon kosher salt, plus more
    as needed

1 large egg

¼–½ cup water

FOR THE SPINACH AND HERB FILLING

3 tablespoons extra-virgin olive oil

1 medium yellow onion, peeled and
    finely chopped

2 leeks, white parts only, finely chopped

1 small garlic clove, peeled and finely
    chopped

2 pounds fresh spinach, boiled, drained,
    and finely chopped

¼ cup finely chopped fresh parsley

1 tablespoon finely chopped fresh dill

2 large eggs, beaten

Kosher salt and freshly ground black
    pepper

1. Make the dough: Combine the flour and salt in a food processor or mixing bowl and mix well. Add the butter in small pieces to the food processor and continue to mix. Add the egg and mix briefly. Slowly add the water while mixing the dough. Continue adding water until the dough is clumpy and flaky. Wrap the dough in plastic wrap and refrigerate for at least 1 hour.

2. Make the filling: Heat the oil in a pan over medium-high heat and sauté the onion until soft and transparent, 5–7 minutes. Reduce the heat and add the leeks and garlic, stirring constantly until the leeks are soft. Remove from the heat, pour the contents of the pan into a mixing bowl, and add the remaining ingredients.

3. To assemble: Heat the oven to 375°F. On a flat surface roll out the dough until it is ¼ inch thick. Cut out 4-inch rounds, add about 2 tablespoons of filling to each, and then fold in half. Use a fork to press and seal edges.

4. To bake: Arrange the empanadas on a baking sheet, brush with oil, and bake until golden, 12–14 minutes.

Pollo Luis de Santángel

Luis de Santángel (d. 1498) was a prominent converso in Renaissance Spain who was instrumental in convincing Queen Isabella the Catholic to fund Christopher Columbus's voyage. The voyage was the result of a juncture of decisive circumstances. The Jews of Spain were expelled in 1492, the same year in which La Reconquista took place, allowing Catholic Spain to establish itself as a nation around a single religion. And that was the year when Antonio de Nebrija, another converso, who taught at the University of Salamanca, published his *Gramática de la lengua española*, an effort to make Spanish the language of the newly created nation.

The life of Santángel has often been the stuff of fiction. He amassed considerable amounts of money. Silently, he might have persuaded the queen to support Columbus in an effort to find an alternative to the Jews escaping Spain. Eventually, after his four voyages, Columbus was granted the island of Jamaica, where a number of crypto-Jews are known to have settled. In that sense, he is a messianic figure. One of Santángel's relatives was burned at the stake. However, because of his relationship with King Ferdinand, he and his family were spared from persecution. There is a bust of Santángel in the Alameda of Valencia.

Little of the diet of Luis de Santángel is known. However, the chicken dish below is named in honor of him, as a sign of gratitude for his effort to open new doors in the Jewish diaspora. Why chicken in particular isn't known either. Fowl was a fixture of European food, but not necessarily of Jewish cuisine. Quail, pheasant, and partridge are common in the Spanish diet. Chicken and hen were favored by the nobility. Ilan tried the Pollo Luis de Santángel at the home of a Lebanese Jewish family in Mexico City with whom he learned Ladino in the early 1980s. This variation is likely a fusion produced by entrepreneurial immigrants. It includes annatto, a tropical orange-red condiment derived from the achiote tree that is believed to have originated in Mexico and Brazil. The flavor is sweet, peppery, and nutty.

....

SERVES 4–6

Preparation time: 30 minutes,
  plus marinating
Cooking time: 35 minutes

⅓ cup extra-virgin olive oil

⅓ cup fresh orange juice

2 tablespoons fresh lime juice

1 small white onion, roughly chopped

4 medium garlic cloves, peeled and roughly chopped

2 tablespoons ground annatto (achiote)

1 tablespoon kosher salt

1 tablespoon ground cumin

2 teaspoons ground coriander

2 teaspoons smoked paprika

2 teaspoons dried oregano

½ teaspoon freshly ground black pepper

½ teaspoon ground chipotle chile

4 pounds bone-in chicken thighs or drumsticks, trimmed of excess skin

Vegetable oil, for greasing

1. In a large bowl, whisk together the olive oil, orange juice, lime juice, onion, garlic, annatto, salt, cumin, coriander, paprika, oregano, black pepper, and chipotle chile. Add the chicken pieces and turn to coat. Cover the bowl and refrigerate, turning the bowl once or twice, for at least 4 hours and up to overnight. Before cooking, allow the chicken to sit at room temperature for about 30 minutes.

2. Heat the oven to 400°F. Line 2 large baking sheets with aluminum foil, then brush with a little oil. Arrange the chicken pieces on the baking sheets in a single layer, removing and discarding the garlic and onion. Bake until the internal temperature reaches 165°F on a digital thermometer, 30–35 minutes. Remove from the oven and let cool slightly before serving.

3. Alternately, heat a grill to medium high and brush the grates with a little oil. Add the chicken to the grill, skin-side down, and grill, flipping once halfway through, until the internal temperature reaches 165°F on a digital thermometer, 10–15 minutes total. Remove from the grill and let cool slightly before serving.

Zabludovsky's Stuffed Poblano Chiles con Brisket y Patatas

Born in Mexico to Yiddish-speaking Polish Jewish immigrants, Jacobo Zabludovsky Kraveski was Mexico's most influential journalist during the last third of the twentieth century, the host of the news program *24 Horas*, produced by Televisa, the country's most successful network. At the time, Mexico was ruled by a single party, Partido Revolucionario Institucional, or PRI, in power uninterruptedly almost since the end of the Mexican Revolution of 1910. The PRI was known to control Zabludovsky, who every night delivered to the nation only the news that whoever was el presidente wanted people to hear. Not surprisingly, Zabludovsky was simultaneously feared and hated. By synecdoche, those feelings were associated with Mexican Jews in general. For Mexican Jews, Zabludovsky was a symbol of the ambiguity of belonging to two not-always-compatible traditions. This dish, which combines a Yiddish and a picante flavor and is loved by those who eat it, memorializes that ambiguity.

Originating from Puebla, poblano chiles have been popular in Mexican cuisine since the Aztec Empire. Stuffed poblanos, like most stuffed pepper dishes, include hollowed-out poblano chiles filled with beef, rice, beans, corn, cheese, and other vegetables after allowing the peppers to *sudar*—sweat—in the roasting process. One popular form of stuffed poblanos features the colors of the Mexican flag: poblano chiles stuffed with meat filling and topped with pomegranate seeds and Mexican crema. We suggest serving these stuffed chiles with a side of beans and warm corn tortillas.

. . . .

SERVES 4–6
Preparation time: 45 minutes
Cooking time: 45 minutes

8 poblano chiles

1½ cups shredded leftover brisket

1½ cups Yukon Gold potatoes, cooked and mashed

8 thin slices Chihuahua or Oaxaca cheese

8 medium plum tomatoes (about 2 pounds), seeds removed, roughly chopped

¼ small white onion, roughly chopped

1 medium garlic clove, roughly chopped

1 cup water

1¼ teaspoons kosher salt, plus more as needed

2 tablespoons vegetable oil

8 tablespoons Mexican crema

1. Heat a large comal or griddle over high heat. Add the poblano chiles and cook, occasionally turning with tongs, until soft and blistered all over, about 20 minutes total. Transfer the hot chiles to a large paper bag, close, and let rest until cool enough to handle, about 15 minutes. Take the chiles out of the bag and carefully peel off and discard the skins. Using a paring knife, cut a slit on one side of each chile and remove the seeds.

2. Stuff each chile with a layer of brisket and a layer of mashed potatoes, then close with toothpicks. Arrange the filled chiles in a 9 × 13-inch baking dish and top with the cheese.

3. Heat the oven to 350°F. Combine the tomatoes, onion, garlic, water, and salt in a blender and blend until smooth. Heat the oil in a medium pot set over medium heat. Pour in the tomato mixture, bring to a boil, and cook, stirring occasionally, until slightly thickened, about 10 minutes. Taste and add more salt, if needed.

4. Pour the tomato sauce into the baking dish, taking care not to pour it directly on top of the chiles. Drizzle 1 tablespoon of crema on top of each chile. Bake until the tomato sauce thickens slightly and the cheese melts, 30–45 minutes. Serve hot.

Milanesa con Patatas

Milanesa, thin steak cutlets battered and pan-fried, has been a favorite comfort meal for Jewish families in Mexico for decades. The cutlets can be of poultry, beef, or lamb. But milanesa didn't originate as a dish of either Ashkenazic or Ottoman emigrants. They found it in Latin America (Argentina is surely a place to try an array of varieties of this recipe, where it is served with eggs, tomatoes, and fruit pairings) because Italian emigrants, with their inclination for crisp and tender meat, brought it with them in the second half of the nineteenth century.

This version was ubiquitous in Ilan's childhood home. It is accompanied by halved red grapes and lemon wedges and often comes with a mixed salad. The purpose is to juxtapose the milanesa with an assortment of greens. Supposedly, the grapes are an invocation of the wineries in the Land of Israel, which Jewish immigrants supported after its creation as a state in 1948. Some people cover the milanesa with tomato sauce or with melted Swiss cheese. We also recommend it topped with freshly prepared pico de gallo.

SERVES 4
Preparation time: 20 minutes
Cooking time: 20 minutes

2 large eggs

1½ cups panko

½ teaspoon kosher salt, plus more
   for sprinkling

¼ teaspoon freshly ground black
   pepper

2 medium garlic cloves, minced, grated,
   or pushed through a press

Vegetable oil, for frying

1 pound skirt steak, cut into 4 pieces
   and pounded to ¼-inch thick

1 large russet potato, peeled and
   thinly sliced

1 teaspoon ground cumin

Halved red grapes, for serving

Lemon wedges, for squeezing

Pico de Gallo (page 159), for topping,
   optional

1. Whisk the eggs together in a shallow bowl. Spread the panko on a large plate, sprinkle with the salt, pepper, and garlic, and use your hands to combine.

2. Heat ¼ inch of oil in a large frying pan set over medium heat, and line a baking sheet with a layer of paper towels. Working in batches of 2, dredge the steak cutlets in the egg on both sides, allowing the excess to drip off, then dip into the seasoned bread crumbs, turning and pressing to coat both sides with panko.

3. Fry the steaks, turning once, until golden brown on both sides, 4–6 minutes total. Transfer the steaks to the paper towels to drain.

4. Add the sliced potato and a sprinkle of salt to the pan and fry, stirring occasionally, until softened and golden, 8–10 minutes. Add the cumin and stir until fragrant, about 1 minute. Transfer the fried potatoes to the paper towels to drain.

5. Arrange the fried potatoes and steaks on a serving platter and garnish with a pile of grapes and lemon wedges. Top with pico de gallo, if desired. Serve immediately.

Red Wine Beef Fillets with Farfel and Artichoke

Farfel is an Ashkenazi dish composed of small, pellet-shaped egg pasta, similar to the Middle Eastern dish couscous. This recipe was created by Irma Appel, fusing her love of artichokes with cooking lessons from Lebanese chef Elaine Abumbrad, who taught her more about using wine in making meat and fish sauces. While Irma has always had a playful and experimental approach to cooking, she benefited from Elaine's attention to exactness and experimentation with spices. Most of the students were, like her, *idii-shikas*, Ashkenazi women. These classes widened the spectrum of flavors and emotions for them. But the story of how this dish ended up combining farfel, beef, and artichoke was accidental. Irma didn't have any rice in her pantry, so she played with alternatives. She was surprised at how well farfel integrated with the red wine sauce. After stumbling into this juxtaposition of flavors, she laughs and remembers the role reversal of the discovery: student teaching chef.

SERVES 4–6
Preparation time: 20 minutes
Cooking time: 50 minutes

Irma Appel in her kitchen,
Mexico City, January 2023.

2 ounces marrow, scooped from about 1 pound of beef bones and soaked in cold water overnight

¾ teaspoon kosher salt, plus more as needed

Freshly ground black pepper

¼ cup plus 2 tablespoons extra-virgin olive oil, divided

4 small shallots, finely chopped

4 medium garlic cloves, 2 finely chopped and 2 minced, grated, or pushed through a press

1 sprig fresh thyme

14 ounces dried farfel

3½ cups beef broth

2 cups dry red wine

1 (14-ounce) can artichoke hearts, peeled and finely chopped, divided

4 (6-ounce) beef fillets

1. Put the marrow in a small saucepan and cover with fresh water. Sprinkle generously with salt, then place over high heat and bring to a boil. Boil for 5 minutes until opaque, then drain. If there are any larger pieces, chop them, and set the marrow aside.

2. Heat ¼ cup of the oil in a large soup pot set over medium heat. Add the shallots and cook, stirring often, until softened and lightly golden, 8–10 minutes. Add the chopped garlic and thyme and cook, stirring, until fragrant, about 1 minute. Add the farfel and cook, stirring, until golden, about 5 minutes.

3. Stir in half of the broth, raise the heat to medium high, and bring to a boil. Lower the heat to medium and add the red wine, the remaining broth, ¾ teaspoon salt, and a generous amount of pepper. Raise the heat to medium high and cook, stirring, until the farfel thickens, about 30 minutes.

4. Stir in half the marrow and half the artichoke hearts, taste and add more salt, if needed, then remove from the heat.

5. Heat the grill or a grill pan to medium high. Rub the beef fillets with the remaining 2 tablespoons of oil and the minced garlic. Grill, turning once, until seared outside and cooked medium inside, about 5 minutes per side.

6. Transfer the beef fillets to serving plates and top each with a portion of farfel and the remaining marrow and artichoke hearts to taste.

Niddo Vegetable Lasagna

Mexican Jewish chef and restaurateur Karen Drijanski shares her recipe for vegetable lasagna, a dish her family has enjoyed over Shabbat meals and one she offers seasonally at her restaurant Niddo, which began with a single location in Colonia Juárez, and currently has five locations open across Mexico City. Although the menu at Niddo is known for its Jewish-leaning menu (babkas, bagels and lox, latkes), it emphasizes vegetable-forward, soul-hugging foods: *comida que apapacha*. Karen is parent to three adult children—some living in Mexico and others in the United States—and sister to Pati Jinich, who is also featured in this book. Pati and Karen are two of the four daughters of Moises Drijanski, a Mexico City restaurateur whose father emigrated from Poland. Karen abundantly shares her spiritual approach to food as a source of deep connection, joyfully exclaiming that *Sabor Judío* has reunited family lines. Through the Drijanski family, Margaret learned she is part of the same genealogy. Karen exudes warmth, presence, and deep intentionality around eating and flavor in conversation. Although this lasagna preparation includes zucchini, Karen also rotates in asparagus and recommends choosing what is in season and incorporating that into this dish.

....

SERVES 6–8
Preparation time: 30 minutes
Cooking time: 1½ hours

½ small head cauliflower (about ½ pound), cored and cut into small florets

2 medium zucchini (about ¾ pound), ends trimmed, halved crosswise, and sliced into ½-inch planks

1 small butternut squash (about 1 pound), peeled and sliced into ½-inch-thick rounds

8 ounces fresh baby bella mushrooms, stems removed, thickly sliced

2 teaspoons dried thyme

⅓ cup plus ¼ cup extra-virgin olive oil, divided

Kosher salt and freshly ground black pepper

½ medium white onion, finely chopped

6 medium garlic cloves, peeled and chopped

1 (24½-ounce) bottle tomato purée (passata)

1 (14½-ounce) can crushed tomatoes

½ cup water

1 (9-ounce) package no-boil lasagna noodles

2 cups (8 ounces) shredded Monterey Jack cheese

1 cup (4 ounces) shredded Grana Padano or Parmesan cheese

1. Heat the oven to 400°F and line 2 large baking sheets with parchment paper. Add the cauliflower, zucchini, squash, mushrooms, and thyme to a large bowl. Drizzle with ⅓ cup of oil and season generously with salt and pepper, then mix to combine.

2. Divide the vegetables between the 2 baking sheets and roast, stirring once, until tender and golden, but not falling apart, 25–30 minutes. Remove from the heat and set aside to cool slightly.

3. Meanwhile, heat the remaining ¼ cup of oil in a medium-size saucepan set over medium heat. Add the onion and garlic and cook, stirring occasionally, until softened and golden, 6–8 minutes. Stir in 2 teaspoons of salt and ¼ teaspoon pepper, then stir in the tomato purée, crushed tomatoes, and water. Bring the mixture to a low simmer, then turn heat to medium low and cook, stirring often, until slightly thickened, 10–15 minutes. Taste and add more salt and pepper, if needed.

4. Lower the oven temperature to 350°F while assembling the lasagna. Spoon approximately one-third of the tomato sauce into the bottom of a 9 × 13-inch baking dish. Top with a layer of noodles, followed by half of the roasted vegetables and half of the Monterey Jack. Spread another one third of the sauce over the cheese, then top with another layer of noodles, the remaining roasted vegetables, and the remaining Monterey Jack.

5. Top with a final layer of noodles (you might not use the whole package), then spread the remaining third of the tomato sauce over top and sprinkle evenly with the Grana Padano. Wrap the baking dish tightly with aluminum foil and bake until bubbling, about 45 minutes. Remove the foil and continue baking until the top is browned, 10–15 minutes. Remove from the oven and allow to cool for 10–15 minutes before serving.

Bravocado

AGUACATES—from the Nahuatl word *āhua-catl*, in English "avocado"—is a domesticated Mesoamerican fruit (yes, a fruit) used by the Aztecs as garnish and even as butter. In the past century, it has acquired a protagonist role in Jewish Mexican cuisine. You find it in the omnipresent guacamole, which La Comunidad seasons with horseradish, hard-boiled egg, onion, and even garlic. Some guacamoles might include everything bagel seasoning.

"Everyone loves avocados—even anti-Semites!" a Mexican Jewish pun goes. People call them bravocados.

The fruit is said to have magical powers. But even if you don't believe in legend, its shades of green make it an appealing companion. You will also spot it on toast—called tartines—as well as in soups, salads, tacos, quesadillas, and huaraches. It might show up in the desayuno next to your eggs, in your torta de queso at una comida, and as a stand-alone ingredient, with salt and pepper, during the cena.

Calibrating whether an avocado is ripe is both an art and a science. Such is the passion for avocados that Mexican Jews know simply by looking at it when it will have a place at the table today. If when touching its peel its interior is hard, it still has a day or two to go. If on the other hand it feels too soft, it is likely overripe.

Even the avocado peel is put to use. As it dries up, it creates cloudlike shapes in the inside that some claim might help them foresee the future. Or offer an explanation as to why life is senseless. Or the pit or peel of the avocado might be used to inscribe a message in times of oppression.

The story goes that Luis de Carvajal the Younger (1566–1596), the most famous crypto-Jew to be put on trial in Mexico by the Holy Office of the Inquisition and burned at the stake in an auto-da-fé, was imprisoned, along with his mother and sister, for a number of years. The inquisitors would always bring him his meals not on a plate but in an avocado peel. Carvajal would deny the food, saying he wasn't hungry, and ask them to give it to his mother and sister, who were in nearby cells. He would carve messages to them in the inside of the peel and cover them with the food. It was the text messaging of the time.

The inquisitors caught him but pretended they didn't know. The avocado peels were disposed of, but all of Carvajal's messages survived, having been transcribed by one of the prison guards.

Holy Guacamole! •

Palacio de la Inquisición,
Mexico City, January 2023.

CENA

x x x x x x x x x x x x x x x x x x x x x x x x x x x x x x x x x x

The last meal of the day takes place relatively late, around 9:00 p.m., at a time when many people in other parts of the globe are already asleep. It isn't as sophisticated as la comida, yet it involves delicate, at times contrasting, flavors. The objective is to conclude the day satisfied without overwhelming the stomach with intense ingredients.

You might start with Tamarind Street Corn Cups. They are light and refreshing. Mexicans of all backgrounds eat these as a snack. Or you might eat an Israeli salad con queso Oaxaca—cucumber, tomato, and onion and finely chopped.

If you're feeling somber, the way to patiently satisfy your appetite is with caldo verde with corn and matzah balls, a variation of the famous matzah ball soup. La Comunidad has gently adapted it by giving this soup a spicier taste with rich mouthfeel. Another way into the cena is with leek fritters. The dish is a bit more festive and rich, with flavors you might get at a neighborhood fair.

One option for a starter that Mexican Jews love is snapper ceviche con maror. There are all kinds of ceviches in Mexican coastal cuisine, such as Veracruz, Oaxaca, and Guerrero. This version introduces an essential Passover ingredient to give it a memorable twist. Or perhaps you might prepare sopes de picadillo "Rabino Apóstata." This recipe comes from seventeenth-century conversos.

The main course of the cena might be squash blossom quesadillas, mushroom huaraches con pepitas, or pineapple black bean tlacoyos. A certain informality ties together these foods; eating with your hands is encouraged. To savor them in full, you will need one or more types of salsa and a smear of crema fresca.

People say that your *último bocado*, your last bite, will define the nature of your dreams. If you surround yourself during the cena with happy flavors, your imagination will transport you to *el jardín de las delicias*, which is what Mexican Jews call paradise. •

Baba Ganoush Jerusalén con Chile

Baba ganoush is a traditional Middle Eastern dip made from roast eggplants and tahini. The Arabic word *baba* translates to "father" and *ghanoush* translates to "spoiled" or "pampered," so the name of the dish is literally "pampered father." The folklore behind the name suggests that the dish was prepared for elderly men who relied on soft foods for nutrition. But this recipe is inspired by Margaret's aunt Cara in California, who is committed to vegan foods, regular opportunities for the extended family to gather around the dinner table, and her Israeli roots (her brother Berty Richter is the chef for the San Antonio restaurant Ladino, celebrating Jewish Balkan cuisine). While the eggplant enthusiasts might want to eat this directly from a spoon, we recommend pairing it with a variety of other dips and salads (cilantro mousse, Israeli salad, Mediterranean couscous, hummus). What we adore about this recipe is that it can be easily made ahead or doubled, if desired.

. . . .

SERVES 6
Preparation time: 15 minutes
Cooking time: 40 minutes

2 small eggplants (about 2 pounds), unpeeled and halved lengthwise

2 tablespoons extra-virgin olive oil, plus more for brushing and drizzling

1 Anaheim chile

1–2 small garlic cloves, minced, grated, or pushed through a press

2 tablespoons fresh lemon juice, plus more as needed

¼ cup well-stirred tahini

¾ teaspoon kosher salt, plus more as needed

½ teaspoon ground cumin

Roughly chopped parsley, for serving

1. Heat the oven to 425°F and line a large baking sheet with aluminum foil. Prick the eggplant skin in several spots with a fork and brush the cut sides lightly with olive oil. Place the eggplants on the prepared baking sheet, cut side down. Add the Anaheim chile to the baking sheet.

2. Roast, turning the chile once or twice, until the eggplants and chile are very tender and charred in spots, 30–40 minutes. Remove from the oven and let cool.

3. Once cool enough to handle, remove and discard the chile seeds. Scoop out the eggplant pulp, discarding the skin.

4. Add the chile and eggplant to a large bowl and mash with a fork to combine. Add 2 tablespoons of oil, garlic, lemon juice, tahini, salt, and cumin and mix well to combine. Taste and add more salt or lemon juice, if needed.

5. Transfer the mixture to a serving bowl, drizzle with a little more olive oil, and sprinkle with parsley.

CENA

Tamarind Street Corn Cups

Esquites, corn kernels mixed with mayonnaise and spice and traditionally served in small cups, is one of the most popular street foods in Mexico. This sweet and spicy adaptation features Tamalitoz, tamarind hard candies, and was created by the candy company's co-owners Jack Bessudo, of Mexican Jewish descent, and his husband, Declan Simmons, originally from the United Kingdom. The couple started making candy in Mexico City in 2015, fusing the flavors of their families: British sweets with traditional Mexican flavors. Tamalitoz candies are named after their shape—tiny tamales—in homage to the handmade quality and slight variation of each individual candy. The couple, in conversation about cultural values, home foods, and joyful pride, developed the candy concept into a brand that would appeal to US consumers. Although the original candy store in Mexico did not survive the pandemic, their Texas-based distribution reaches across the States.

. . . .

SERVES 4
Preparation time: 40 minutes

FOR THE CORN

3 tablespoons unsalted butter

½ large white onion, finely chopped

2 medium garlic cloves, peeled and finely chopped

½ serrano chile, seeds removed, if desired, and finely chopped

1¼ teaspoons kosher salt, plus more as needed

2 fresh epazote leaves (whole), or 1 teaspoon dried oregano

5 cups fresh corn kernels (from about 10 cobs of corn, or use frozen corn kernels)

2½ cups water

¼ cup mayonnaise

FOR SERVING

Crumbled Cotija cheese

Crushed chile piquín or red pepper flakes

Crushed Tamalitoz candies, tamarind flavor

Fresh lime juice

1. Melt the butter in a large frying pan set over medium heat. Add the onion and garlic and cook, stirring occasionally, until soft and translucent, about 5 minutes.

2. Add the serrano chile, salt, and epazote leaves, followed by the corn kernels and the water. (The water should barely cover the mixture.) Raise the heat to high and bring to a boil, then lower the heat to medium and cook, stirring occasionally, until the corn is tender and the liquid has almost completely evaporated, 30–35 minutes. Taste and add more salt, if needed.

3. Remove from the heat and discard the epazote. Add the mayonnaise and stir to combine.

4. Divide the corn mixture into four tall cups. Top with the Cotija cheese, chile piquín, and crushed tamarind candies, to taste. Drizzle each cup with a little lime juice just before serving.

Note: To crush the Tamalitoz candies, place them on a large cutting board and roll over them with a sturdy rolling pin.

Israeli Salad con Queso Oaxaca

Jewish communities in the Middle East began to make refreshing salads from cucumber and tomato in the nineteenth century, and by the mid-twentieth century the dish became popular across Israel and the surrounding region. Ilan first tried a variant of this recipe in the late 1970s, when he worked in Kibbutz Tel Katzir, in northern Israel, south of the Sea of Galilee. This adaptation shared with us from La Comunidad reflects adaptation with local ingredients, the queso Oaxaca imparting a distinctive texture and flavor from the more familiar feta cheese variety.

. . . .

SERVES 4
Preparation time: 15 minutes

1 small red bell pepper, seeds removed, chopped (about ½ cup)

1 small yellow bell pepper, seeds removed, chopped (about ½ cup)

1 small orange bell pepper, seeds removed, chopped (about ½ cup)

3 large plum tomatoes (about 1 pound), seeds removed, finely chopped

1 small red onion, finely chopped

5 small cucumbers, chopped

1 cup chopped fresh parsley

4 tablespoons extra-virgin olive oil

2 tablespoons fresh lemon juice

½ cup crumbled Oaxaca cheese

½ teaspoon kosher salt, plus more as needed

¼ teaspoon freshly ground black pepper, plus more as needed

1. In a large bowl, combine the diced vegetables and herbs.

2. In a smaller bowl, combine the oil, lemon juice, salt, and pepper and mix thoroughly.

3. Pour the dressing into the bowl of vegetables and toss to combine with the crumbled cheese. Refrigerate until chilled before serving.

Mediterranean Couscous with Chipotle Salsa

The Jewish Mexican fusion of flavors in this recipe is exceptional, combining the Mediterranean landscape with the unique smokiness of Mexican chiles and the refreshing bite of fresh cilantro and lime. Couscous first appears in Arabic cookbooks from the thirteenth century and is thought to have been first prepared by the Berber people of North Africa. Traditionally, Jewish communities cooked couscous with salt water and oil, and Sephardic Jews often serve the grain with root vegetables and Middle Eastern spices. It was Ottoman Jews who brought couscous, along with tabouli, to Mexico.

. . . .

SERVES 4–6
Preparation time: 30 minutes

FOR THE SALSA

- 1 (14-ounce) can diced fire-roasted tomatoes

- 2 chipotle chiles in adobo, roughly chopped

- 2 medium garlic cloves, peeled and chopped

- ½ lightly packed cup roughly chopped fresh cilantro

- 2 teaspoons fresh lime juice, plus more as needed

- ½ teaspoon kosher salt, plus more as needed

- ¼ teaspoon freshly ground black pepper, plus more as needed

FOR THE COUSCOUS

- 2 cups water

- ¾ teaspoon kosher salt

- 1 tablespoon butter or vegetable oil

- 1 (10-ounce) box couscous (1¾ cups)

- 1 large tomato, peeled, seeds removed, finely chopped

- 2 medium cucumbers, peeled, seeds removed, and finely chopped

- 3 tablespoons chopped parsley

1. Make the salsa: Mix the fire-roasted tomatoes, chipotle chiles, and garlic in a small saucepan set over medium heat. Bring to a simmer and cook, stirring occasionally, until slightly thickened, 7–10 minutes.

2. Remove from the heat, add the cilantro, lime juice, salt, and pepper, and use an immersion blender to blend the mixture into a textured salsa. Taste and add more lime juice, salt, and pepper, if desired. Transfer to a serving bowl and set aside.

3. Make the couscous: Add the water, salt, and butter to a medium saucepan and bring to a boil over medium-high heat. Remove from the heat, stir in the couscous, cover, and steam (off the heat) for 5 minutes. Gently fluff with a fork and transfer to a medium-size serving bowl along with the tomato, cucumbers, and parsley. Mix to combine.

4. Serve the couscous warm or at room temperature, with the salsa alongside for drizzling. Alternatively, stir a generous amount of the salsa into the cooked couscous mixture, serving the remainder alongside.

Caldo Verde with Corn and Matzah Balls

Matzah ball soup is a favorite cure-all, and this festive Mexican Jewish adaptation incorporates spice, savory herbs, and sweet corn. It is a dish that asks us to contemplate the boundaries between our Judaism and our Mexicanness: Where does one begin and the other end? In 2007, Margaret stumbled onto Alejandro Springall's movie *My Mexican Shivah*, shown as part of the Atlanta Jewish Film Festival when she was a graduate student at Emory. Although a parody of Mexican Jewish life, the film created for Margaret the strange sensation of being transported into a distorted mirror of her own family life: having attended family shivahs in Mexico City and participated in a religiosity that was more foreign than the Spanish made the film especially indelible. The film is based on Ilan's novella of the same time, although it was almost a decade later that Margaret and Ilan first met in person when she invited him to lecture on the history of crypto-Jews. The processional of food, family, and close quarters evoked by *My Mexican Shivah* is recalled in this warming matzah ball soup.

. . . .

SERVES 6
Preparation time: 30 minutes,
  plus chilling
Cooking time: 1½ hours

FOR THE MATZAH BALLS

1½ cups matzah meal

6 large eggs, lightly beaten

⅔ cup sparkling mineral water
  (ideally Tehuacán Brillante)

2 tablespoons schmaltz or
  vegetable oil

¾ teaspoon kosher salt, plus more
  for boiling

FOR THE SOUP

1 poblano chile

½ packed cup fresh parsley
  (stems okay)

½ packed cup fresh cilantro (stems
  okay), plus more for garnish

1 packed cup fresh spinach

½ medium white onion, finely chopped

2 medium garlic cloves

6 cups chicken broth, divided

¾ teaspoon kosher salt, plus more
  as needed

½ teaspoon freshly ground black
  pepper

16 ounces frozen corn kernels

Lime slices, for serving

1. Make the matzah balls: In a large bowl, stir together the matzah meal, eggs, mineral water, schmaltz, and salt. Cover and refrigerate for 30 minutes. Meanwhile, bring a pot of salted water to a boil, then reduce the heat to a simmer.

2. Using moistened hands to prevent sticking, scoop out heaping tablespoons of the mixture and form into 1-inch balls. Gently drop the balls into the simmering water while continuing with the remaining mixture. Cover the pot and cook until the matzah balls are cooked through, about 1 hour.

3. Meanwhile, make the soup: Heat the oven broiler on high and place the poblano chile on a baking sheet. Broil, turning the chile with tongs every 4–5 minutes, until all sides are blistered. Place the charred chile in a small bowl and cover with a plate to let steam and cool for about 10 minutes, then peel off the skins, remove and discard the stem and seeds, and roughly chop the poblano.

4. Add the charred poblano to a blender along with the parsley, cilantro, spinach, onion, garlic, and 2 cups of the broth and blend until smooth. Transfer the mixture to a soup pot set over medium-high heat along with the remaining 4 cups of broth and the salt and pepper. Bring the mixture to a simmer, then add the corn, cook for 5 minutes more, and remove from the heat.

5. Add the desired number of matzah balls to bowls and ladle the soup over top. Serve hot, garnished with fresh cilantro, and with limes alongside for squeezing.

Leek Fritters

Leeks are commonly served as part of Jewish new year celebrations, symbolizing a fresh start and protection from enemies. Leeks in the form of fritters come from the Sephardic tradition, commonly part of Hanukkah menus—fried foods always being the centerpiece—but also enjoyed throughout the year, holding their own as well as part of festive holiday menus or as weeknight late snacks. Los Angeles–based poet Rachel Kaufman writes eloquently about her Sephardic ancestry bound in food, with poems inspired by wisdom of the kitchen and records of the Mexican Inquisition, as in this excerpt from "Inquisition Letters":

> words scratched on
> peach and avocado pits
> wrapped in taffeta
> and hidden in melons, or
> wrapped in ribbons and pocketed
> inside banana's skin.

The flavor of leeks is sweet and subtle in this recipe and accented by lime and salty pecorino cheese.

. . . .

MAKES ABOUT 20 FRITTERS
Preparation time: 20 minutes
Cooking time: 1 hour

1 large russet potato (about ½ pound), peeled and cut into chunks

1 pound leeks, both white and light green parts, cleaned well and finely chopped

4 large eggs, lightly beaten

¼ cup matzah meal

¼ cup grated pecorino cheese

1¼ teaspoons kosher salt

½ teaspoon freshly ground black pepper

Vegetable oil, for frying

Lime wedges, for serving

1. Place the potato chunks into a small saucepan and cover with 1 inch of water. Set over medium heat, bring to a boil, and cook, stirring occasionally, until the potatoes are tender, 20–30 minutes. Drain the potatoes and mash until smooth, then transfer to a large bowl.

2. Add the leeks, eggs, matzah meal, pecorino cheese, salt, and pepper to the bowl with the mashed potatoes and stir to fully combine.

3. Heat ¼ inch of oil in a large frying pan set over medium heat until shimmering. Meanwhile, line a large plate or baking sheet with paper towels.

4. Working in batches of 5–6, scoop out heaping tablespoons of the leek mixture, roll into balls (moisten hands if the mixture is sticking), and place in the hot oil, gently flattening into patties. Fry, turning once, until golden brown on both sides and cooked through, 4–6 minutes per batch. Transfer to the paper-towel-lined sheet to drain while frying the remainder.

5. Serve hot, with lime wedges alongside for squeezing.

Chelmelquitengo Lamb Tacos with Raisins and Pomegranate

Although there is a city in southeastern Poland called Chelm, the town is also a mythical concoction of eastern European Jewish folklore. Also spelled Khelem, in this place all the residents believe themselves to be very wise, whereas in reality they are all fools.

Through immigration, Chelm entered Mexican Jewish folklore. Rumor has it that a select number of Chelemites, escaping pogroms, settled near Toluca, not far from Mexico City, where they invited only the wisest, most intelligent scholars, among them Talmudists, kabbalists, and other authorities. Their site is called Chelmelquitengo. They have incorporated all kinds of Mexican culinary traditions, such as eating tacos, with ingredients they have borrowed from the slow-cooked stew known as cholent and other Polish Jewish dishes.

This is one of Chelmelquitengo's favorite recipes. It is said that that after eating Lamb Tacos with Raisin and Pomegranate, you can memorize an entire page of the Talmudic tractate Bava Metzia, which, in its early chapters, deals with watching over another person's property without being remunerated. According to the people of Chelmelquitengo, a *shomer hinam*, the unpaid watchman, can become rich simply by adding raisins and pomegranate seeds to the dish.

It is all fantasy—except the taste of this delicious dish. Try it! We aren't fooling you.

. . . .

SERVES 4–6
Preparation time: 15 minutes
Cooking time: 35 minutes

FOR THE FILLING

2 tablespoons extra-virgin olive oil

1 medium white onion, finely chopped

1 pound ground lamb

½ teaspoon ground cardamom

¼ teaspoon kosher salt

¼ teaspoon freshly ground black pepper

¾ cup water

¼ cup dark raisins

FOR THE SPICE MIXTURE

¼ cup finely chopped fresh cilantro

¼ medium white onion, very finely chopped

¾ teaspoon ground cinnamon

⅛ teaspoon ground cloves

¼ teaspoon kosher salt, plus more as needed

¼ teaspoon freshly ground black pepper

FOR SERVING

12–16 (6-inch) corn tortillas, warmed

Fresh pomegranate seeds, for sprinkling

Honey, for drizzling

1. Heat the oil in a large frying pan set over medium heat. Add the onion and cook, stirring occasionally, until softened and lightly browned, 6–8 minutes. Add the lamb and cook, stirring often and breaking up large pieces, until browned, about 8 minutes. Stir in the cardamom, salt, pepper, and water.

2. Cover the pan, turn the heat to medium low, and cook, stirring occasionally, until the meat is tender and cooked through, about 20 minutes, adding the raisins during the last 5 minutes of cooking. Drain the meat mixture, discarding the cooking liquid or reserving for another use, and transfer the meat to a serving dish.

3. While the meat simmers, make the spice mixture: Combine the cilantro, onion, cinnamon, cloves, salt, and pepper. Stir it into the still-hot meat mixture. Taste and add more salt, if needed.

4. To serve, place a couple of heaping tablespoons of the lamb mixture over pairs of tortillas, sprinkle with pomegranate seeds, and drizzle with honey. Serve hot or warm.

Stuffed Poblanos with Guacamole and Gribenes

In making schmaltz, the skin and fat of poultry is cooked to isolate the fat and flavors. Small pieces of remaining skin become crispy and rendered in this process, and these are referred to as gribenes, sometimes called "Jewish bacon" or chicarrón de pollo. To add flavor and texture, gribenes can be added to a variety of dishes. Irma Appel remembers eating avocado tacos when she was a little girl. Only later, when she was a mother, did she come up with the idea of sprinkling gribenes on top of guacamole. This happy accident has brought her many friends. In fact, it is the gribenes, she says, that have helped her expand her clientele. Irma frequently gives away bottles of gribenes for people to add to the matzah ball soup they prepare for Passover.

Irma reminds us that poblano chiles en escabeche—that is, cooked or pickled, in an acidic sauce, usually with vinegar, and colored with paprika, citrus, and other spices—is a well-kept secret and that approach to timing tells you a lot about the cook. Many of her dishes have benefited from the conversations with her staff of Mexican cooks, including Jaime Ramón Lorenzo, María Cruz Ramírez, and Gabriel (Gabo) Valdéz Rojas. Jaime's specialty is desserts and marmalades. María has perfected the art of cooking borscht, helzalaj, and stuffed cabbages. Gabo, for instance, learned to cook cholent from Irma, and he pushed her to incorporate new uses of chiles in many of her dishes, including this one.

. . . .

SERVES 6
Preparation time: 25 minutes,
  plus overnight resting
Cooking time: 1 hour

FOR THE POBLANOS

6 poblano chiles

2 cups white vinegar

1 cup water

2 tablespoons kosher salt

¼ cup granulated sugar

2 medium garlic cloves, smashed
  and peeled

2 medium carrots, peeled and sliced

FOR THE GRIBENES

1 pound chicken skins, rinsed, patted dry, and cut into ¼-inch pieces

½ teaspoon kosher salt, plus more for sprinkling

1 large white onion, peeled and thinly sliced

FOR THE GUACAMOLE

3 medium avocados, peeled, pitted, and roughly chopped

½ small white onion, finely chopped

Juice of 1 lime

1 medium garlic clove, minced, grated, or pushed through a press

¼ cup finely chopped fresh cilantro

½ teaspoon kosher salt, or more as needed

Ground white pepper and Maggi seasoning, to taste, optional

. . . .

1. Heat the oven to 425°F and place the poblano chiles in a baking dish. Roast, turning every 5 minutes, until soft and blistered all over, 20–25 minutes total. Transfer to a bowl and cover loosely with a clean tea towel. Once cool, carefully cut off and discard the tops, and slice the chiles along one side to remove the seeds. Set aside.

2. Combine the vinegar, water, salt, sugar, and garlic in a small saucepan set over medium-high heat. Bring to a boil, stirring to dissolve the salt and sugar, then remove from the heat and let cool for about 10 minutes.

3. Arrange the chiles and sliced carrots in a small baking dish. Add the vinegar mixture, cover the baking dish, and refrigerate overnight.

4. The following day, make the gribenes: Place the chicken skins in a large nonstick frying pan set over medium-low heat and sprinkle with 1 teaspoon of water and the salt. Cook, stirring often, until the fat melts and pools at the bottom of the pan and the skin darkens and begins to curl up at the edges, 20–30 minutes.

5. Add the onion and cook, stirring constantly, for 5 minutes. Remove the pan from the heat and strain any rendered fat into a glass jar. (This fat, called schmaltz, can be stored in the fridge and used for cooking.)

6. Return the skins and onion to the frying pan and season with a little more salt. Set the pan over medium heat and continue cooking, stirring often, until the skins and onion are deeply browned and crispy, 15 to 25 minutes. (Watch carefully so they don't burn.) Transfer the gribenes to paper towels to drain. Keep the mixture at room temperature.

7. Make the guacamole: Place the avocados in a medium-size bowl and mash with a fork until a chunky paste forms. Add the onion, lime juice, garlic, cilantro, and salt and stir to combine. Taste and add more salt if needed. If desired, season the guacamole with white pepper and Maggi seasoning to taste.

8. Remove the chiles and carrots from the fridge, strain, and pat dry. Carefully stuff the peppers with the guacamole, then garnish with the gribenes and carrots. Serve immediately.

¡Que Viva el Chile!

A JEWISH MEXICAN JOKE states that, in 1523, as Spanish conquistador Hernán Cortés was subduing Tenochtitlán, what is today Mexico City, he captured and then tortured Cuauhtémoc, the last Aztec emperor. In pain, Cuauhtémoc heroically confided to one of his generals that even if the Aztec people were completely subdued, one day they would reverse their curse through spice. "Con chile," he said. Through chiles.

To which a Mexican Jew standing nearby added: "Poor Cuauhtémoc! Those thoughts only come when you are already chopped liver."

There are about sixty different types of chiles in Mexico, including jalapeño, poblano, chile de árbol, chilaca, mirasol, manzano, chipotle, pasilla, piquín, guajillo, ancho, mulato, habanero, serrano, and cascabel, to name a few. Jewish Mexican cuisine uses them all.

You will feel the curse of Cuauhtémoc in your desayuno as you savor huevos divorciados. Or in the salsas you spread on your tacos. Or in the chipotle that makes a brisket torta taste divine. In soups, you can add them to caldo verde or, as Pati Jinich does, you may mix mushrooms and jalapeños in matzah ball soup. Either way, they always add a spicy flavor that makes the Jewish and Mexican connection a fortunate one.

A popular dish is chilaquiles, made of tortillas and chile verde salsa. The Jewish Mexican variety reinvents it with matzah. It is served not only on Passover but throughout the year. The chile condiment makes the unleavened bread taste, well, blasphemous.

The best way to appreciate chiles and not suffer is to walk around a mercado. Marchantes specializing in chiles pile them up in enormous quantities. They also sell them in ready-made paste for mole and other delicacies.

Mexican Jews are even known to eat chile with their paletas, particularly those made of piquín. Or in snacks with elotes (the Mexican word for corn), jicama, cucumber, mango, and other fruits and vegetables.

There is a story about a Jewish immigrant from Warsaw who couldn't learn Spanish slang fast enough to feel at home in his new country. A marchante at the mercado suggested he eat a spoonful of chile ancho that night. The moment he tried it, he let out a scream: "¡Órale cabrones! ¡Viva México! ¡Y que viva el Chile!" •

Chile Relleno Yiddish

The fusion of Jewish Mexican cuisine is handsomely projected in this recipe. Letters, diaries, and other historical documents reference how, at the turn of the twentieth century, Ashkenazic immigrants, bamboozled by the picante nature of Mexican cuisine, hesitated to embrace a new diet. Instead, they stuck to their mores, eating traditional European dishes. But as assimilation took place, they combined the two traditions. Chile Relleno Yiddish thus became a model of integration.

A staple of Mexican cuisine, chile relleno is a dish of stuffed poblano chiles, battered and fried. They are generally coated with egg and stuffed with minced meat. It is a versatile dish—said to have originated in the state of Puebla in 1858 among a group of nuns who used walnut sauce, pomegranate, and parsley—that shows up as breakfast, lunch, and dinner. The Jewish variation foregrounds homemade queso Yiddish.

· ·

SERVES 4
Preparation time: 30 minutes
Cooking time: 40 minutes

4 large pasilla chiles (or substitute poblanos)

About 2 cups Queso Yiddish (page 21)

2 large eggs, beaten

5 tablespoons all-purpose flour, divided

¼ cup vegetable oil, plus more for frying

4 medium plum tomatoes (about 1 pound), cored and roughly chopped

1 cup vegetable broth

2 medium garlic cloves, roughly chopped

1 tablespoon dried Mexican oregano

1 teaspoon kosher salt, plus more as needed

1. Heat the oven to 425°F and place the pasilla chiles in a baking dish. Roast, turning the chiles every 5 minutes, until soft and blistered all over, 20–25 minutes total. Transfer to a bowl and cover loosely with a clean tea towel. Once cool, carefully slit the chiles along one side and remove the seeds.

2. Stuff approximately ½ cup of Queso Yiddish into each chile, roll it up, and keep closed with toothpicks or tie with thin kitchen twine.

3. Whisk the eggs and 1 tablespoon of the flour together in a medium-size bowl. Heat ¼ inch of oil in a medium frying pan set over medium heat. Working in batches of 1–2, carefully dip the stuffed chiles into the egg mixture, letting the excess drip off and fry, turning once, until golden brown on both sides, 5–6 minutes per batch. Set aside on a paper-towel-lined plate to drain.

4. Combine the tomatoes, vegetable broth, garlic, oregano, and salt in a blender and purée until smooth. Set aside.

5. Heat the ¼ cup of oil in a large frying pan set over medium-low heat. Stir in the remaining 4 tablespoons of flour and cook, stirring constantly, until toasted and golden. Add the tomato mixture and cook, stirring often, until thickened and warmed through, about 5 minutes. Taste and add more salt, if needed.

6. Transfer the stuffed chiles to a serving plate and pour the tomato sauce over top. Serve hot.

Falafel Taquitos

"Vamos a echarnos unos taquitos" was a phrase often made as an inside joke in Margaret's family, her mom laughing about the difficulty of translating this commonly used expression back to English—the hunger for food literally moving you to throw food in your face. Taquitos are more commonly prepared with chicken or beans, but this innovative dish incorporates the Middle Eastern street food falafel made from chickpeas and a delicious array of herbs. This recipe blends two deep-fried traditions to produce a savory and spiced meal that can be served both as appetizer and as main course. Although this recipe calls for baking over frying, with results that still produce a satisfying crunch, home cooks can deep-fry the taquitos as an alternative.

SERVES 6
Preparation time: 30 minutes, plus
   soaking and chilling
Baking time: 20 minutes

FOR THE TAQUITOS

½ pound dried chickpeas, soaked overnight in water, then rinsed and drained

½ medium yellow onion, roughly chopped

2 tablespoons roughly chopped fresh parsley

2 tablespoons roughly chopped cilantro

2 medium garlic cloves, roughly chopped

1 teaspoon kosher salt, plus more as needed

1 teaspoon ground cumin

½ teaspoon ground coriander

⅛ teaspoon cayenne

Vegetable oil, for brushing

12 (6-inch) corn tortillas

FOR THE TAHINI SAUCE

½ cup well-stirred tahini

¼ cup fresh lemon juice

¼ cup cold water

1. Add the chickpeas to a food processor bowl along with the onion, parsley, cilantro, garlic, salt, cumin, coriander, and cayenne. Pulse, scraping down the sides of the bowl as needed until a textured paste forms. Taste and add more salt, if needed. Transfer to a bowl and refrigerate the mixture for 30 minutes.

2. Heat the oven to 400°F and brush a 9 × 13-inch baking dish with about 1 tablespoon of oil. Lay one tortilla on a flat surface and place a scant ¼ cup of the filling along one edge, nudging it into a line. Roll up the tortilla tightly and place it seam-side down in the prepared baking dish. Repeat the process with the remaining tortillas and filling.

3. Brush the tops of the tortillas with more oil and bake until crispy and golden, 15–20 minutes. Meanwhile, whisk together the tahini, lemon juice, and water. Serve the taquitos hot, drizzled with tahini sauce.

Chicken Kreplach Soup con Tomatillo Salsa

"Ándale, Ilan," Bobe Miriam would often say, "Él que no sabe comer, no sabe vivir"—he who doesn't know how to eat doesn't know how to live. Her fame, though, was the result of the high marks she consistently got for the family meals she prepared for Shabbat and the High Holidays. Everyone would congregate in her apartment. The bacchanals would last four or five hours. Grandchildren would play dreidel, *lotería*, and other games. Or even more exciting, the family would walk to the park, where the kids played *escondidillas*, hide and seek, while the adults would debate politics of Israel and Palestine or Mexico's most recent, never-disappointing political scandal.

It is strange, therefore, to remember that at heart Bobe Miriam was somewhat shy. Ilan remembers her sitting quietly on his living room sofa, looking attentively as the children ran from one corner to another. After an hour or so, she would stand up and make her way to the kitchen. She never liked to cook in someone else's house. Her own kitchen was a sacred space where she reigned uncontested. Yet she always found ways to prolong the power she exerted in the kitchen by preparing dishes she would bring with herself as presents as she visited relatives up and down Mexico City. Ilan especially remembers a variety of soups. They would arrive in hermetically sealed Tupperware. On the surface of each, she would attach a name and detailed list of ingredients. If and when Bobe Miriam opened the refrigerator and got her soups ready, children would know automatically that playtime was now over. The most important part of the day had arrived: tasting grandmother's latest succulent concoction. Her recipe of Chicken Kreplach Soup with Tomatillo Salsa comes from Ilan's cousin Anat Nurko and her daughter.

SERVES 6
Preparation time: 1 hour
Cooking time: 2½ hours

FOR THE SOUP

8 skin-on, bone-in chicken thighs

1 large yellow onion, peeled and halved

2 large carrots, peeled and halved

1 medium celery stalk, halved

2 medium zucchini, ends trimmed and halved

1 chayote, peeled and roughly chopped (optional)

2 garlic cloves, peeled and roughly chopped

1 lightly packed cup fresh dill (stems okay)

1 tablespoon kosher salt, plus more as needed

½ teaspoon freshly ground black pepper

FOR THE DOUGH

2 large eggs

3 tablespoons vegetable oil

1 teaspoon cold water

½ teaspoon kosher salt

1½ cups all-purpose flour, plus more as needed

FOR THE TOMATILLO SALSA

6 small tomatillos (about ½ pound), paper skins removed

1 large garlic clove, peeled

1 medium serrano or jalapeño chile, halved lengthwise and seeds removed

½ bunch roughly chopped fresh cilantro

½ teaspoon kosher salt, or more to taste

1. Make the soup: Place the chicken, onion, carrots, celery, zucchini, chayote (if using), garlic, and dill in a tall, 8-quart soup pot and cover with 1 inch of water. Bring to a boil over high heat, then turn the heat to low. Partially cover the pot and simmer, skimming off any foam that accumulates, until the chicken is very tender and falling off the bone, 1½–2 hours. The soup should roll along at a very gentle bubble, not a rapid boil.

2. Remove the chicken pieces from the pot and set aside to cool. Remove and discard the larger vegetable pieces, then strain the broth through a fine-mesh sieve into a large bowl, discarding the solids. Return the strained broth to the pot.

3. Set aside 2 of the cooked chicken thighs for the kreplach filling. Remove the meat from the rest, roughly chop into bite-size pieces, and return to the soup pot along with the broth. Stir in the salt and pepper, then taste and add more salt, if needed. Set aside, or let cool, cover, and refrigerate for up to 3 days.

4. Make the dough: Whisk together the eggs, oil, water, and salt in a medium-size bowl until frothy. Add the flour in 2 batches and stir until a shaggy dough forms. Transfer to a flat surface and knead until smooth. If the dough is too wet or sticky, knead in a little more flour. Wrap the dough in plastic wrap or parchment paper and let rest for 1 hour.

5. Meanwhile, make the tomatillo salsa: Heat a comal or grill pan over medium-high heat. Add the tomatillos, garlic, and serrano chile and cook, turning occasionally with tongs, until charred and softened, 7–10 minutes.

6. Add the charred vegetables to a food processor along with the cilantro and salt and pulse until a smooth salsa forms. Taste and add more salt, if needed. Remove the meat from the reserved chicken thighs, shred with your fingers, and place in a medium-size bowl. Stir in some of the salsa, until the chicken is coated but the filling isn't runny or wet. (Reserve the remaining salsa for another use.)

7. Form and boil the kreplach: Bring a large pot of water to a boil. Meanwhile, on a lightly floured surface, roll out the dough to ⅛-inch thickness (ideally thinner, if possible). Use a 3-inch cookie cutter to stamp out as many rounds of dough as possible. Spoon a rounded teaspoon of the chicken filling into each circle. Run a wet finger around the outside edges of the rounds, then fold each in half, enclosing the filling inside, and press the edges firmly to seal. If desired, reroll the dough scraps and stamp out more rounds.

8. Add the kreplach to the boiling water and gently stir. When they float, continue cooking for 15 minutes, stirring occasionally, then remove from the boiling water and let drain.

9. Finish the soup: Bring the chicken soup to a simmer. Divide the boiled kreplach among serving bowls, and top with the soup. Serve hot.

Note: The kreplach can be frozen. Defrost and reheat in chicken soup or boiling water.

Snapper Ceviche con Maror

Thought to have originated during the Incan empire in Peru, ceviche—the word was first documented in 1820 in the Peruvian soldier song "La Chicha," but its etymology also connects with *escabeche*, meaning "meat cooked in vinegar"—has since evolved to be a popular dish across Latin America and the United States. Ceviche makes use of fresh seafood: kosher and nonkosher varieties. The use of maror, or horseradish, in this recipe was an invention during a Passover Seder in Mexico City, creating a savory contrast among the fish, the jalapeño, and the horseradish. The symbolism is enthralling: Can you imagine the Israelis, as they crossed the Red Sea, cooking ceviche on their way to a forty-year itinerant life in the desert before they settled in Canaan? The best ceviche is refreshing and original in that it imagines new combinations of flavors, and the chilled dish pairs beautifully with hot weather. The seafood is cooked with the acid of a citrus marinade, as opposed to heat, and served with garnishes including bell peppers, onions, chiles, and herbs such as basil, cilantro, and parsley. Ceviche is not a make-ahead dish. Ideally, it should be served within an hour of when it is made.

. . . .

SERVES 6
Preparation time: 25 minutes,
  plus chilling

¾ cup fresh lime juice

¼ cup fresh lemon juice

1 small jalapeño chile, seeds removed, finely chopped

1 small red bell pepper, seeds removed, finely chopped (about ½ cup)

1 small yellow bell pepper, seeds removed, finely chopped (about ½ cup)

½ small red onion, thinly sliced

1 small garlic clove, minced, grated, or pushed through a press

⅛ teaspoon ground cumin

½ teaspoon kosher salt

1 pound red snapper fillets, skin removed

2 tablespoons finely chopped fresh cilantro

1 teaspoon extra-virgin olive oil

Prepared horseradish, for topping (optional)

1. In a large bowl, stir together the lime juice, lemon juice, jalapeño chile, red and yellow bell peppers, red onion, garlic, cumin, and salt.

2. Using a sharp knife or kitchen shears, cut the fish fillets into ½-inch pieces and add to the citrus mixture, stirring to combine. Cover the bowl and refrigerate for 30 minutes.

3. Just before serving, stir in the cilantro and oil. Serve immediately, dolloped with horseradish, if desired.

Sopes de Picadillo "Rabino Apóstata"

Mexican Jews, like other Mexicans, love to use the diminutive in their speech as a sign of affection: a lover is an *amorcito*, a meal is a *comidita*, and a party is a *fiestecita*. This helps in understanding the meaning of *antojito*. In popular parlance, it means an irresistible urge. Much of Mexican Jewish cuisine might fall under that description, yet in Mexico street food in general is what is called *un antojito*. And among street food, sopes have a leading role.

Sopes are made of a fried masa base with some kind of topping. One measure of the nation's inventiveness is the wide spectrum of sope toppings. They might be in a kosher style made of shredded beef, refried beans, picadillo, fish, or chicken, topped with tomato, lettuce, and avocado. Or non-kosher and wildly popular braised pork or shrimp, topped with veggies, cheese, or Mexican crema. If you know your way around Mexico, you're likely to have your favorite sope stands, just as you will have your preferred torta and taco joints.

Mexican Jews have emphatically incorporated sopes into their diet. Starting with its name, this particular dish isn't always kosher (bring on the cheese). In fact, it goes out of its way to test faith, invoking an apostate believer ready to indulge in the earthly pleasures. This dish comes to us from a Jewish Mexican family in Colonia Roma. The suggestion for topping the sopes with horseradish comes from several recipes across La Comunidad and provides an invigorating second layer of spice.

SERVES 4–6
Preparation time: 30 minutes,
  plus resting
Cooking time: 45 minutes

FOR THE PICADILLO

3 medium plum tomatoes (about ¾ pound), stems removed and roughly chopped

1 medium white onion, peeled and roughly chopped

1 medium garlic clove, peeled and roughly chopped

1 tablespoon chipotle paste

1 teaspoon granulated sugar

1¼ teaspoons kosher salt, plus more as needed

½ teaspoon freshly ground black pepper

2 tablespoons vegetable oil

1 medium carrot, peeled and finely chopped

1 small Yukon Gold potato, peeled and finely chopped

¾ pound lean ground beef

½ cup frozen green peas

FOR THE SOPES

2 cups masa harina

2½ teaspoons kosher salt

1½ cups water

1 tablespoon vegetable oil, plus more for frying

FOR SERVING

Canned or homemade Refried Beans (page 29), warmed

Shredded lettuce

Queso fresco

Prepared horseradish

1. Make the picadillo: Combine the tomatoes, onion, garlic, chipotle paste, sugar, salt, and pepper in a blender and blend until smooth. Set aside.

2. Heat the oil in a large frying pan set over medium heat. Add the carrot and potato and cook, stirring occasionally, until softened, 6–8 minutes. Add the ground beef and cook, stirring often and breaking up large pieces of meat, until browned, about 5 minutes.

3. Pour the tomato mixture over the beef mixture. Add the peas and cook, stirring often, until the mixture thickens, 8–10 minutes. Taste and add more salt, if needed, then set aside.

4. Make the sopes: In a large bowl using a sturdy spoon, stir together the masa, salt, water, and 1 tablespoon oil until a soft and slightly sticky dough forms. Let the dough rest at room temperature for 10–15 minutes (it should firm up enough to roll).

5. Scoop out approximately ¼ cup of the dough and roll it into a ball. (Lightly moisten your hands to prevent sticking.) Using your fingertips, press the dough into a circle that is approximately 3 inches in diameter and ½ inch thick. Gently pinch all around the edges of the tortilla to make a concave shape. Place the tortilla on a large plate and repeat with the remainder of the dough.

6. Heat ½ inch of oil in a large nonstick frying pan. Working in batches of 4–5 and adding more oil as necessary, place the sopes in the pan and cook, turning once, until lightly fried, 3–4 minutes total.

7. To serve: Spoon a heaping tablespoon of warm refried beans into the bowl of the fried sopes. Top with the seasoned meat mixture, then garnish as desired with lettuce, queso fresco, and horseradish. Serve immediately.

Mushroom Huaraches con Pepitas

Another antojito and a close cousin of sopes, this recipe is one of our favorite vegetarian offerings. Part of the joy of this dish is in the assembly: conversation as the dough comes together and the banter of a couple of friends or family members who help roll out the dough and arrange toppings.

Huaraches can be easily personalized with variation in the balance of refried beans, the mushrooms dependent on season or geography, and abundant or minimal handfuls of cheese, avocado, and toasted pepitas to garnish. If possible, we encourage spreading out the toppings as part of the dinner table—mushrooms in one large bowl, other small dishes containing garnishes of cheese, lettuce, tomatoes, and pepitas—allowing guests to customize their plates. Over the bowl of pepitas, you might recall the long history of the seeds, a staple of regional cuisine in Mexico long before rice and beans.

The comal referenced in this recipe and others across the book is usually made of heavy cast iron. We find evidence of comales used across Mexico, dating back even to the Olmec people.

. . . .

SERVES 6
Preparation time: 30 minutes,
   plus brief resting
Cooking time: 30 minutes

2 cups masa harina

2 teaspoons kosher salt

1½ cups warm water

1 tablespoon vegetable oil, plus
   more for frying

About ⅓ cup canned or homemade
   Refried Beans (page 29)

3 tablespoons unsalted butter

½ medium white onion, finely
   chopped

1 pound fresh mushrooms (assorted),
   stems removed and finely chopped

3 medium garlic cloves, finely chopped

1 teaspoon dried Mexican oregano

1 teaspoon sherry vinegar

½ teaspoon kosher salt, plus more
   as needed

FOR SERVING

Diced avocado

Shredded lettuce

Diced tomatoes

Crumbled Cotija cheese

Toasted pepitas

1. In a large bowl using a sturdy spoon, stir together the masa, salt, water, and 1 tablespoon of oil until a soft and slightly sticky dough forms. Let the dough rest at room temperature for 10–15 minutes (it should firm up enough to roll).

2. Divide the dough into 6 equal portions and roll into balls. Working one at a time, press each ball into a 4-inch circle. Spread about 1 tablespoon of refried beans evenly over the top, then roll up the circle into a cylinder, using your hands to smooth any cracks. Using a tortilla press, huarache press, or rolling pin, flatten the cylinder until it is approximately ½ inch thick.

3. Heat 2 tablespoons of oil in a large comal or frying pan set over medium heat. Working in batches, add the filled huaraches and cook, turning once, until golden brown, 3–4 minutes per side, adding more oil if needed. Transfer to a serving platter and set aside while making the mushroom topping.

4. Wipe out the frying pan, then add the butter and melt over medium heat. Add the onion and cook, stirring occasionally, until softened and lightly browned, 6–8 minutes. Add the mushrooms and garlic and continue cooking until golden brown, 8–10 minutes. Stir in the oregano, vinegar, and salt. Taste and add more salt, if needed.

5. Top the fried huaraches evenly with the mushroom mixture, then sprinkle with the avocado, lettuce, tomatoes, Cotija cheese, and pepitas. Serve warm or at room temperature.

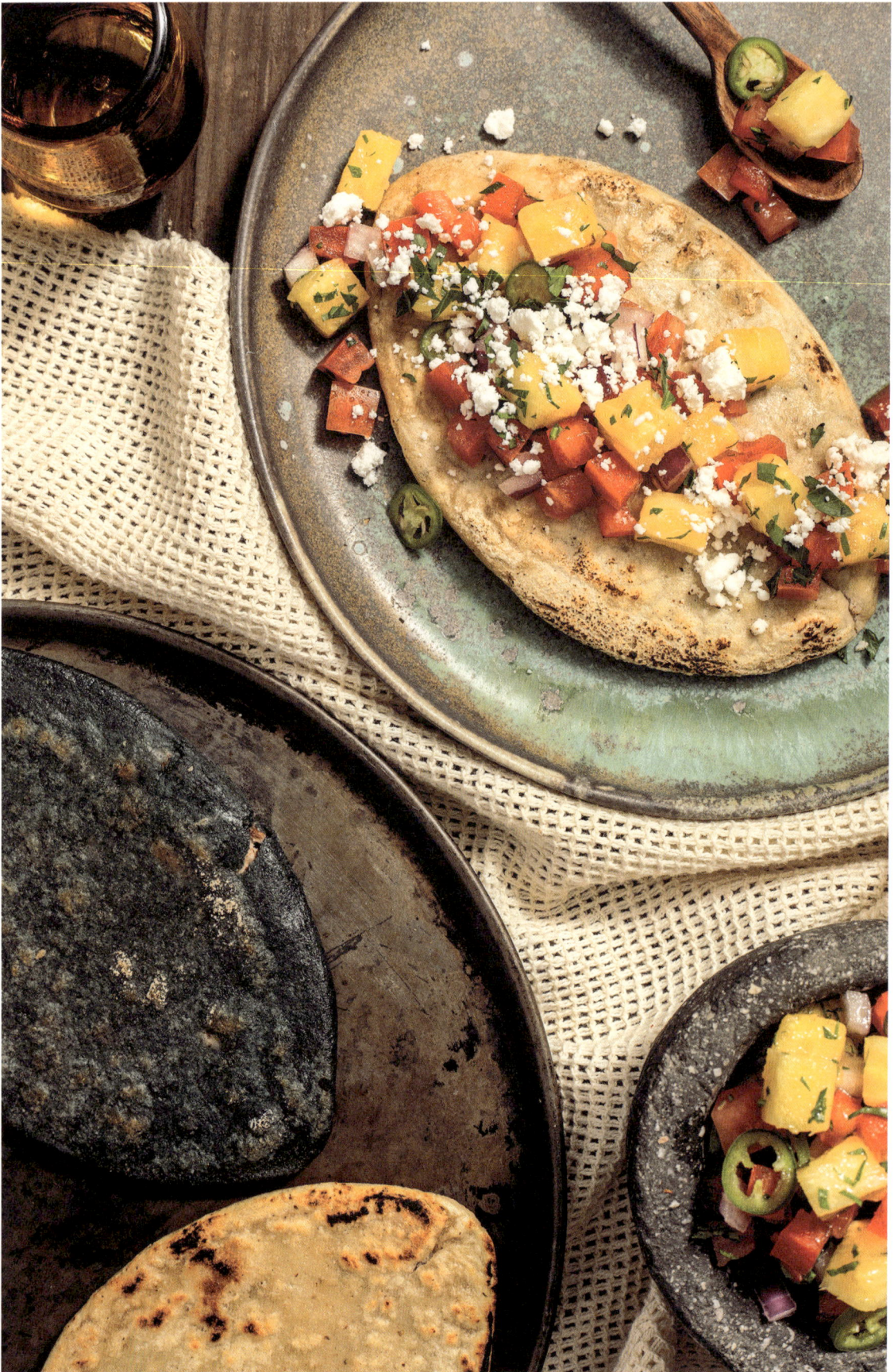

Pineapple Black Bean Tlacoyos

One more celebrated vegetarian antojito, tlacoyos can be prepared with a variety of corn masas, ranging from deep blue to fine white, from mass-produced to local heirloom varieties, depending on preference and what is in your pantry. In our conversations with Jewish Mexican chefs and home cooks, we learned that most families have their favorite varieties, and we encourage experimentation and even play with contrasting-color doughs as part of the liveliness of the recipe. Just as with huaraches, this is a dish that favors assembly by groups around a kitchen table, everyone creating a perfect balance of flavors as the texture of pineapple salsa complements the smooth filling of refried black beans. The history of pineapple through the region can be traced to the Mayan people, and the fruit is found in a number of recipes across this book, as well as in other popular dishes including sweet tamales.

MAKES ABOUT 12 TLACOYOS
Preparation time: 45 minutes
Cooking time: 25 minutes

FOR THE SALSA

2½ cups diced fresh pineapple, or 1 (20-ounce) can diced pineapple, drained well

2 medium plum tomatoes, seeds removed, finely chopped

1 jalapeño chile, seeds removed, if desired, and thinly sliced

¼ large red onion, finely chopped (about ½ cup)

1 medium garlic clove, finely chopped

⅓ cup finely chopped fresh cilantro

1½ tablespoons fresh lime juice

½ teaspoon kosher salt

FOR THE TLACOYOS

1½ cups masa harina

½ teaspoon kosher salt

1¼ cups warm water

1 tablespoon vegetable oil, plus more for frying

About 1 cup canned or homemade Refried Beans (page 29)

FOR SERVING

Crumbled queso fresco

1. Make the salsa: Combine the pineapple, tomatoes, jalapeño, red onion, garlic, cilantro, lime juice, and salt in a medium-size bowl and mix well. Cover and refrigerate until needed.

2. Make the tlacoyos: In a large bowl using a sturdy spoon, stir together the masa, salt, water, and 1 tablespoon of oil until a soft and slightly sticky dough forms. Let the dough rest at room temperature for 10–15 minutes (it should firm up enough to handle).

3. Scoop out 2 rounded tablespoons of the dough and roll into a ball (lightly wet or oil your hands to prevent sticking). Flatten the masa ball with your palms into a 2½-inch disk. Add about 1 tablespoon of the refried beans to the center, then fold the dough in half like a taco to seal, gently flattening and shaping the dough into a football shape. Set the filled tlacoyo aside while continuing with the remaining dough and filling.

4. Heat ¼ inch of oil in a large nonstick frying pan or griddle over medium heat. Working in batches, use a thin metal spatula to carefully transfer the stuffed tlacoyos to the pan and fry, turning once, until lightly browned and warmed through, 2–3 minutes per side. Add more oil to the pan if needed.

5. Serve hot, topped generously with the pineapple salsa and queso fresco.

Roasted Eggplant Frittata

Eggplant, referred to as "Jew's apple" in the seventeenth and eighteenth centuries, appears across a number of recipes in this book, a reflection of the centrality of the vegetable across Ashkenazi and Sephardic traditions. Frittatas have deep imprints in Jewish Mexican literature, likely because the dish is easy to prepare, is readily customizable, and can be served casually throughout the day. Prominent Jewish Mexican writer Myriam Moscona writes at length about a Sephardic recipe for cheese frittata in her novel *Tela de Sevoya*. And in *León de lidia*, she writes about Mexican Bulgarian Sephardic identity, taking up the topic of memory and foods, inspiring the dish below. Myriam hosted Margaret and Ilan in her apartment in Mexico City one afternoon in 2023—an apartment building from the 1960s with an almost identical architecture to Margaret's great-grandmother's home, down to hallway tile and spacing. Myriam prepared for us a richly spiced Turkish coffee after a lunch of eggplant, black beans, and nopales. We three talked with fervor about the library of books in her light-filled living room, the labyrinth of Judeo-Spanish, Yiddish, and ties that bind them in food, literature, diaspora, and memories.

. . . .

SERVES 4–6
Preparation time: 30 minutes,
     plus standing
Baking time: 40 minutes

1 small eggplant (about 1 pound),
     unpeeled and cut into ½-inch cubes

1¼ teaspoons kosher salt, divided

¼ cup extra-virgin olive oil, plus more
     as needed

1 medium yellow onion, finely chopped

1 large garlic clove, finely chopped

7 large eggs, lightly beaten

4 ounces crumbled feta cheese
     (about ¾ cup)

3 tablespoons matzah meal

¼ cup plain yogurt

½ teaspoon freshly ground
     black pepper

1. Add the eggplant pieces to a strainer set over a bowl, sprinkle with 1 teaspoon of the salt, and mix with your hands to combine. Let the eggplant stand for 1 hour, then discard any liquid and pat the eggplant pieces dry with a paper towel.

2. Heat the oven to 350°F and lightly grease an 8 × 8-inch baking dish.

3. Heat the oil in a large frying pan set over medium heat. Add the onion and cook, stirring occasionally, until softened and lightly browned, 6–8 minutes. Add the eggplant pieces and continue cooking, stirring occasionally and adding a drizzle more oil if the pan looks dry, until the eggplant is softened and browned, 10–12 minutes. Add the garlic and cook until fragrant, about 1 minute. Remove from the heat and transfer to a mixing bowl to cool slightly.

4. Add the eggs, feta, matzah meal, yogurt, the remaining ¼ teaspoon of salt, and the pepper to the eggplant mixture and stir to combine.

5. Transfer the mixture to the prepared baking dish and bake until puffed and golden brown, 30–40 minutes. Remove from the oven and let cool a bit. Serve warm or at room temperature.

Pierogi con Pico de Gallo

These semicircular dumplings originated in eastern Europe more than 400 years ago, and this filling marries the Old World simplicity of potatoes and sweet onions with a bright and flavorful salsa. Ashkenazi Jews in Poland, where the pierogi is a national dish, incorporated it into their diet (there is a controversy about its origins actually being Ukrainian). Given that pierogi feel like a kind of empanada, it is no surprise that the dumplings have entered the cuisine of Mexican Jews. Warm pierogi with chilled salsa is particularly delicious, the flavors enhanced by the contrast in temperatures. This recipe comes from Galia Nurko, the great-granddaughter of Miriam Slomianski, Ilan's grandmother. For another way to serve these Pierogi con Pico de Gallo, Galia also recommends mole. She says that Jewish Mexicans are always looking to add "a kick of spice" to meals.

. . . .

MAKES 20–24 PIEROGI
Preparation time: 1½ hours
Cooking time: 10 minutes

FOR THE PICO DE GALLO

4 medium plum tomatoes (about 1 pound), seeds removed, finely chopped

½ medium white onion, finely chopped

1 medium jalapeño chile, seeds removed, finely chopped

¼ cup finely chopped fresh cilantro

1 tablespoon fresh lime juice, plus more as needed

½ teaspoon kosher salt, plus more as needed

⅛ teaspoon freshly ground black pepper

FOR THE DOUGH

2 cups all-purpose flour, plus more as needed

2 large eggs

1 teaspoon kosher salt

5–6 tablespoons water

FOR THE FILLING

2 medium russet potatoes, peeled and cut into chunks

3 tablespoons vegetable oil, plus more for boiling

2 small white onions, finely chopped

2 medium garlic cloves, minced, grated, or pushed through a press

½ teaspoon kosher salt, plus more as needed

1 large egg, beaten

1. Make the pico de gallo: Combine the tomatoes, onion, jalapeño, cilantro, lime juice, salt, and pepper in a medium-size bowl and mix well. Taste and add more lime juice or salt, if desired. Cover and refrigerate until needed.

2. Make the dough: In a large bowl, combine the flour, eggs, salt, and 5 tablespoons of water and stir until a shaggy dough forms.

3. Turn the dough out onto a flat surface and knead a few times to form a smooth dough. If the dough is too dry, add up to 1 more tablespoon of water, a little at a time, until the desired texture is reached. If the dough is too wet or sticky, sprinkle over additional flour, a little at a time, and continue kneading. Place the dough in a bowl, cover, and let rest for 30 minutes.

4. Meanwhile, make the filling: Bring a medium saucepan of water to a boil over high heat. Add the potatoes and cook, stirring occasionally, until tender. Drain, return to the saucepan, and mash until smooth. Let cool slightly.

5. Heat the oil in a large frying pan set over medium heat. Add the onions and cook, stirring often, until deeply golden, 15–20 minutes. If the onions are beginning to burn, nudge the heat down and add a small splash of water to the pan. Add the garlic and salt and cook, stirring, until fragrant, about 1 minute.

6. Stir the browned onions, along with any oil in the pan, into the mashed potatoes. Taste and add more salt, if needed. Add the egg and stir to combine.

7. Form the dumplings: Bring a large pot of water set over high heat to a boil. Once boiling, add a little salt and 1 tablespoon of oil to the pot.

8. On a large, flat surface, roll out the dough into a large ⅛-inch-thick rectangle (or thinner, if possible). Trim the edges, then cut the rectangle into 3 × 3-inch squares. Place 1 rounded tablespoon of the filling in the center of a square. Fold the 2 opposite corners together to make a triangle, then press the edges with your fingers or the tines of a fork to seal. Repeat the process with the remaining dough squares and filling.

9. Gently slip the dumplings into the boiling water and boil, stirring occasionally, until cooked, about 10 minutes. Remove with a slotted spoon and transfer to a serving bowl. Serve topped with pico de gallo.

Cilantro Mousse

This is an ideal appetizer—it comes together quickly and results in lots of compliments.

Mexican Jewish chef Irma Appel first tried a smoked oyster mousse in Mexico City at the elegant San Ángel Inn, a former seventeenth-century hacienda on Calle Diego Rivera that was converted to a restaurant in 1963. She asked the waiter for the recipe, and before she knew it, she was talking with the restaurant chef. Since she has many clients that are kosher and thus don't eat seafood, she tried adapting the recipe with cheese and finally settled on cilantro. This mousse pairs well with almost everything and is one of the most requested items on her menu, beloved by generations of her clients. The recipe can be considered a savory adaptation of the Mexican gelatinas. We especially enjoy this spread with all varieties of quesadillas; it also pairs well with fruit.

SERVES 8
Preparation time: 15 minutes,
  plus chilling

½ cup plain yogurt

1 banana pepper (chile güero), seeds removed, finely chopped

1 small garlic clove, finely chopped

2 tablespoons fresh lemon juice

1 tablespoon granulated sugar

2 cups finely chopped fresh cilantro (about 2 medium bunches)

½ teaspoon kosher salt

¼ teaspoon freshly ground black pepper

1 packet (¼ ounce) unflavored gelatin

¼ cup boiling water

1. Combine the yogurt, banana pepper, garlic, lemon juice, sugar, cilantro, salt, and pepper in a high-powered blender and blend into a smooth purée.

2. Stir together the gelatin and boiling water in a medium-size bowl until completely dissolved and let sit for 30 seconds. Add the cilantro purée and mix well to combine. Pour the mixture into a long, thin mold (such as a terrine mold), cover, and refrigerate until firm, at least 4 hours. Serve chilled.

Squash Blossom Quesadillas

Margaret enjoyed quesadillas on the menu many nights in her childhood. It was one of the first dishes she learned to prepare herself and one of the first dishes her kids could confidently make with minimal supervision. Although cheese plus tortilla is deeply satisfying, incorporating squash blossom when in season elevates the dish in flavor and color. This is not to suggest that the dish should be viewed as in any way gourmet: squash blossom quesadillas are on standard offer from street vendors who prepare quesadillas en masse on large griddles with baskets of squash blossom flowers at their side.

A few notes on ingredients: Queso Oaxaca is a stringy Mexican cow's milk cheese similar to mozzarella but worth sourcing from your local market. Blossoms can be picked from squash in late spring and early summer (another reason to grow zucchini in the garden), and squash blossoms are sometimes sold in heaps at farmers' markets. The flowers can be served as part of fillings, as in this recipe, or if you have extra, they are also enjoyed stuffed with cheese or as the star ingredient in soups. For the quesadillas, tortillas can be made by hand or store-bought as time allows.

MAKES 4 QUESADILLAS
Preparation time: 10 minutes
Cooking time: 10 minutes

1 tablespoon unsalted butter

½ small white onion, finely chopped

1 medium garlic clove, finely chopped

12 squash blossoms

¼ teaspoon kosher salt

8 (6-inch) corn tortillas

1¾ cups shredded Oaxaca cheese

Vegetable oil, for frying

1. Heat the butter in a large frying pan set over medium heat. Add the onion and garlic and cook, stirring often, until fragrant and translucent, 2–3 minutes.

2. Add the squash blossoms and salt and cook, stirring gently, until tender and wilted, 2–3 minutes. Remove from the heat and transfer to a bowl to cool slightly. Wipe out the frying pan and set aside.

3. Assemble the quesadillas: Spread about one-quarter of the cheese onto a tortilla, then top with one-quarter of the squash blossom filling and a second tortilla. Continue the process until all the cheese, filling, and tortillas are used. Alternatively, use single tortillas and fold in half.

4. Heat 1 teaspoon of oil in the frying pan over medium heat, swirling to coat the bottom. Working in batches, fry the quesadillas, flipping once, until golden brown outside and the cheese has melted, 3–5 minutes per batch. Add oil as needed.

5. Transfer the cooked quesadillas to a cutting board and let cool slightly, then cut into wedges. Serve warm.

Schmoozing

IN OUR EXPLORATION of Jewish Mexican food, we ate at the home of dozens of generous hosts, not only in Mexico, but in various cities of the United States. Aside from the exquisite flavors, of course, it was the schmoozing that left a deep impression.

We were regaled with all kinds of stories: about *clápers*, door-to-door tchotchke salesmen; about Jewish *celestinas*, matchmakers coupling young men and women as soon as they disembarked their ship (*La Celestina: The Tragicomedy of Calisto and Melibea* is a classic Spanish work written by a converso in 1499 about a matchmaker and her wiles); and someone told us about Diego Rivera's strong friendship with a Polish poet, Isaac (Itzjok) Berliner, and how the two collaborated in a collection of Yiddish poems called *Shtot fun palatsn* (City of palaces).

An essential aspect of that schmooze was the assortment of languages. In their daily life, Mexican Jews might be said to live in their own Torre de Babel, Tower of Babel. You can even see it in the recipes we received. While we have unified them all in a single tongue, English, they arrived in, or were sprinkled with, Spanish, Yiddish, Ladino, Arabic, Turkish, Portuguese, Greek, Hungarian, Polish, Bulgarian, Romanian, Ukrainian, Russian, Hebrew, English, French, and other tongues.

Spanish, obviously, is everyone's lingua franca. The immigrant generation, Ashkenazic and Ottoman, quickly learned Cervantes's language. Crypto-Jews communicated *en español*, leaving the entirety of their accounts in that tongue. But Ladino was also a feature in the New World.

Early twentieth-century Ottoman immigrants brought Arabic, French, and Greek. Ashkenazim introduced Yiddish, Polish, Russian, and other central and eastern European languages. Although their children quickly learned Spanish, *lluego lluego*, immigrant languages didn't vanish. Jewish schools, Yidishe Shule, Yavne, Naye Yidishe

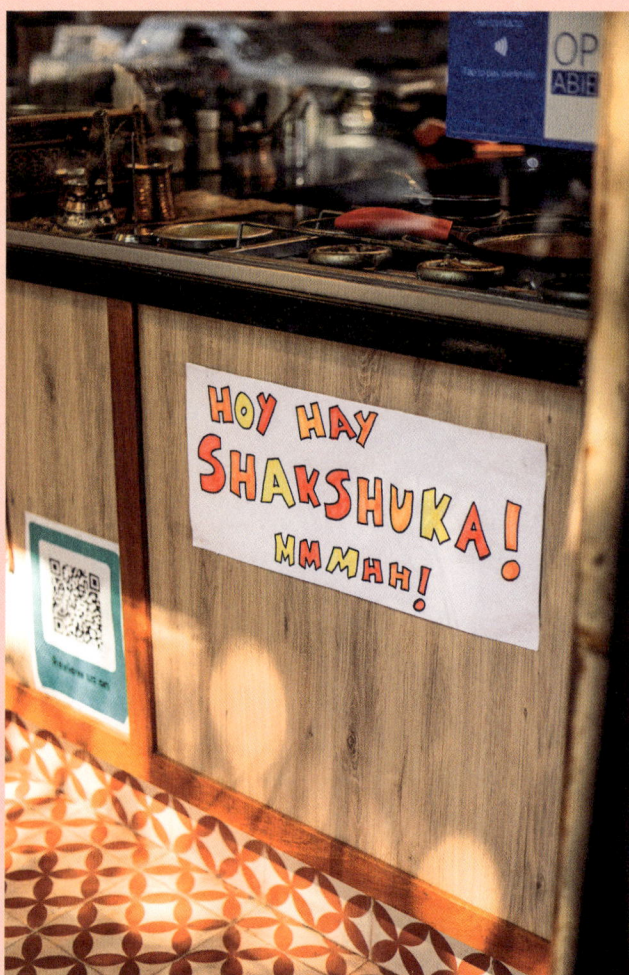

Shule, and others, taught Yiddish until at least the 1970s, when, with retiring teachers and very few replacements, but also as a result of the growing influence of the nascent state of Israel, Hebrew was embraced as one of the languages of instruction.

In the 1970s, Jewish Mexican parents started enrolling their children in American schools, where the primary languages of instruction were English and Spanish. In part, this was a response to a feeling that Yiddish wasn't a viable language for the future. This was the case for Margaret's mother, Gina, who returned from Los Angeles to Mexico City to live with her grandparents during high school.

In Mexico per se, while Yiddish and Ladino no longer have the status they once enjoyed, they are still important in La Comunidad. Cultural events rotate around them. Scholars study the development of these languages in the Mexican habitat. And a new generation that is nostalgic for the past looks to revitalize them.

In Ilan's memoir *On Borrowed Words*, he discusses the tensions among languages among Mexican Jews. Each chapter of this memoir is about another family member and the language that their life, or at least a portion of it, rotated around: Bobe Bela, Ilan's paternal grandmother, a Yiddish-speaking young woman who immigrated to Mexico City from Warsaw in 1919 and whose transition into Spanish catered the way for the family to assimilate into Mexican culture; her second son, Ilan's father, Abraham, who became a famous telenovela and theater actor, known for his physical versatility—the language of the body—on stage and beyond; Ilan's brother Darián, a musician, for whom sound, rhythm, and harmony were a form of grammar; and Ilan himself, whose quest to become a writer pushed him to switch languages: from Yiddish and Spanish to Hebrew and English.

Around the dinner table it is common to hear Mexican Jews switching between languages seamlessly, clinking glasses with "Salud" and "L'Chaim" in a single toast. Jewish Mexican dishes are enriched by the multilingual traditions they represent. •

brownie smore

SOBREMESA

Although the word *sobremesa* means "dessert," it also refers to the conversation people have at the end of a plentiful meal. And oh, do Mexican Jews know how to engage in wholesome sobremesa! A quintessential companion is wine and good poetry.

This type of conviviality might extend for a couple of hours, featuring a range of topics, from political debates to family anecdotes. But don't be fooled. This type of conversation might be hefty. In her autobiography, Sor Juana Inés de la Cruz, Mexico's most distinguished colonial poet, suggests that it is in the art of conversing after a good *guisado* that lasting philosophical systems are forged.

After a meal, dialogue includes *bastante humor*, lots of jokes. Indeed, Mexican Jews might be described as jokesters, especially at times of collective anxiety. It is said that in times of trouble, a Mexican Jewish joke is likely to arrive faster, and is more trustworthy, than the police.

Likewise, what levels both Jews and Mexicans is their sweet tooth. Jewish desserts are legendary in both Sephardic and Ashkenazic cuisine. And Mexican *repostería* is known worldwide for its apparently infinite possibilities. All this to say that a scrumptious Jewish Mexican meal is faithfully followed by a flavorful dessert: varieties of tarts, cakes, and cookies. And of course we can hear our *tías* and *abuelas* reminding us these sweets can be served at any time of day.

There are abundant fillings and braiding techniques for babkas. While we highlight cinnamon churro and Mexican chocolate varieties of babka, we have tasted babkas flavored with pistachio and cardamom and with hibiscus za'atar (these two are Chicago bakery Masa Madre best-sellers), as well as babkas infused with cajeta, cheese, poppy seed, and so many fruits. Here, too, we count on puddings, including flan and arroz con leche.

Some desserts are fried, most famously churros and buñuelos, with cinnamon and sugar. Sor Juana lived in a convent in downtown Mexico City, where she is known as one of the most prolific intellectuals of her time, engaged with theological debate, the rights of women, science, philosophy, and cooking. Long after her death, a recipe notebook compiled by Sor Juana was found. Most of its content is related to sobremesa. It includes a recipe for buñuelos. We have modernized it here.

An irreplaceable companion in the Mexican Jewish sobremesa is the digestif. Hibiscus teas and aguas. Kahlúa with condensed milk or horchata is a favorite option. Others include herbal liqueurs such as Chartreuse or Cynar, or Damiana from Baja California, bitter amaro or orange peel varieties, sweet ones such as limoncello and Grand Marnier, fortified wines such as vermouth or sherry, and aged liquor, including whiskey and brandy. Ilan frequently opts for Mexican digestifs such as Cazcabel, made with blanco tequila, Amargo-Vallet Angostura, made with cherries, cloves, and angostura bark, and ancho chile liqueur.

It is often said that when strangers sit at the table listening to Mexican Jews converse, a whole collective history unfolds. Genealogies are traced: which ancestor came from what town in Aleppo, Syria, or what shtetl in Ukraine. You never really know who you are until you experience your family's journey during sobremesa. •

Tequila with Basil
"El Pogrom"

The word *pogrom* comes from Russian. It describes a violent antisemitic outburst often resulting in a massacre of Jewish people. The word entered European lexicons from the eighteenth century onward, as pogroms spread in different parts of the continent, particularly in the Pale of Settlement, the portion of land in central and eastern Europe where the Russian czar had allowed the Jews to settle in shtetls and urban ghettos.

There were pogrom-like outbursts before that time. In fourteenth-century Spain, antisemitism was rampant. For instance, in 1391 there was a Jewish massacre in Seville and Castile during the reign of Peter the Cruel. Latin America, in spite of its relatively short history concerning the Jews—a bit over five hundred years old—has also had a pogrom-like incident. Called Semana Tragica (Tragic Week) because of its duration, this labor dispute occurred in Buenos Aires in 1919. Jewish businesses were targeted as symbols of an immigration wave that radical forces described as watering down the nation's traditions. Exactly how many victims were lost remains a subject of debate: some suggest that 700 people died, 2,000 were injured, and 45,000 people were arrested.

Many Mexican Jews are descendants of immigrants escaping pogroms and other antisemitic attacks in Europe and the Ottoman Empire. Since humor is a component of their character, remembrances of such incidents occasionally show up in food. This Tequila with Basil cocktail is connected with a number of incidents, including the pogrom that took place in Kishinev, now modern Moldova, in 1905, memorialized by Hebrew poet Hayim Nahman Bialik in his poem "In the City of Slaughter." Other references are a L'Chaim to the death of the seventeenth-century antisemitic Cossack Bohdan Khmelnytsky, who, along with his army, massacred thousands of Jews between 1648 and 1649, in Ukraine, in what remains as one of the darkest days in Jewish history.

. . . .

SERVES 2
Preparation time: 5 minutes

6 fresh basil leaves

4 ounces fresh lemon juice (from 1–2 lemons)

3 ounces gold tequila

1 ounce simple syrup

Ice, for serving

Bitters, to taste

1. Muddle the fresh basil leaves to release their oil, then place them in a cocktail shaker.

2. Add the lemon juice, tequila, and simple syrup to shaker.

3. Shake passionately, then pour over ice. Add bitters to taste.

Miriam's Cinnamon Sugar Beer Cookies

As a child, Ilan had other motives for his sweet tooth: he pretended that through Bobe Miriam's beer cookies, he was being introduced to the extraordinarily rich world of Mexican alcoholic beverages, in particular beers such as Corona, XXX, and Negra Modelo. Somehow he did, although he only got drunk with them in the figurative sense. Variations of these soft and chewy cookies were sent to us from a number of families across Mexico, including an almost identical recipe from Baba Malka, this one infused with the crunch of cinnamon sugar and the extra maltiness of Negra Modelo, introduced in Mexico in 1925 and still perceived as the working-class beer.

MAKES ABOUT 30 COOKIES
Preparation time: 10 minutes
Baking time: 15 minutes

FOR THE COOKIES

2½ cups all-purpose flour

½ teaspoon kosher salt

1 teaspoon baking powder

1 teaspoon baking soda

1 cup (2 sticks) unsalted butter, softened

1¼ packed cups light brown sugar

⅓ cup dark beer

1 large egg

1 teaspoon vanilla extract

FOR THE TOPPING

¼ cup turbinado sugar

1 tablespoon ground cinnamon

1. Heat the oven to 350°F and line 2 large baking sheets with parchment paper.

2. Sift together the flour, salt, baking powder, and baking soda in a medium-size bowl and set aside.

3. In a separate large bowl, beat together the butter and brown sugar until smooth. Add the beer, egg, and vanilla and mix until well combined. (The mixture will look curdled at this stage.) Add the dry ingredients to the wet in 2 batches, stirring after each, until a smooth dough forms.

4. Make the topping: In a small bowl, stir together the turbinado sugar and cinnamon.

5. Scoop out rounded tablespoons of the dough and roll into balls. (Wash and dry your hands periodically while forming the cookies to keep the dough from sticking.) Roll the dough balls into the cinnamon-sugar topping, then place on the prepared baking sheets.

6. Bake, rotating the baking sheets back to front and top to bottom halfway through, until golden and puffed, 13–15 minutes. Transfer the cookies to wire racks to cool.

Malka's Mexican Chocolate Babka

Malka traveled from Mexico City to Los Angeles throughout Margaret's childhood. Frozen *babkes* wrapped in foil always filled at least one of her suitcases, and her family would store and thaw babkas at set intervals in between her visits to and from Mexico. Baba Malka would pack at least one babka for each member of the family, and they would in turn fill her empty suitcase with assorted oddities that she loved from the United States: Solo poppy seed cake filling, L'Oreal hair dye, a modest dress from Robinsons-May department store.

Babkas are prepared with yeast-leavened dough, rolled out and braided, incorporating a variety of ingredients including chocolate, cheese, dried fruit, nuts, and spice before they are baked in the oven. We can trace recipes for sweet braided babka to Ashkenazic communities in Poland and the Ukraine in the eighteenth century. Babkas are wildly popular in Israel and in the Jewish diaspora around the world, with battles for best chocolate babkas fought across Brooklyn bakeries today.

This version of chocolate babka uses Mexican chocolate, a blend of cacao, chiles, cinnamon sugar, and other spices. As Baba Malka knew well, babkas bake and freeze well, so consider doubling this recipe to share or store.

. . . .

MAKES 1 ROUND BABKA
Preparation time: 40 minutes,
  plus rising
Bake time: 35 minutes

FOR THE DOUGH

1 packet (2 ¼ teaspoons) active dry yeast

1 teaspoon plus ⅓ cup granulated sugar, divided

½ cup warm water

2 ½–2 ¾ cups all-purpose flour, plus more for rolling and shaping

½ teaspoon kosher salt

1 large egg

½ cup (1 stick) unsalted butter, cut into pieces and softened, plus more for the pan

1 teaspoon vegetable oil

FOR THE FILLING

1 cup raisins (golden or dark)

¾ cup walnuts

¾ cup granulated sugar

4 tablespoons unsalted butter, softened

4 ounces Mexican chocolate, roughly chopped

FOR THE TOPPING

1½ tablespoons granulated sugar

1 teaspoon ground cinnamon

1 large egg

· ·

1. Make the dough: In a large bowl, stir together the yeast, 1 teaspoon of sugar, and the warm water. Let sit until foaming, about 5 minutes.

2. Meanwhile, whisk together 2½ cups of the flour, the remaining ⅓ cup of sugar, and the salt in a medium-size bowl.

3. Stir the egg into the yeast mixture. Add the flour mixture and gently stir until the dough begins to come together. Turn the dough out onto a floured surface and knead well, adding the softened butter pieces a few at a time, and adding up to ¼ cup more flour as needed, until you have a supple, slightly tacky dough, about 10 minutes. You might not need all of the flour. (The kneading can also be done in a stand mixer fitted with a dough hook, 5–7 minutes.)

4. Grease a large bowl with the oil, add the dough, and turn to coat. Cover the bowl with a clean tea towel and let it sit in a warm place until nearly doubled in size, about 2 hours.

5. Meanwhile, make the filling: In a food processor, combine the raisins, walnuts, sugar, butter, and Mexican chocolate and pulse until smooth.

6. Generously grease a round 10-inch Bundt pan with butter and set aside.

7. Gently punch down the dough, turn out onto a lightly floured surface, and roll into a large, ¼-inch-thick rectangle.

8. Spread the filling onto the dough, leaving a ¼-inch border around the edges. Starting at one of the long sides of the rectangles, roll up the dough tightly like a jelly roll. Using a sharp knife, trim the ends off each roll and discard. Halve the roll lengthwise. You should now have 2 long strands of dough, with the layers of filling exposed. Twist the strands together and pinch at the top and bottom to seal. Lay the twist into the Bundt pan, cover with a clean tea towel, and let rise until puffed, 1 hour.

9. Meanwhile, heat the oven to 350°F. To make the topping, stir together the sugar and cinnamon in a small bowl, and beat the egg with a splash of water in another small bowl. Brush a layer of the egg wash over the top of the babka (you will not use all of it), then sprinkle with the cinnamon sugar mixture.

10. Bake until golden brown and cooked through, 30–35 minutes.

Cinnamon Churro Babka

Masa Madre—in Spanish, "mother dough"—is a Mexican Jewish artisanal bakery based in Chicago. The founders and owners are bakers Tamar Fasja Unikel and Elena Vasquez Felgueres, longtime friends who grew up near each other in Mexico City. In their words, they blend their "shared Mexican heritage and Tamar's Jewish roots through flavors inspired by [their] grandmothers' kitchens." Both recent immigrants, they add, "We missed the taste of home and found bread to be the key to connection and community."

Tamar and Elena are extraordinarily creative in their combinations: hibiscus-spiced challah, tres leches babka. The recipe they share with us here connects the sweet braided bread that originated in Ukraine and Poland with the flavor of churros, a fried dough that Mexico inherited from Spain, made with choux pastry piped into hot oil. During the Christmas holidays, you can get churros on street corners everywhere in Mexico. They are coated with either sugar or melted chocolate. The combination of babka and churro pushes the palate into new dimensions. This recipe asks for Ceylon cinnamon, which is regarded as a more delicate, subdued, and sweet version of the spice and is the preferred cinnamon in traditional Mexican cuisine. If you use a stronger-flavored cinnamon, we suggest you reduce the amount to two teaspoons.

. . . .

MAKES 2 LOAVES
Preparation time: 40 minutes,
  plus rising
Baking time: 35 minutes

FOR THE DOUGH

1 packet (2¼ teaspoons) active
  dry yeast

1 tablespoon granulated sugar

¾ cup warm water

4–4¼ cups all-purpose flour

1 teaspoon kosher salt

½ cup vegetable oil

4 large eggs, divided

1 tablespoon honey

FOR THE FILLING

½ cup (1 stick) unsalted butter or
  nonhydrogenated margarine,
  softened

1 packed cup light brown sugar

1 tablespoon ground cinnamon
  (preferably Ceylon)

1. Make the dough: Combine the yeast, sugar, and warm water in the bowl of a stand mixer fitted with a dough hook and allow the yeast to bloom, about 5 minutes.

2. Meanwhile, whisk together 4 cups of the flour and the salt in a medium-size bowl, and set aside.

3. Add the oil, 3 of the eggs, and the honey to the yeast mixture and beat on low to combine. Add the flour mixture and let the mixer run, scraping down the sides of the bowl and adding up to ¼ cup more flour as needed, until the dough is supple and elastic, but not sticky, 7–8 minutes. (You might not need all of the flour.) Cover the bowl and let the dough rise for 1 hour.

4. Make the filling: Add the softened butter, brown sugar, and cinnamon to a medium-size bowl and use a sturdy spoon to mix it together until smooth.

5. Grease two 9 × 5-inch loaf pans, or line them with parchment paper, and set aside.

6. Gently punch down the dough and turn it out onto a lightly floured surface. Divide into 2 equal pieces. Working with one piece at a time, roll out the dough with a floured rolling pin into a large rectangle about ¼ inch thick.

7. Evenly spread half of the filling onto the dough, leaving a ¼-inch border around the edges. Starting with one of the long sides, roll the dough up tightly like a jelly roll. Using a sharp knife, slice the roll lengthwise. You should now have 2 long strands of dough, with the filling exposed. Twist the strands together and pinch at the top and bottom to seal. Carefully transfer it to one of the loaf pans, tucking it in to fit, if needed. Repeat the process with the remaining dough and filling. Loosely cover the loaves with a clean tea towel and let rise for 30 minutes.

8. Meanwhile, heat the oven to 350°F.

9. Beat the remaining egg in a small bowl and evenly brush the loaves with a layer of egg wash (you will not use all of it.) Bake, rotating the pans front-to-back halfway through, until golden brown and cooked through, 30–35 minutes. Remove from the oven and set on wire racks to cool.

Lime Macaroons

According to some historians, the macaroon, a cookie made from ground almonds, coconut, or maybe potato, popped up in Italian monasteries in the eighth century. Macaroons are a staple of Passover meals, since they don't require the leavening of flour in baking. They come in different types, including the beloved chocolate-dipped variety. This recipe relies on a meringue base that is used abundantly, in many macaroon recipes. Margaret's aunt Eve is known for her chocolate-inflected variety and is a gentle coach in observing egg whites transmuting to stiff peaks.

This recipe appears in Ilan's grandmother's recipe book. He would visit her a day or two before Passover to watch her prepare them, along with other dishes for the holiday. As she would mix the ingredients, Bobe Miriam would talk about going to different mercados in downtown Mexico City, either with her daughters or with a couple of friends, to find the particular marchante, Dona Toñita, the stand seller who sold the best flaked coconut, eggs, and limes. The citrus flavor is emblematic of the Mexican Jewish palate, and this recipe is quick to prepare and very forgiving, making it a special delight to prepare with young children.

MAKES ABOUT 2 DOZEN COOKIES
Preparation time: 20 minutes
Baking time: 25 minutes

14 ounces unsweetened, flaked coconut

1 cup sweetened condensed milk

1 teaspoon vanilla extract

2 packed teaspoons grated lime zest

2 large egg whites

¼ teaspoon kosher salt

1. Heat the oven to 325°F and line 2 large baking sheets with parchment paper.

2. In a large bowl, mix together the coconut, condensed milk, vanilla, and lime zest.

3. In a stand mixer fitted with a whisk attachment (or using a handheld electric mixer), beat together the egg whites and salt until stiff peaks form. Gently fold the egg whites into the coconut mixture until no streaks remain.

4. Scoop out rounded tablespoons of the coconut mixture and form into small mounds on the baking sheets, leaving 1 inch of space around each cookie.

5. Bake, rotating the baking sheets back to front and top to bottom halfway through, until golden around the edges and on top, 20–25 minutes. (The cookies will be soft but will firm up as they cool.) Remove from the oven and carefully transfer to wire racks to cool.

Mexican Alfajores: Morir sin Sufrir

Or should it be *sufrir sin morir*, to suffer but not die? Although these cookies—the name derives from the Arabic word *al-fakhir*, meaning "luxurious"—are regarded as a traditional Argentinian sweet, they date back to the eighth-century Middle East. They later flourished in Andalusia and were brought to Latin America during colonization. Alfajores are usually present during the end-of-the-year holidays. This recipe comes from La Comunidad and is often enjoyed at birthday celebrations accompanied by a mariachi soundtrack. The added moniker "Morir sin sufrir" is a humorous statement suggesting that the best way to face death is while eating a life-affirming sweet.

MAKES ABOUT 20 COOKIES
Preparation time: 35 minutes, plus cooling
Baking time: 12 minutes

1½ cups pastry flour, plus more for rolling

½ cup cornstarch

1 teaspoon baking powder

½ teaspoon kosher salt

10 tablespoons (1¼ sticks) unsalted butter, softened

½ cup confectioners' sugar, plus more for dusting

1 teaspoon grated orange zest

2 large egg yolks

1 teaspoon vanilla extract

Cajeta and orange marmalade, for filling

1. Whisk together the pastry flour, cornstarch, baking powder, and salt in a medium-size bowl and set aside.

2. Add the butter, confectioners' sugar, and orange zest to the bowl of a stand mixer fitted with a paddle attachment and beat until pale and fluffy, 3–4 minutes. Add the egg yolks, one at a time, followed by the vanilla, beating to incorporate after each addition.

3. Add the flour mixture to the butter mixture in 2 batches, beating on low to combine, until a smooth dough is formed. Form the dough into a disk and wrap well in parchment or plastic wrap and refrigerate for 1 hour.

4. Heat the oven to 350°F and line 2 large baking sheets with parchment paper. Turn the dough out onto a lightly floured work surface and, using a lightly floured rolling pin, roll the dough out to ¼-inch thickness. (Don't roll the dough thinner or the cookies will break when you fill them.) Using a 2-inch round cookie cutter, stamp out as many circles of dough as possible, and transfer them to the baking sheets. Gather and reroll the dough and stamp out more circles.

5. Bake until very lightly golden and just set, 10–12 minutes. Transfer the cookies to wire racks to cool completely.

6. Gently spread about 1 teaspoon of cajeta over the flat side of one cookie, then top with about ½ teaspoon of marmalade. Carefully top the filling with a second cookie and transfer to a serving plate. Repeat the process with the remaining cookies and filling. Dust the tops of the cookies with confectioner's sugar just before serving.

Poppy Seed Flan

Flan as custards have many regional variations across Latin America, including Venezuelan flan and island-inspired coconut flan. In different parts of the Caribbean, like the Dominican Republic and Venezuela, flan is called *quesillo*. In Ilan's and Margaret's families, different variations of flan were served depending on the occasion, from more traditional caramel and chocolate to fruit-infused varieties, such as mamey. No matter the flavor, flan was frequently the closing number to a succulent meal.

There is a science connected with the consistency of flan. Some prefer it thicker, almost like queso blanco. Others opt for a more delicate texture more malleable than gelatin that is at once soft and elegant. The colors of flan are also essential. A good flan must be a visual treat, offering a range of hues that erase the borders between each other.

This variation incorporates poppy seeds, an ingredient central in Middle Eastern and eastern European cuisines, and the favorite of Margaret's grandfather Ruben. The poppy seeds provide a nice counterbalance of taste and texture to the familiar sweetness of this custard.

SERVES 8
Preparation time: 15 minutes,
    plus chilling
Baking time: 45 minutes

1½ tablespoons poppy seeds, plus
    optionally more for topping

1 cup granulated sugar

¼ cup water

4 large eggs

½ packed cup light brown sugar

2 teaspoons vanilla extract

½ cup heavy cream

1½ cups whole milk

1. Heat the oven to 325°F. Lightly grease or spray eight 6-ounce ramekins and arrange them inside a large baking dish (or two baking dishes if they don't all fit in one).

2. Add the 1½ tablespoons of poppy seeds to a spice grinder or coffee grinder and briefly grind until cracked but not floury. Set aside.

3. Stir together the sugar and water in a medium-size heavy-bottomed sauce-pan set over medium-low heat. Let the mixture cook, stirring as little as pos-sible, until an amber-colored caramel forms, 5–10 minutes. (Watch carefully so the caramel doesn't burn.) Immediately divide the hot caramel among the rame-kins, coating the bottom of each with a layer of caramel.

4. In a large bowl, whisk together the eggs, brown sugar, vanilla, and ground poppy seeds.

5. Heat the heavy cream and milk together in a microwave in 30-second increments, or on the stovetop over medium heat, until just steaming but not boiling.

6. Whisking constantly, gradually add the heated milk mixture to the egg mixture. (Add just a tablespoon at a time at first, to temper the eggs so they do not scramble.) Divide the custard evenly between the ramekins.

7. Carefully pour enough water into the baking dishes to reach halfway up the ramekins. Cover the baking dishes with aluminum foil and bake until the centers of the custard are just set, 25–35 minutes. Remove from the oven and let cool, then cover each ramekin and let them chill in the refrigerator for at least 4 hours before serving.

8. To serve, run a knife along the outside of the custards and unmold by inverting the ramekins onto serving plates. Sprinkle each with more poppy seeds, if desired.

Sor Juana's Ricotta Buñuelos

The family of Sor Juana Ines de la Cruz (1648–1695), one of whose ancestors had Jewish blood, was from Nepantla. When she chose monastic life, she resided in a couple of convents. One of them is where the Claustro de Sor Juana stands today, not far from the Inquisition Palace, where the Holy Office held its trials against Jews, Muslims, heretics, witches, and various categories of others considered to be deviants. Some scholars believe Sor Juana's grandmother was a conversa. How much of the family's Jewish tradition passed on to her is subject of debate. What is unquestionable is that one of Sor Juana's varied interests was the art of cooking. In the convent of San Jerónimo, which is where the Claustro stands now, she monitored, in meticulous detail, the ingredients acquired to prepare meals for the nuns. And in her autobiographical *Response to Sor Filotea de la Cruz*, a letter to the Bishop of Puebla, Manuel Fernández de Santa Cruz (published posthumously in 1700), she writes passionately about the right for women to have access to education, and across her writing she makes a reference to cooking as a kind of knowledge: "If Aristotle had cooked, he wouldn't have written." Sor Juana's ricotta buñuelos come from a small recipe book she compiled. It includes mostly desserts that were served in her convent; we have updated her recipe for today's home kitchen.

MAKES 10–15 FRITTERS
Preparation time: 40 minutes, plus resting
Cooking time: 30 minutes

1 cup ricotta cheese

6 egg yolks

¼ cup granulated sugar, plus more for serving

2½ teaspoons ground anise

3 cups all-purpose flour, plus more for rolling

1½ teaspoons baking powder

Vegetable oil, for frying

Jam, for serving

1. Combine the ricotta, egg yolks, sugar, and ground anise in the bowl of a stand mixer and beat on low until combined. Whisk together the flour and baking powder in a medium-size bowl.

2. Add the flour mixture to the ricotta mixture in stages, beating on low and scraping down the sides of the bowl as necessary, until a thick and sticky dough forms. Cover the mixing bowl and let rest at room temperature for 1 hour.

3. On a large, floured work surface using a floured rolling pin, roll out the dough to ⅛-inch thickness. Use a sharp knife and a plate or bowl with a 4–5-inch diameter to cut out circles. Gather the scraps and repeat the rolling and cutting process, if desired.

4. Heat ¼ inch of oil in a medium frying pan set over medium heat until it reaches 350°F on a digital thermometer, and line a large baking sheet with paper towels. Working with one circle of dough at a time, slip it into the hot oil and fry, turning once, until puffed and golden, 30–60 seconds per side.

5. Transfer the fritters to the paper towels to drain and cool slightly. Serve warm, sprinkled with more sugar or dolloped with jam.

Kamish Bread con Cajeta

This is another one of Ilan's wife Alison's recipes, passed down from her great grandmother, who first baked it in Lviv, in western Ukraine, and brought kamish bread along as an immigrant to the United States. The name comes from Ukrainian *kamishbrot*. In Yiddish, it is *mandelbroyt,* also known as mandel bread, which literally means "almond bread," a reference to a common ingredient used in this recipe by Ashkenazi Jews but not by Alison. The Italian variety is called biscotti.

During Hanukkah, the moment she announces she is about to start baking kamish bread, the entire house descends to the kitchen to participate in the ritual. It is a joyful occasion. Dipping the kamish bread in cajeta is Ilan's addition.

MAKES ABOUT 20 LONG COOKIES
OR 40 SHORTER COOKIES
Preparation time: 20 minutes
Baking time: 1 hour, 25 minutes

½ cup (1 stick) unsalted butter, softened

1 cup plus 2 tablespoons granulated sugar, divided

3 large eggs

1 teaspoon vanilla extract

3 cups all-purpose flour

1 teaspoon baking powder

½ teaspoon kosher salt

1 teaspoon ground cinnamon

Cajeta, for serving

1. Heat the oven to 350°F and line 2 large baking sheets with parchment paper.

2. In a stand mixer fitted with the paddle attachment (or using a handheld mixer and a large bowl), beat the butter and 1 cup of sugar together on medium speed until light and fluffy. Add the eggs and vanilla and beat to combine.

3. Add the flour, baking powder, and salt and beat on low to form a soft, spread-able batter.

4. Scoop half of the batter into the center of each baking sheet. Using a butter knife or offset spatula, spread into oval-shaped loaves, about 8 inches in length. Mix together the remaining 2 table-spoons of sugar with the cinnamon and sprinkle half of the mixture over each loaf. Bake until just set enough to slice, about 25 minutes.

5. Remove from the oven and let the loaves cool slightly. Meanwhile, lower the oven temperature to 250°F. Slice the loaves crosswise into ¾-inch-thick pieces and space the pieces out onto the sheets. If shorter cookies are desired, each piece can be cut in half.

6. Return the cookies to the oven and bake until they are hard and dried out, about 1 hour. Remove from the oven and transfer to wire racks to cool.

7. Serve the cookies with cajeta along-side for dipping or spread a little cajeta onto each slice.

Ilan's Arroz con Leche

Ilan's family lived in Copilco, a neighborhood in the southern part of Mexico City, adjacent to the campus of UNAM (Universidad Nacional Autónoma de México), the largest public university in Latin America and one of the most respected. He credits this recipe with luring many of his high school friends, who lived in faraway parts of the city, to his house after class for a succulent portion of arroz con leche. Even though the dessert is a constant in Mexican cuisine, *un no sé qué* in the way it was made in Ilan's home—lemon zest, a cinnamon stick, golden raisins—and how it made people experience myriad reactions. Although it has the texture of a pudding, the key is to allow the rice to preserve its integrity and not disintegrate.

SERVES 4
Preparation time: 40 minutes

¾ cup short-grain white rice
  (such as bomba or arborio)

2½ cups water, plus more as needed

1 cinnamon stick

¾ cup whole milk

½ cup sweetened condensed milk

¼ cup golden raisins

1½ teaspoons vanilla extract

1 packed teaspoon grated lemon zest

Ground cinnamon, for dusting

1. Put the rice, water, and cinnamon stick in a medium saucepan set over medium-high heat. Bring to a boil, then lower the heat to medium and cook, stirring occasionally (and more frequently as the liquid reduces, to prevent burning), until the rice is tender and the liquid has evaporated, 15–20 minutes.

2. Meanwhile, whisk together the whole milk, condensed milk, raisins, vanilla, and lemon zest in a medium-size bowl. Pour the milk mixture into the saucepan and continue cooking, stirring often, until the mixture thickens, 5–10 minutes. (It will continue to thicken as it cools, so err on the soupy side.) Remove and discard the cinnamon stick.

3. Transfer to serving bowls and serve warm, dusted with ground cinnamon. Or let fully cool, then cover and refrigerate until chilled.

Ofelia's Dulce de Leche Churros

Ilan's sweet tooth comes from his mother, Ofelia, a connoisseur of confectionary dishes. As soon as she entered a bakery, her eyes would target the arrays of cakes and tarts. She wanted to know how each was made, how the recipes had evolved, what kind of clientele went for one type of cake and not the other. Bobe Miriam, Ofelia's own mother and Ilan's grandmother, frequently said that as a little girl her daughter wanted to grow up to be an ice cream taster and that, if ice cream tasting didn't work out, she wanted to learn how to bake elaborate holiday cakes.

Although Ofelia became a psychotherapist, her passion for sweets never diminished. She would always have spare candy in her purse to give people, especially if they found themselves in challenging situations. We think of the sweet as response to sadness as another characteristic of the Jewish Mexican condition, hard candies circulated among congregants at the end of Yom Kippur, cakes and vials of sprinkles shared and offered to mourners.

Ofelia's Dulce de Leche Churros is a glutton's dream. She would serve it on cold nights, accompanied with chocolate caliente, a cup of hot Mexican chocolate. On the table, there would be assorted fresh fruit—guava, mango, and prickly pear. Whenever Ilan's father was in the middle of rehearsing a new play, she would also bring her churros for actors to savor at the end of the session.

This type of churro is available in Mexican mercados around Día de los Muertos and at the end of the year, during Navidad and Día de Reyes.

· ·

SERVES 8–10
Preparation time: 1½ hours

½ cup water

¼ cup granulated sugar, plus more for dusting

½ cup (1 stick) unsalted butter, softened

1 teaspoon vanilla extract

2 cups all-purpose flour

4 large eggs

Vegetable oil, for frying

Ground cinnamon, for dusting

1 (15-ounce) jar dulce de leche, for dipping

1. Combine the water, sugar, butter, and vanilla in a large saucepan set over low heat. Heat, stirring occasionally, until the ingredients are melted and well mixed.

2. While still on the heat, gradually add the flour, mixing with a sturdy spoon to form a batter that doesn't stick to the pan. Transfer the batter to a stand mixer fitted with a paddle attachment and beat at medium speed until smooth. Add the eggs, one at a time, beating to fully incorporate after each addition, to form a thick paste.

3. Heat 2 inches of oil in a medium-size saucepan set over medium heat until the oil reaches 350°F on a deep-fry thermometer. Meanwhile, line a large plate with paper towels and set aside.

4. Transfer the churro paste to a pastry bag fitted with a large star tip. Working in batches of 4–5, squeeze the paste into the heated oil, using scissors to cut each churro to the desired length. Fry, turning once, until puffed and golden, 1–3 minutes per batch, depending on the length and thickness of the churros. Transfer the fried churros to the paper-towel-lined plate to briefly drain.

5. Mix a little more sugar with cinnamon in a bowl (at whatever your desired ratio) and sprinkle the churros with the cinnamon sugar while still warm. Serve warm with dulce de leche alongside for dipping.

Cheesecake con Guayaba

Variations on pay de queso, sweet Mexican cheese pie, abound. This recipe is truer to the flavor profile of an East Coast sour cream cheesecake and comes to us from a Jewish Mexican family in Miami. This family incorporates the guava (*guayaba* in Spanish) glaze cheesecake with stories about Shabbat dinners, tiny grandchildren, and the movement across borders and generations. While it is possible to serve a plain cheesecake with squares of prepared guava paste as a complement, we recommend preparing the guava sauce with fresh fruit if possible and drizzling it artfully over the cheesecake or individual servings.

· ·

SERVES 8

Preparation time: 30 minutes,
   plus resting and chilling
Baking time: 1¼ hours

FOR THE CHEESECAKE

2 cups finely crushed graham cracker crumbs (from about 20 whole graham crackers)

½ cup (1 stick) salted butter, melted and slightly cooled

1 cup plus 3 tablespoons granulated sugar, divided

4 (8-ounce) packages cream cheese, softened

¾ cup sour cream

2 teaspoons all-purpose flour

½ teaspoon kosher salt

4 large eggs plus 1 large egg yolk

2 teaspoons vanilla extract

FOR THE GUAVA SAUCE

1½ pounds ripe guavas, peeled, seeds removed, and quartered

2 tablespoons honey

1. Make the cheesecake: Heat the oven to 350°F and lightly grease a 9-inch springform pan.

2. Mix together the graham cracker crumbs, melted butter, and 3 table-spoons of sugar in a medium-size bowl. Transfer the crumb mixture to the greased springform pan, then press it evenly across the bottom to create a thick layer of crumbs. Bake until lightly golden, about 10 minutes, then remove from the oven and let cool while making the filling.

3. In a stand mixer or using a handheld electric mixer, beat the softened cream cheese, sour cream, flour, remaining 1 cup of sugar, and salt until creamy and smooth. Add the eggs, egg yolk, and vanilla and beat until smooth. Pour the mixture over the graham cracker crust, smoothing the top.

4. Bake for 70 minutes, then turn the oven off and leave the cheesecake inside for 15 minutes more. (It will puff up dramatically, then fall once out of the oven.) Remove from the oven and let cool to room temperature, about 2 hours, then cover and refrigerate until chilled, 2–3 hours.

5. Meanwhile, make the sauce: Combine the guava and honey in a medium-size saucepan set over medium heat. Bring the mixture to a bubble and cook, stirring often, until the mixture thickens, about 20 minutes. Remove from the heat and use an immersion blender to blend into a smooth purée. Let cool.

6. To serve: Gently open the springform pan and transfer the cake to a serving plate. Serve the cake sliced, with the guava sauce alongside for drizzling.

Paletas de Jamaica con Limón

You could call them ice pops or popsicles, but then you would be missing the complex culture around paletas in Mexico. These multiflavored, liquid-based frozen bars defy the imagination. No wonder the *paleterías*, shops specializing in the creation and sale of paletas, have become increasingly popular both in Mexico and in the United States over the decades.

Paletas are created of all sorts of concoctions: guacamole, enchiladas, tequila, cactus fruit, crickets, sugar skulls, and anything else in between. The most common flavors are lemon, strawberry, hibiscus, and coconut, but who wants to be traditional in a realm where the possibilities are literally infinite? This recipe combining hibiscus and lime is wildly popular at Mexican taquerias, and the tart flavor is a refreshing balance to any savory meal or just a cooling treat during a hot day.

In Mexican Jewish households, just as in every Mexican home, people seek to be unique by creating their own recipe. During the making of this volume, we savored many varieties, both at homes of different hosts and in paleterías: cucumber in vodka, pineapple with cilantro, mango with chile piquín, mint and lime, café con leche, margarita, tacos al pastor, cookies and cream, and a thousand others.

MAKES 6 PALETAS
Preparation time: 40 minutes,
 plus chilling

3 cups water

1 cup granulated sugar

½ cup dried hibiscus flowers

2 tablespoons fresh lime juice

1. Combine the water and sugar in a medium saucepan set over medium-high heat. Bring to a boil, stirring often to dissolve the sugar.

2. Add the hibiscus flowers, lower the heat to medium, and simmer, stirring occasionally, until the mixture thickens a bit, about 5 minutes. Remove from the heat and let cool.

3. Strain the liquid through a mesh sieve into a bowl, discarding the hibiscus flowers. Stir in the lime juice, then divide the mixture evenly between 6 paleta or flat popsicle molds. Freeze until solid, at least 5 hours.

Ruben's Gogol Mogol

A traditional Ashkenazi recipe, similar to eggnog, traditionally served warm for a therapeutic effect akin to chicken soup as curative for a cold. Though Margaret's grandfather Ruben was loath to let illness slow him down— "I've got plenty what to do"—he was an emblematic hustler-mensch. Ruben was born in Veracruz and grew up and spent his early adulthood in Mexico City, studying architecture and designing buildings, including the apartment building where his parents lived.

In the early 1960s, he moved his young family (including Margaret's mother) to Los Angeles. Margaret heard stories about the egg-cure from parents and grandparents, but it wasn't until the end of his life that Ruben taught Margaret to make this drink late one evening, just as he had learned it from his parents. Now we cherish those evening conversations and fondly prepare the drink as a remedy and reminder to slow down.

SERVES 1
Preparation time: 5 minutes

1½ teaspoons granulated sugar

1 egg yolk

1 ounce brandy

¾ cup warmed whole milk

1. Whisk together the sugar and egg yolk in a mug until the sugar has mostly dissolved.

2. Stir in the brandy, then gently pour over the warmed milk, stirring constantly. Serve immediately.

Café de Olla con Licor

Café de olla, which translates literally to "coffee from a pot," is a traditional Mexican beverage mixing coffee, spices, and sugar. The drink was also thought to be a favorite of Emiliano Zapata, a key player in the Mexican Revolution of 1910, which was the first major upheaval of its kind in the twentieth century. Zapata called for land reform, returning farmable land to workers. You might sip the coffee and mull over the words *tierra y libertad*, "land and freedom."

In whichever metropolitan center you live, you will likely know where and when to find the best marchantes of café de olla. In Mexico City, for instance, some of our favorite stands are in the downtown area, Hipódromo, Roma, Coyoacán, Iztapalapa, and Xochimilco. If you arrive too early, the marchante might still be setting up; if too late, your cup will be filled with the muddy-tasting sediment at the bottom of the tank.

Mexican Jews like all kinds of cafés de olla, and they are enjoyed as frequently in the kitchen as they might be after Shabbat services. The one with liquor adds a little punch. Some also mix with chocolate: chile-chocolate, a drink that dates back to the Aztecs and is made with hot chiles, and the warm beverages chocolate caliente or champurrado.

SERVES 2
Preparation time: 25 minutes

5 cups water

3 cinnamon sticks

4 whole cloves

2 star anise pods

1 tablet piloncillo sugar, or
  ½ cup dark brown sugar

¾ cup espresso ground coffee

4 ounces almond liqueur

2 tablespoons heavy cream or
  condensed milk

1. Combine the water, cinnamon sticks, cloves, star anise, and sugar in a small saucepan. Bring slowly to a boil over medium heat, stirring occasionally to break up the sugar. Reduce the heat and simmer for 20 minutes. Remove from the heat, stir in the coffee, cover, and steep for 5 minutes. Strain the coffee through a filter or press.

2. To serve each glass: Add almond liqueur (roughly 2 ounces) and top with café de olla. Add heavy cream or condensed milk to taste (roughly 1 tablespoon). This beverage can be enjoyed hot or chilled over ice.

Fondas and Cafés

AMONG OTHER THINGS, Mexican Jews are known for the outstanding eateries they have opened over almost a century. A number of our recipes in this volume come from the chefs of those restaurants.

As soon as immigrants settled down, it was the women who, in almost no time, transformed their kitchens into Jewish *fondas* (makeshift restaurants) and opened their doors in downtown Mexico City. They would shop in nearby kosher butcher shops, visit La Merced for fruits and legumes, and cook not only for their immediate family but for members of La Comunidad. News of these fondas traveled by mouth. One of the early ones was on Calle Academia, no. 42.

Margo Glantz, in her memoir *The Family Tree*, describes, in handsome detail, El Carmel, her immigrant parents' restaurant in Zona Rosa, which opened to much acclaim in the 1960s. Elizabeth Shapiro, Glantz's mother, was the force behind the restaurant. Her husband was Jacobo Glantz, a Russian-born Jewish poet who witnessed the Bolshevik Revolution. He was known for writing impressionistic Yiddish poetry. He looked like Leon Trotsky. For one of Diego Rivera's murals, the painter asked the poet to pose. The menu fused Israeli cuisine of the 1960s—falafel, tahini, tomato and cucumber chopped salad—with salsas, Mexican fruits such as mango, papaya, and mamey, and cakes that combined eastern European and Mexican elements.

Over time, fondas mutated into sophisticated restaurants, bakeries, and cafés. On one of our trips to Mexico City, we visited the headquarters for a tour of the AJLA Gourmet, a kosher Mediterranean-style bakery that celebrates making babka a landmark in Mexico City. Observing the team of pastry chefs and bakers, we were surrounded by the scents and sights of trays of cookies recently baked and in process, other rooms full of dough proofing, and the highlight of watching pita puff over a wood-fire stove with bakers singing mariachi in the background.

Mexican Jews own taquerías, mezcalerías, and paleterías. We enjoyed extended lunch and conversation at Niddo in Colonia Juaréz, sampling a variety of breakfast foods, including shakshuka, chilaquiles, molletes with refried beans, squash blossoms and salsa, avocado-topped bagels, and a variety of fruits, juices, coffees, and teas.

We also sampled falafel and paletas from small vendors across the city and hunted down the famed kosher quesadillas from La Muertita's food truck. Our friends told us that the best New York Jewish deli could now be found in the Mexico City neighborhood La Condesa: Mendl's Delicatessen, run by Sephardi chef Monserrat Garza Garduño.

And we laughed about Mishiguene ("crazy" in Yiddish), an eatery with its first location in Buenos Aires, Argentina, and a more recent branch in Pedregal, in the southern part of Mexico City. The menu—like so many across this vibrant landscape—showcases immigrant and diaspora Jewish cuisine from around the globe.

We also enjoyed learning about the legendary galletas Taifeld, cookies that have been a staple on Jewish Mexican tables for generations. The Taifeld family opened a bakery that made challahs available early on Fridays. They launched in the 1970s with the traditional favorite panecillos de Salvado con miel de abeja y avena, bran muffins with honey and oatmeal. The bakery has adapted to modern tastes and demands, more recently including vegan cookies and high-protein offerings.

Just like everywhere else, eating out for La Comunidad is almost a sport. The moment a new spot opens up, people are eager to sample dishes, passing on their opinion with fervor. The joy of eating and the art of critiquing go hand in hand. Is there anything more Jewish? •

Outdoor seating at Niddo Dresde in Mexico City, January 2023.

FIESTAS JUDÍAS

✕✕✕✕✕✕✕✕✕✕✕✕ ✕✕✕✕✕✕✕✕✕✕✕✕✕✕

As is the case around the globe, the calendar of La Comunidad rotates around set rituals. There is the solar year starting in January and the lunar year that begins in Tishrei. There are all kinds of Jews in Mexico: from orthodox to agnostic, passing through conservative and reform. Observing the holidays starts with Shabbat, considered to be the holiest of all festivities in the calendar. Every Friday night, observant Mexican Jewish families congregate at home at sunset to light candles, break challah, and bless wine. A succulent meal follows, and then a round of sweets. Folks can linger around the table until 11:00 p.m.

During the High Holidays of Rosh Hashanah and Yom Kippur, Mexican Jews of all denominations are visible in Polanco, Tecamachalco, Hipódromo, Las Lomas, Santa Fé, and other neighborhoods. Before starting the fast, they often eat a light meal involving fruits. For the breaking of the fast, some might begin with a cup of tea accompanied by crackers or with sweet candies collected in a purse for the end of a service. With family at home, an array of savory dishes can be found.

The festival of Purim is a joyful occasion to dress up not only like Haman in the book of Esther but in costumes reminding people of the gallery of villains in Mexican history: dictator Porfirio Díaz, President Carlos Salinas de Gortari, El Chupacabra, and others. Visiting a mercado, particularly the section of piñatas, chocolates, and dulces cristalizados, might be an activity in which children are part. Marchantes in mercados such as La Merced, Coyoacán, Del Valle, Portales, and Hipódromo are commissioned—in spite of the prohibition against images—to design paraphernalia depicting biblical characters (Kings David and Solomon, for instance), as well as ancient and contemporary Jewish heroes such as Bar Kochba of the Masada rebellion, Maimonides, Anne Frank, the leader of the Warsaw ghetto uprising Mordecai Anielewicz, and Zionist figures including Theodor Herzl, David Ben Gurion, and Golda Meir. There are also effigies of recognizable Mexican historical characters like Sor Juana Inés de la Cruz, Frida Kahlo, Emiliano Zapata, Subcomandante Marcos, and others.

During Passover (Pésaj, in Spanish), Mexican Jews combine elements of the Exodus narrative that serves as blueprint for the occasion, with motifs in Mexican history about resistance and survival. These include references to the plight of Indigenous leaders such as the final two Aztec emperors, Moctezuma and Cuauhtémoc, or the antireligious president Benito Juárez. Passover often brings families together for two consecutive Seders, in which remembering the departure from Egypt is an opportunity to talk about freedom, bondage, resistance, and new beginnings. The Seder meal features all sorts of fusion dishes.

Hanukkah allows for inspiring cross-fertilization. Mexicans love candles, and the Festival of Lights is a suitable opportunity for displaying not only different models of menorahs but multicolored candles. Indeed, the making of original menorahs has no end. Mexican Jews create them with an assortment of materials. Those playing with dreidels connect with non-Jewish neighbors using tops called *trompos*. The Mexican tradition of Posadas, which memorializes the itinerant journey of José and María, parents of Jesus, as they sought refuge before she gave birth, gathers people on successive evenings to eat and drink together. Although the activity is beyond the purview of Jewish tradition, less observant Mexican Jews are frequently invited to participate.

Driven by a desire to build bridges across religious traditions, younger Mexican Jews have incorporated elements of Día de los Muertos into their routines. The sugar skull makes an appearance in Jewish gatherings, using words that might refer to the ten kabbalistic sefirot, Talmudic lessons, Israeli iconography, and other aspects of Jewish life.

Sinagoga Justo Sierra, Mexico City, January 2023.

Throughout the decades, the departure of younger Mexican Jews to Israel as well as the United States and Canada, along with the arrival in Mexico of Israelis who have come to resettle, has incorporated fresher elements to the crossbreeding traditions. Numerous falafel bars have sprung up in Mexican cities, as well as elegant restaurants showcasing Mediterranean cuisine, specialty markets, and other Israeli-style venues. •

Pomegranate Margarita

The flower known in Spanish as *margarita*, "daisy," has given its name to what is arguably the best-known drink from the Hispanic world (Cuba libre comes in a distant second). The margarita features tequila, triple sec, and lime juice. Everyone seems to have a say in its origin story: some trace it to Tijuana in 1937, and others to Ensenada, Baja California, in 1941; the name might have been inspired by a Ziegfield dancer named Marjorie King who liked tequila but was allergic to other spirits or by Margarita Henkel Cesena, a Mexican German cantina customer.

The fact is that the cocktail has become a ubiquitous presence at fiestas and other occasions, not to say a best-selling drink at bars and restaurants. It is Mexican, Mexican American, and, thanks to Mexican Jews, a luscious combination of traditions.

One way for La Comunidad to prepare it is with pomegranate. In Sephardic households, pomegranate is enjoyed on the second day of Rosh Hashanah as a symbol of righteousness, knowledge, and wisdom in the new year. Throwing in a handful of pomegranate seeds invokes the sense of new beginning that Rosh Hashanah invokes.

Other ways to prepare it include incorporating pineapple, peach, and watermelon. Another combination called mojarita, part margarita and part mojito, mixes tequila and mint. There are spicy margaritas that contain not only a halo of salt or sugar but chile piquín. Ilan has been present at parties where that piquant rim is described as "the trace of a yarmulke."

. . . .

SERVES 2
Preparation time: 2 minutes

8 ounces unsweetened
  pomegranate juice

4 tablespoons fresh lime juice

3 ounces tequila

1 ounce orange liqueur

FOR SERVING

Coarse salt   Ice

Lime wedges   Pomegranate
                           seeds

1. Place some coarse salt on a small plate. Rub the rim of each glass with lime and dip in the salt.

2. Combine the drink ingredients in a cocktail shaker, add ice, and shake vigorously, then strain into the prepared glass. Garnish with pomegranate seeds and a lime wedge.

Latkes con Mole

One of the most delicious Jewish Mexican dishes, this recipe of latkes with mole was created by Alison Sparks, Ilan's wife. When Alison first traveled to Mexico in the 1980s, she learned from her *shviger* (mother-in-law), Ofelia, how to make mole. She soon discovered that in Mexico mole is served on everything, from eggs to chicken and tacos to enchiladas. Why not put mole on a latke? At the next Hanukkah celebration, she was quick to combine this ubiquitous sauce with the sumptuous latke. A classic was born.

The word *mole* derives from the Nahuatl *molli,* "sauce." Nahuatl was the language spoken by the Aztecs when the Spaniards arrived in the early sixteenth century. It is fitting that the Aztec rebellion against the conquistadors is here connected with the Jewish festival in which the Maccabees resisted Seleucid oppression.

After peeling, the russet potatoes are ground using the largest side of the grinder in order for the shreds to have a solid consistency. They are mixed with shredded onions, egg, potato starch, and salt. The deep-frying in oil speaks to the miracle in the Hanukkah story, in which a tiny quantity of oil let candles burn for eight nights. Although latkes are delicious in warming winter meals, they are also wonderful year-round as part of breakfast or an appetizer.

"The Hanukkah celebration is especially cheery because of the ritual candle lighting that takes place each night," says Alison. "I am always certain to include this special Spanish blessing: *Que nada brille más que la flama de la vela*—nothing should shine brighter than the candle flame."

. . . .

SERVES 8
Preparation time: 1½ hours

FOR THE LATKES

4 pounds russet potatoes, scrubbed and peeled

1 medium yellow onion, peeled

½ cup potato starch

1 tablespoon kosher salt

4 large eggs, lightly beaten

Vegetable oil, for frying

FOR THE MOLE

2 tablespoons vegetable oil

1 small white onion, finely chopped

1 (8-ounce) jar prepared mole

3 cups chicken or vegetable broth

2 ounces bittersweet chocolate, roughly chopped

FOR SERVING

Crumbled queso fresco

1. Make the latkes: Line 2 large baking sheets with several layers of paper towels and set aside.

2. Grate the potatoes and onion on the large holes of a box grater. (Or cut them into quarters and shred using the shredding disc of a food processor.) Working in batches, wrap the shredded potatoes and onion in a clean tea towel and squeeze out as much water as possible.

3. Add the shredded potatoes and onion to a large bowl along with the potato starch, salt, and eggs. Mix until fully incorporated.

4. In a large frying pan, heat ¼ inch of oil over medium-high heat until shimmering but not smoking. Working in batches of 4–5, drop ¼ cup of batter into the pan and press gently with a spatula to flatten slightly. Cook, flipping once, until browned on both sides and cooked through, 6–8 minutes per batch, then transfer to the prepared baking sheets to drain.

5. Continue with the remaining latke mixture, adding more oil as necessary and adjusting the heat up or down if the latkes are browning too quickly or not quickly enough. The latkes can be kept warm in the oven while preparing the mole.

6. Make the mole: Heat the oil in a large saucepan set over medium heat. Add the onion and cook, stirring often, until softened, 6–8 minutes.

7. Add a heaping tablespoon of the prepared mole, stirring to combine it with the onion, then add 1 cup of the broth. Bring to a boil, then lower the heat to medium low and cook, stirring often, until the mixture reaches the consistency of thick soup.

8. Continue adding the prepared mole and the remaining broth, a little at a time, until both are completely used up. Continue cooking the mixture, stirring often, until it turns into a thick, rich sauce. Add the chocolate, stirring to melt, then remove from the heat.

9. Serve the latkes hot, topped with mole and crumbled queso fresco.

On prepared mole: For readers in Los Angeles, we shout out Guelaguetza Restaurant, specializing in Oaxacan food, and their excellent jars of mole starters ready for purchase in person or online.

Chipotle Chicken Noodle and Matzah Ball Soup

Matzah balls take center stage at Passover—and, if we're honest, throughout the year at our homes—each recipe blending matzah meal, egg, and fat (most frequently chicken fat, schmaltz, or vegetable oil) to form a soft dumpling ready to absorb the flavors of a comforting broth. The chicken broth, egg noodles, and matzah balls will be familiar to many Ashkenazi households, but this Mexican Jewish variety relies on the irreplaceable and smoky satisfaction of the chipotle chile. Take care, though—it's easy to warp the recipe by going overboard with the chipotle.

The key is to remember what Ofelia, Ilan's mother, frequently said about it: chipotle is like perfume. A simple drop does wonders! Today he adds chipotle to his breakfast eggs, milanesa con patatas, and many other dishes. There is a variation of shakshuka that features, but isn't overwhelmed with, chipotle.

. . . .

SERVES 6
Preparation time: 30 minutes,
  plus resting
Cooking time: 30 minutes

¼ medium white onion, roughly
  chopped

¼ packed cup roughly chopped
  fresh cilantro (stems okay)

1 chipotle chile in adobo, chopped

4 large eggs

2 tablespoons vegetable oil

¾ teaspoon kosher salt

1 cup matzah meal

2 quarts chicken broth

2 cups water

2 medium carrots, peeled and
  thinly sliced

1 medium parsley root, peeled
  and thinly sliced

2 celery stalks, thinly sliced

1 large garlic clove, finely chopped

1–2 teaspoons adobo sauce

1 teaspoon kosher salt

Cooked egg noodles, for serving

1. Combine the onion, cilantro, chipotle chile, eggs, oil, and salt in a blender and blend until smooth. Transfer the mixture to a bowl and stir in the matzah meal. Cover and refrigerate for at least 30 minutes.

2. Meanwhile, bring a large pot of salted water to a boil over high heat, then turn the heat down to medium and keep at a steady simmer. With lightly moistened hands, scoop out rounded tablespoons of the matzah ball mixture, roll into balls, and drop into the simmering water. Cover the pot and cook, undisturbed, until puffed and cooked through, 20–25 minutes.

3. In a second large pot set over high heat, bring the broth and water to a boil. Add the carrots, parsley root, celery, garlic, desired amount of adobo sauce, and salt. Turn the heat down to medium and cook, stirring occasionally, until the vegetables soften, about 15 minutes.

4. To serve: Add the desired amount of matzah balls and egg noodles to individual bowls, and top with the soup. Serve hot.

Gefilte Fish en Salsa Roja

Gefilte fish with salsa—this variety relying on habanero, garlic, and cream—is a traditional Shabbat dish in La Comunidad. Made from ground whitefish, seasonings, eggs, and starch, the dish originated in eastern Europe as a way for poor Jewish women to serve meals during Shabbat while observing the tenets of the day of rest, which forbade removing bones from the fish. By the nineteenth century, gefilte fish was a staple of Ashkenazi cuisine. Mexican Jews have further adapted the dish, challenging the reputation of gefilte fish as flavorless with the addition of local ingredients.

Anat Nurko, who emigrated from Mexico City to Cleveland, Ohio, says that when the Spaniards conquered Mexico and settled in Veracruz, they brought with them new ingredients such as tomatoes, capers, and olives, which natives of Veracruz combined with chiles to make the celebrated Salsa Veracruzana, then added it to local fish like red snapper (huachinango) or robalo (snook).

Anat shares this recipe and remembers first eating this dish as part of Bar Mitzvah Kiddush lunches. She recalls soaking challah bread in salsa and says that the dish is a staple at family holiday meals, converting even the gefilte fish skeptics into enthusiasts.

. . . .

SERVES 6–8
Preparation time: 30 minutes
Cooking time: 1¼ hours

FOR THE POACHING BROTH

2 large carrots, peeled and
roughly chopped

1 large yellow onion, peeled
and roughly chopped

1 leek, halved lengthwise and
cleaned well

1 medium turnip, peeled and
roughly chopped

1 medium kohlrabi bulb, peeled
and roughly chopped

1 celery stalk, roughly chopped

12 cups water

1 tablespoon kosher salt

FOR THE FISH

12 ounces grouper fillets, skin
removed and cut into chunks

12 ounces red snapper fillets, skin
removed and cut into chunks

4 large eggs, lightly beaten

1 cup matzah meal

1 tablespoon vegetable oil

1 teaspoon granulated sugar

¾ teaspoon kosher salt

¼ teaspoon ground white pepper

FOR THE SALSA

4 large plum tomatoes (about 2 pounds),
cored and roughly chopped

1 medium white onion, peeled and
roughly chopped

1 large garlic clove, roughly chopped

½ habanero chile, seeds removed, if
desired, and roughly chopped

¾ cup heavy cream

1 teaspoon dried oregano

1¼ teaspoons kosher salt, plus more
as needed

¼ teaspoon freshly ground black
pepper

1. Make the poaching broth: Add the carrots, onion, leek, turnip, kohlrabi, celery, water, and salt to a large soup pot set over high heat. Bring to a boil, then lower the heat to medium low and simmer, partially covered, for 30 minutes.

2. Remove the vegetables from the pot with a slotted spoon, discarding the solids or reserving them for another use. Cover and set aside, off the heat.

3. Make the fish: Add both kinds of fish to a food processor and process until finely chopped. Add the eggs, matzah meal, oil, sugar, salt, and white pepper and pulse to fully combine.

4. Return the poaching broth to a simmer over medium heat. Meanwhile, scoop out ¼ cup of the fish mixture and, using lightly moistened hands, roll it into an oval-shaped ball. Set aside on a plate and continue with the remaining fish mixture.

5. Add the fish balls to the simmering broth. Cover, turn the heat to medium low, and simmer until firm and cooked through, about 30 minutes.

6. Meanwhile, make the salsa: Wash and dry the food processor, then add the tomatoes, onion, garlic, and habanero chile. Blend until smooth, then pour the mixture into a large saucepan set over medium-high heat. Stir in the heavy cream, oregano, salt, and black pepper. Bring to a boil, then lower the heat to medium and cook until slightly thickened, about 15 minutes. Taste and add more salt, if needed.

7. Transfer the cooked gefilte fish balls to the salsa and let cook, basting the gefilte fish with the salsa, until warmed through, 5–10 minutes. Serve hot or warm.

Variation: Baked Gefilte Fish. Do not make the poaching broth. Place the formed gefilte fish balls in a lightly greased baking dish and pour the salsa over top. Cover the baking dish with aluminum foil and bake at 350°F until bubbling and the fish is cooked through, 40–60 minutes.

Avocado Egg Salad

Margaret's parents hosted the breaking of the fast gathering at the conclusion of Yom Kippur for her maternal grandparents, aunts and uncles, cousins, and other family and friends. Hosting meals throughout this busy holiday season often rotated among family members in adjacent parts of Los Angeles. As the family would attend synagogue, it was often easier to have a variety of pre-prepared options at the ready for the end of the day: bagels, lox, and cream cheese and this avocado egg salad, first made by Baba Malka in Mexico City. Her no-fuss dish was a favorite during the breakfast and would rotate in for sandwiches or spreads with crackers throughout the year. It's a welcome adaptation of egg salad that makes good use of creamy avocados.

SERVES 2–4
Preparation time: 10 minutes

3 large avocados, peeled, pitted, and roughly chopped

2 tablespoons mayonnaise or Greek yogurt

2 teaspoons fresh lime juice, plus more as needed

¼ teaspoon kosher salt, plus more as needed

⅛ teaspoon freshly ground black pepper

4 hard-boiled eggs, peeled and chopped

1. In a medium-size bowl, use a fork to mash together the avocado, mayonnaise, lime juice, salt, and pepper.

2. Fold in the chopped eggs. Taste and add more lime juice or salt as desired. Serve immediately.

Colonias

AS WITH OTHER DIASPORAS, Jewish Mexican history is traceable through *colonias*, Mexican Spanish for "neighborhoods." It is the equivalent of looking at the life of a tree by studying the concentric lines of its trunk. Each of these colonias is the stage of extraordinary stories about fusion dishes that ultimately became a staple of Jewish Mexican cuisine, along with fondas and other restaurants where that food became a staple of La Comunidad.

Crypto-Jews also lived in the Mexican states of Nuevo León, Veracruz, and Puebla, but the headquarters of the Holy Inquisition were in downtown Mexico City, which, ironically, is where Jewish immigrants first settled.

By 1910, when the Mexican Revolution started, a new wave of Jewish immigrants was arriving in Mexico: from the Pale of Settlement as well as from the crumbling Ottoman Empire. Veracruz, in the Gulf of Mexico, was the port of entry. The majority migrated to the nation's capital, settling in downtown, around the streets of Manzanares, San Antonio Tomatlán, Rodríguez Puebla, Jesús María, and Loreto.

Ashkenazi and Ottoman Jews settled not far from one another, in and around Calles Justo Sierra and adjacent downtown streets. The first synagogue was on Calle Jesús María and República de Uruguay. It also functioned as a community center and an aid society. Schools, mikvahs, kosher butchers, and challah and matzah bakeries sprang up nearby. While each of them made sure to continue their traditions, they made unexpected partnerships, particularly through shared philanthropic organizations.

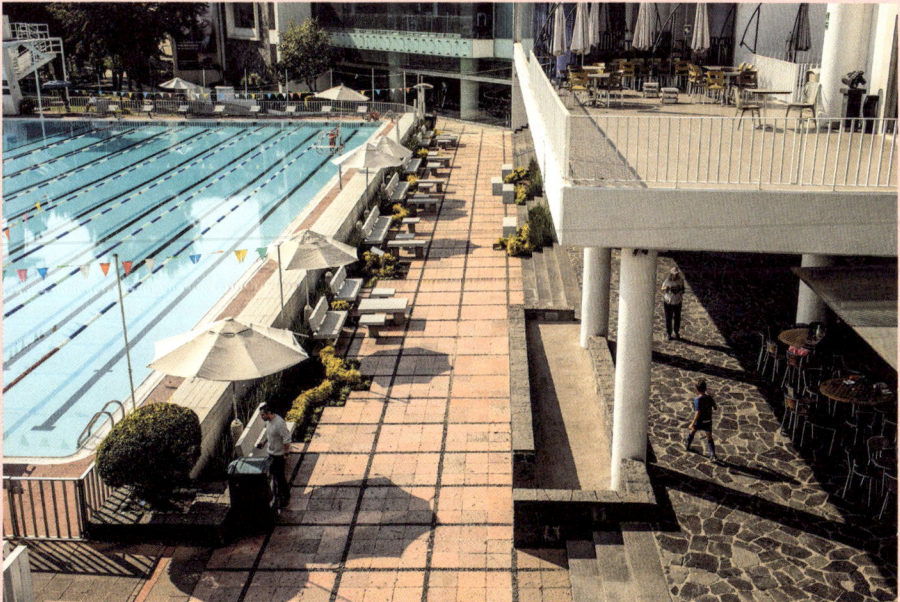

Centro Deportivo Israelita, Mexico City, January 2023.

Still, the differing religious traditions among immigrants carried over beyond life. Jewish cemeteries are separated to this day: Ashkenazim bury their dead in one place, Sephardim and Ottoman in another. In subsequent decades, as immigrants and their offspring entered the middle class, they moved to farther colonias such as Condesa, Hipódromo, Roma, and del Valle. In the 1960s, Jews relocated to Polanco, Tecamachalco, and Las Lomas. This move was consolidated when the majestic Centro Deportivo Israelita (known as CDI) was built in the northern part of the metropolis, on Avenida Constituyentes. Originally built in 1950 and led by a team of twenty-four, including Margaret's great-grandfather Elias, the CDI, despite its name, isn't only a sports center.

It actually includes spaces for multiple activities, from a library and a theater to a banquet hall commonly used for weddings and Bar Mitzvahs. A mural painted in this space in 1957 by Fanny Rabel, a student of Diego Rivera, depicts the stories of Jews from biblical times to Israel, the Spanish Inquisition, and the Holocaust. It includes images of Einstein and Freud meeting Abraham and Moses. The institution is a magnet to Jews of all ethnic backgrounds and religious denominations.

These urban waves were also accompanied by the expansion or reinvention of state-of-the-art synagogues around which different congregations rotated: Templo Bet El and Templo Monte Sinai, among others. New markets, bakeries, and butcher shops emerged in these neighborhoods to satisfy the demand for more secular Jewish families. Yet religion, although at first appearing to be a casualty, wasn't abandoned altogether. By the 1980s, a branch of Chabad had opened in the Mexican capital, followed by other cities.

In the demographically dense Mexico City, traffic makes it difficult to move from one place to another. As a result, Mexican Jews attend synagogue and engage with most aspects of Jewish daily life within a twelve-mile perimeter from home. •

Mango Noodle Kugel

For some reason, whenever Ilan eats pasta kugel with mango he visualizes the life of his maternal family in the early twentieth century in the small town of Yashinovka, Poland, which he has never visited. Ilan has seen about half a dozen photographs, though, enough to spark the imagination. He assumes that the family in Yashinovka ate kugel, an Ashkenazi casserole often baked with noodles or potatoes, because sometime in childhood Ilan heard a story about how they prepared it for Jewish holidays and other festive celebrations. He knows that the recipe had neither cinnamon nor raisins, as would be traditional in most sweet preparations. Ilan's grandmother Bobe Miriam—in Spanish, María—must have added the mango, in one of the iterations of the recipe moving from Yashinovka to Mexico, after spending time with marchantes at the mercado.

During peak mango season in Mexico, between May and June, mangos are plentiful and readily affordable. But mangos are not native to Mexico; they arrived in the eighteenth century from the Philippines and Southeast Asia, most probably originally from India. There are four kinds: Manila when relating to the Filipino variety, Ataulfo, Tomi, and Manglova. The most popular, and the one Bobe Miriam preferred, is Manila; the sweet and juicy Manglova might also be used for this recipe.

Clearly, once in Mexico, Jewish immigrants infused pasta kugel with new flavors, experimenting at every turn.

SERVES 8–10
Preparation time:
20 minutes
Cooking time:
1 hour

16 ounces wide egg noodles

7 large eggs, lightly beaten

16 ounces cottage cheese

½ cup (1 stick) unsalted butter, melted and slightly cooled

¾ packed cup light brown sugar

1½ teaspoons ground cinnamon

⅛ teaspoon kosher salt

1 medium ripe mango, peeled and cut into ½-inch pieces (about 1 cup)

3 medium apples, peeled and cut into ½-inch pieces (about 3 cups)

1. Heat the oven to 350°F and lightly grease a 9 × 13-inch baking dish.

2. Bring a large pot of water to a boil over high heat. Add the noodles and cook, stirring occasionally, until al dente. Drain and set aside to cool slightly.

3. In a large bowl, mix the eggs, cottage cheese, butter, brown sugar, cinnamon, and salt. Stir in the cooked and drained noodles, then fold in the mango and apple pieces.

4. Pour the mixture into the baking dish and bake until the kugel is set and the top is golden brown, 45–60 minutes. Transfer to a wire rack to cool, and serve warm or at room temperature.

Cheesy Jalapeño Challah

Challah is a traditional Jewish braided bread made with eggs, typically braided with three strands of dough, and served on Shabbat. Margaret enjoys the meditative practice of braiding the challah and the slowing down the bread baking requires. Many families bake challah every Friday, allowing the dough to rise on Friday morning so that freshly baked bread can initiate Shabbat dinner. Challah is so ubiquitous as part of Jewish ceremony that we sometimes joke it is the gateway drug into the religion.

As with so many ritual foods, challah offers significant variety. Different shapes are served on different holidays: a ladder on Yom Kippur, a circle on Rosh Hashanah. Challah can be garnished with a variety of fillings, and some of our family favorites include sesame seeds, poppy seeds, za'atar, chocolate chips, and grageas (rainbow sprinkles). This distinctly Jewish Mexican favorite, cheese and jalapeño, makes frequent appearances in Ilan's kitchen.

MAKES 1 LARGE LOAF
Preparation time: 20 minutes,
 plus rising
Baking time: 25 minutes

1 packet (2¼ teaspoons) active
 dry yeast

¾ cups warm water

4 cups all-purpose flour, plus
 more for kneading

2 teaspoons kosher salt

⅔ cup vegetable oil

3 tablespoons honey

3 large eggs, divided

1 jalapeño chile, halved, seeds
 removed, and thinly sliced

Grated cheddar cheese, for topping

1. In a large bowl, stir together the yeast and warm water and let sit until foaming, about 5 minutes.

2. Meanwhile, whisk together the flour and salt in a medium-size bowl and set aside.

3. Add the oil, honey, 2 of the eggs, and 1 egg yolk (reserve the egg white for later in the recipe) to the yeast mixture and stir to combine. Add the flour mixture and stir until a shaggy dough forms.

4. Transfer the dough to a flat, lightly floured work surface, and knead until the dough is supple and smooth, about 10 minutes. Sprinkle a little more flour, as needed, to prevent sticking. Place the dough back into the large bowl, cover tightly, and let rise for 2 hours.

5. Gently deflate the dough and divide it into 3 equal pieces. Roll each piece into a long strand, then braid the strands together and place on a parchment-lined baking sheet. Cover with a clean tea towel and let rise for 60 minutes.

6. Meanwhile, heat the oven to 375°F. Brush the risen loaf with the reserved egg white (you will not use all of it) and bake for 20 minutes.

7. Remove from the oven and sprinkle the jalapeño slices and a generous amount of cheddar cheese over top. (Sprinkle the cheese on top of the jalapeño slices to help them stick to the challah as the cheese melts.)

8. Continue baking until the loaf is baked through and the cheese has melted, 5–10 minutes. Remove from the oven and let cool on a wire rack for at least 30 minutes before slicing and serving.

Cognac Chicken Liver Pâté with Tortilla Chips

Chicken liver pâté, or chopped liver, is a traditional Ashkenazi dish, pairing chicken livers with onions, hard-boiled eggs, and a source of fat, often schmaltz. This variety is a centerpiece of Irma Appel's catering business, and a favorite dish of her late husband, Pepe, incorporating apples, Cognac, and spices. As a teenager, Irma began helping Jacobo Glantz's wife, Lucía, cook the kneidlach—matzah balls—and started to dream of becoming a caterer. She built a restaurant and then a catering business, and taught all four of her children to cook. Years later, Irma and Pepe settled in La Escandón, where her mother-in-law, a wonderful cook, became one of her teachers. Irma would take notes as she cooked, admiring her recipes: sweet lekaj (honey cake), strudel, marmalades, and other delicacies. It was after she became an empty nester that she started to cook for Bar Mitzvahs, birthdays, wedding anniversaries, and shivahs. While not everyone loves chicken liver (Ilan doesn't, Margaret does), we found that this was another dish high on nostalgia. For Irma, this dish connects her to her aunts who experimented with various ratios of Cognac, onion, egg, and schmaltz before settling on this signature recipe.

SERVES 6
Preparation time: 15 minutes
Cooking time: 25 minutes

1 pound chicken livers, trimmed and patted dry

3 tablespoons schmaltz or vegetable oil

1 medium white onion, finely chopped

½ medium green apple, peeled and finely chopped

2 tablespoons Cognac

2 hard-boiled eggs, chopped

¼ teaspoon ground nutmeg

½ teaspoon kosher salt, plus more as needed

¼ teaspoon freshly ground black pepper

Toasted sesame seeds, for sprinkling

Tortilla chips (freshly made or store-bought), for serving

1. Heat a cast-iron pan or grill pan over medium heat. Add the chicken livers and sear, turning once, until browned on both sides, 3–4 minutes per side. Transfer to a cutting board and let cool, then roughly chop and set aside.

2. Heat the schmaltz in a medium frying pan set over medium heat. Add the onion and cook, stirring occasionally, until softened and lightly golden, 6–8 minutes. Add the apple and cook until softened, about 5 minutes.

3. Add the chopped livers and cook, stirring often, until cooked through, about 5 minutes. Stir in the Cognac and let cook for about 1 minute, then remove from the heat and let the mixture cool slightly.

4. Transfer the liver and onion mixture to a food processor along with the hard-boiled eggs, nutmeg, salt, and pepper. Pulse, scraping down the sides of the bowl as necessary, until smooth. Taste and add more salt, if needed. Transfer the mixture to a serving bowl, cover, and refrigerate for at least 1 hour or up to overnight.

5. Serve at room temperature, sprinkled with sesame seeds and with tortilla chips alongside for scooping.

Borscht con Crema

Borscht is a vibrant and refreshing beet soup that rose to popularity within eastern European Jewish communities in the late sixteenth century. As Ashkenazi Jews emigrated to the Americas, they brought with them the tradition of borscht alongside rich traditions of pickling and preserving. The soup is a staple for many Ashkenazi families on the first evening of Passover and otherwise a refreshing summertime delight for outdoor lunches and dinners.

Everything in this recipe should be grated using the large holes of a box grater. If you do not have freshly fermented pickles in your home pantry, in US markets we recommend the readily available Bubbies Pickles, free of vinegar and added sugar or preservatives. The soup is topped to taste with sliced eggs and Mexican crema (crema fresca), a richer and slightly more tangy variety of American sour cream.

SERVES 8
Preparation time: 15 minutes,
    plus chilling
Cooking time: 1 hour

4 medium red beets (about 2 pounds),
    tops trimmed

1 small bunch red radishes, trimmed
    and grated

1 medium cucumber, peeled and grated

4 dill pickles, grated (use pickles that
    do not contain vinegar)

¾ cup pickle juice

½ cup finely chopped fresh dill, plus
    more for serving

1 small bunch chives, finely sliced

2 quarts buttermilk

Kosher salt and freshly ground black
    pepper, as needed

Quartered or sliced hard-boiled eggs
    and Mexican crema, for serving

1. Heat the oven to 400°F. Wrap each beet tightly in aluminum foil and place them in a baking dish. Roast until very tender, 40–60 minutes. Remove from the oven and let sit until cool to the touch. Unwrap the beets, peel them, and grate them on the large holes of a box grater.

2. In a large bowl, combine the grated beets along with the radishes, cucumber, pickles, pickle juice, dill, chives, and buttermilk. Taste and add salt, if needed, and a generous amount of pepper. Cover the bowl and refrigerate for at least 1 hour to allow the borscht to chill and the flavors to meld.

3. To serve: Spoon the borscht into serving bowls. Top each bowl with sliced eggs, a dollop of crema, and a little more fresh dill.

Alison's Brisket Tortas

A torta is a Mexican sandwich made from a fluffy roll stuffed with meat and vegetables. It might also include refried beans, avocado slices, sliced or chopped chiles, and other ingredients. Tortas come in multiple sizes and styles. They can be stuffed with shredded pork carnitas or served *ahogada*, dipped in spicy salsa.

This brisket can stand on its own as the main dish on the table. Ilan's wife, Alison, refined a recipe she inherited, along with her mother, from past generations. It can be served for Passover, any Shabbat meal, or other important Jewish occasion. "Over the years, I became dissatisfied with an inherited brisket recipe from the family," Alison says. "My mother and I began to experiment until we had come up with a full-flavored version." She adds, "I enjoy making it with my husband and children. It has become a way for us to remember my mother Joanie."

Alison serves her tortas with the brisket and plenty of sauce from the pan—nothing more. Others have added lettuce, tomato, guacamole, and other desired toppings.

. . . .

SERVES: 8–10
Preparation time: 20 minutes,
 plus overnight chilling
Cooking time: 3 hours

2 tablespoons vegetable oil

1 brisket (about 5 pounds)

Freshly ground black pepper

3 large yellow onions, finely chopped

8 medium garlic cloves, finely chopped

1 cup dry red wine

4 cups beef broth

¾ cup sweet chili sauce

3 tablespoons apple cider vinegar

½ packed cup light brown sugar

2 bay leaves

8–10 bolillos (or other soft rolls)

Thinly sliced jalapeño chiles, for serving
 (optional)

1. Heat the oven to 350°F.

2. Heat the oil in a large roasting pan over medium-high heat. Season the brisket on both sides with pepper, place in the hot pan, and sear, turning once, until well browned on both sides, 3–5 minutes per side. (If the meat doesn't fit in a single layer in the pan, cut it in half and sear in 2 batches.) Transfer the browned meat to a plate.

3. Add the onions and garlic to the pan, turn the heat down to medium, and cook, stirring occasionally, until soft and golden brown, 6–8 minutes.

4. Add the wine and beef broth, raise the heat to medium high, and bring to a low boil. Stir in the chili sauce, vinegar, brown sugar, and bay leaves. Gently return the seared brisket to the pan (along with any juices accumulated on the plate) and spoon the sauce evenly over the meat.

5. Cover the roasting pan and transfer to the oven. Let the brisket cook, undisturbed, until fork tender, 2½ hours.

6. Remove from the oven and let cool. Refrigerate overnight, then slice the meat cold. When ready to serve, reheat the sliced meat and juices in a 350°F oven until bubbling.

7. Make the tortas: Cut the bolillos in half and layer with several pieces of brisket, plus a generous spoonful of the sauce. Top with jalapeño slices, if desired.

Eggplant with Herbed Lamb

Margaret adores historical recipes. In 2020, she was a Fulbright scholar at the López Piñero Institute for the History of Medicine and Science in Valencia researching women's recipes found in medical books, Inquisitional trials, and family collections. Lamb recipes are abundant in many of these early sources. With the expulsion of the Jews from Spain, many of these dishes traveled across the Atlantic. We find them in Mexico and Peru, where conversos were known to have settled. Their daily life was defined by a secret devotion to the religion of their ancestors. This recipe is inspired by eggplant, introduced to the Spanish diet by the Arabic population of Al-Andalus (although it is native to India, Africa, and South Asia), and it then became a staple of the New World. In *Don Quixote de la Mancha* (1605–15), its author, Miguel de Cervantes Saavedra, suggests that the story he narrates originally came from an Arabic author, Cide Hamete Benengeli, a name that plays in Spanish with the word *berenjena*, "eggplant." With this dish, we honor the memory—and the humor—of the crypto-Jews who sought ways to practice their faith in times of persecution. The flavor combination and texture are true to these early recipes.

. . . .

SERVES 6
Preparation time: 40 minutes
Cooking time: 45 minutes

FOR THE EGGPLANTS AND FILLING

2 medium eggplants (about 2½ pounds), unpeeled

4 egg whites (reserve 3 of the yolks)

1 teaspoon kosher salt

½ teaspoon freshly ground black pepper

1½ teaspoons ground cinnamon

1 teaspoon crushed lavender flowers

1 pound ground lamb

FOR THE STEW

2 tablespoons extra-virgin olive oil

1 small yellow onion, finely chopped

4 medium garlic cloves, finely chopped

2 teaspoons dried thyme

1 teaspoon dried fennel

1 teaspoon ground coriander seeds

½ teaspoon saffron threads, crushed

½ teaspoon ground cardamom

½ teaspoon grated fresh ginger

¾ teaspoon kosher salt

2 tablespoons red wine vinegar

2 cups water

1 (15-ounce) can chickpeas, drained

2 tablespoons slivered almonds

FOR THE SAUCE

¼ cup balsamic vinegar

2 tablespoons finely chopped red onion

2 tablespoons roughly chopped slivered almonds

2 tablespoons roughly chopped pine nuts

2 teaspoons rose water

1 tablespoon chopped fresh mint

2 fresh lemon segments, finely chopped

1. Bring a large pot of water to a boil over high heat. Add the eggplants and boil, turning a few times, until scalded on all sides, about 5 minutes. (The eggplants won't look particularly different from how they started.) Remove and set aside to drain and cool.

2. Meanwhile, prepare the filling: In a large bowl, whisk the egg whites until foamy. Whisk in the salt, pepper, cinnamon, and lavender. Add the lamb and mix well with your hands to combine.

3. Using a sharp paring knife, remove the tops and bottoms of both eggplants. Use the knife and a sturdy spoon to cut and scoop out the seeds and pulp, leaving about ¾ inch of flesh around the sides. (The pulp can be reserved for another use.) Stuff the lamb mixture into the cavity of each eggplant and set aside.

4. Make the stew: Heat the oil in a large saucepan or Dutch oven set over medium heat. Add the onion and cook, stirring occasionally, until softened and lightly browned, 6–8 minutes. Add the garlic, thyme, fennel, coriander, saffron, cardamom, ginger, and salt and cook, stirring, until fragrant, 1–2 minutes. Stir in the red wine vinegar, followed by the water, chickpeas, and almonds, and bring to a boil.

5. Nestle the stuffed eggplants into the sauce, turn the heat to medium low, cover the pan, and simmer, turning once, until the eggplant is tender and the filling is cooked through, about 40 minutes. Uncover the saucepan and stir a little of the hot cooking liquid into the 3 reserved egg yolks to temper them. Take the stew off the heat and pour the tempered egg mixture into the pan, stirring to combine.

6. While the stew is simmering, make the sauce: Stir together the balsamic vinegar, red onion, almonds, pine nuts, rose water, mint, and lemon in a medium-size bowl.

7. Transfer the stuffed eggplants to a cutting board and slice into 1-inch rounds. Divide among plates, top with the stew, and drizzle with a little of the sauce. Serve hot.

Plantain Chile Kugel

Although apple and sweet cheese kugels are the cornerstones of many Jewish kitchens, this plantain and chile variety incorporates Mexican ingredients to produce a savory, sweet, and deeply comforting adaptation. The manzano chile is an apple-shaped, bright yellow pepper that imparts a citrus flavor and distinctive heat to the sweet plantains in this dish. This recipe makes an excellent pairing with roast chicken over Shabbat dinner.

SERVES 6–8
Preparation time: 35 minutes
Cooking time: 45 minutes

2½ cups all-purpose flour

½ teaspoon kosher salt

1 large egg, lightly beaten

¼ cup plus 2 tablespoons vegetable oil, divided

¾ cup room-temperature water

2 medium manzano chiles (chiles Perón), seeds removed, finely chopped

2 medium ripe plantains, finely chopped

3 tablespoons granulated sugar, divided

1½ teaspoons ground cinnamon, divided

2 tablespoons plum or apricot jam

1. In a large bowl, whisk the flour and salt together. Add the egg, ¼ cup of oil, and the water and stir with a sturdy spoon until the dough begins to come together. Transfer the dough to a lightly floured work surface and knead until it comes together. Return the dough to the bowl, cover, and let rest while making the filling.

2. Heat the remaining 2 tablespoons of oil in a medium frying pan set over medium heat. Add the manzano chiles and plantains and cook, stirring occasionally, until golden, 6–8 minutes. Stir in 2 tablespoons of the sugar and 1 teaspoon of the cinnamon, then remove from the heat and set aside to cool.

3. Heat the oven to 350°F and lightly grease a round 10-inch Bundt pan. On a lightly floured work surface using a floured rolling pin, roll the dough out into a large, ¼-inch-thick rectangle. Spread the dough evenly with the jam, then spread the cooled plantain and chile mixture over top. Sprinkle with the remaining 1 tablespoon of sugar and ½ teaspoon of cinnamon.

4. Starting with one of the long ends, roll the dough onto itself into a coiled rope. Gently twist the rope a couple of times, then fit it into the Bundt pan, overlapping the ends. Bake until the top is lightly golden and the kugel is cooked through, about 45 minutes. Remove from the oven and let cool before slicing. Serve warm.

Orange Fig Hamantaschen

Hamantaschen are triangle-shaped cookies filled with a variety of fillings, including poppy seed, jams, chocolate, and cheese. The cookies are served during the spring festival of Purim, marking the freedom of the Persian Jewish people from Haman, who sought to annihilate them. The triangle shape of the cookies is thought to represent Haman's three-sided hat. While the flavor combinations of the fillings are infinitely customizable, we highlight here a citrus fig recipe that evokes both the Garden of Eden and gardens of California. Margaret connects these hamantaschen with the teacher who helped her prepare for her Bat Mitzvah, Holocaust survivor and author Edith Singer. In her memoir *March to Freedom* (1993), Edith wrote about her experiences as a sixteen-year-old in the Auschwitz death camp. As a long-time Hebrew school teacher in Los Angeles and lecturer at the Holocaust Museum LA, Edith taught generations of other students across the city. In celebrating Margaret's Bat Mitzvah, Edith and Baba Malka connected primarily via Yiddish, with Spanish intermingling with English and Hebrew. What Margaret remembers most vividly are the afternoons spent deciphering Hebrew letters, diaspora stories, plates of seasonally appropriate cookies exchanged between the student and her beloved teacher—prepared from Edith's kosher kitchen or sourced from a nearby bakery—and the long conversations about remembering, rituals, and joyful living.

....

MAKES ABOUT 30 COOKIES
Preparation time: 40 minutes,
   plus chilling
Baking time: 18 minutes

FOR THE DOUGH

3¼ cups all-purpose flour

2 teaspoons baking powder

2 tablespoons cornstarch

1 teaspoon ground cinnamon

½ teaspoon kosher salt

1 cup (2 sticks) unsalted butter,
   softened

¾ cup granulated sugar

2 large eggs

½ teaspoon vanilla extract

FOR THE FILLING

3 cups dried figs, stems removed
   and finely chopped

¼ cup honey

⅔ cup fresh orange juice

Zest of 1 large orange

1 teaspoon ground cinnamon

1. Whisk together the flour, baking powder, cornstarch, cinnamon, and salt in a medium-size bowl and set aside.

2. In a stand mixer fitted with a paddle attachment (or using a large bowl and a sturdy spoon), beat together the butter and sugar until fluffy. Beat in the eggs and vanilla. Add the flour mixture in 2 stages, beating to combine after each, until a firm but pliable dough comes together. Divide the dough into 2 pieces and form into disks. Wrap each disk well in plastic wrap and refrigerate for at least 1 hour or up to 1 day.

3. Make the filling: Combine the figs, honey, orange juice, orange zest, and cinnamon in a medium saucepan set over medium heat. Bring to a simmer, then turn the heat down to low, cover the saucepan, and cook, stirring often and mashing with a potato masher or the back of a spoon, until it becomes a chunky paste, 10–15 minutes. Remove from the heat and let cool to the touch.

4. Heat the oven to 350°F and line 2 large baking sheets with parchment paper. On a floured surface, using a lightly floured rolling pin, roll one disk of dough into a large, ¼-inch-thick rectangle. Using a 3-inch round cookie cutter, stamp out as many circles as possible and transfer them to the parchment-lined baking sheets. Gather the scraps, reroll, and stamp out additional circles.

5. Place a rounded teaspoon of the filling into the center of a circle, then pinch all three corners to seal and form a triangle. Repeat the rolling, filling, and forming process with the remaining dough and filling.

6. Bake until the hamantaschen are lightly golden, 15–18 minutes. Remove from the oven and transfer to wire racks to cool.

Apricot Almond Charoset Truffles

Charoset combines fruits, nuts, and spices and is served as part of the Seder during Passover. The first reference to it is in the Mishnah. The Seder is a convivial occasion that recalls the gatherings in Athens around sages such as Socrates in which pupils listened to philosophical arguments. The sweetness of the dish represents the hope of the Jewish people, despite their struggles in Egypt. The famous dialogues in Plato's *Symposium* depict such a gathering.

In the Sephardic tradition, charoset is made of dates, raisins, and figs. In other traditions, such as that of the Jews of Turkey, chopped apples and cinnamon are added. These truffles, found in some Jewish Mexican homes as far away as Los Angeles, Barcelona, and Tel Aviv, can be served as a dessert during the holidays but also make wonderful snack treats for families on the go.

MAKES ABOUT 3 DOZEN TRUFFLES
Preparation time: 15 minutes,
   plus chilling

2 cups pitted and chopped
   medjool dates

1 cup chopped dried apricots

1 cup golden raisins

1 cup roasted salted almonds

1 tablespoon honey

3 tablespoons sweet red wine
   (or grape juice)

1. Working in batches, add the dates, apricots, raisins, almonds, and honey to a food processor and pulse until a textured paste forms. Transfer the mixture to a bowl and stir in the wine, 1 tablespoon at a time.

2. Scoop out tablespoons of the mixture and, using lightly moistened hands, roll them into balls. Place the truffles on a baking sheet or large plate lined with parchment paper as you go.

3. Refrigerate the truffles (uncovered is fine) for 2 hours, then transfer to a container with a lid and continue to refrigerate until needed. Serve chilled or at room temperature.

Tahini Brownies

Tahini swirled through rich chocolate is a decadent dessert year-round, but this flourless and unleavened treat is particularly beloved over Passover. Tahini is a paste made from sesame seeds and oil and is a crucial ingredient in Middle Eastern cuisine, with a long history likely dating back to the thirteenth century. This recipe comes to us from Israeli immigrants to Mexico, merging flavors across their homes. They share with us that tahini is also infused into their adaptations of mole, the sesame flavor substituting for more common varieties that rely on peanut or almond.

SERVES 6
Preparation time: 15 minutes
Baking time: 22 minutes

3 tablespoons almond flour

¼ cup cocoa powder

½ teaspoon kosher salt

¼ cup extra-virgin olive oil

½ cup well-stirred tahini

4 ounces baking chocolate, roughly chopped

2 large eggs

½ cup granulated sugar

1 teaspoon vanilla extract

½ cup chocolate chips

Flaky sea salt, for sprinkling

1. Heat the oven to 350°F and lightly grease an 8 × 8-inch baking dish. In a small bowl, whisk together the almond flour, cocoa powder, and kosher salt and set aside.

2. Combine the oil, tahini, and chopped baking chocolate in a small saucepan set over medium-low heat and cook, stirring often, until the chocolate is melted and the mixture is smooth. Remove from the heat and let cool slightly.

3. Meanwhile, in a large bowl, vigorously whisk together the eggs and sugar until frothy, 3–5 minutes. Whisk in the vanilla, followed by the cooled chocolate mixture.

4. Add the dry ingredients to the chocolate mixture and stir to combine, then fold in the chocolate chips.

5. Transfer the batter to the prepared pan, smoothing the top, then sprinkle lightly with flaky sea salt. Bake until a tester inserted in the center comes out clean, 18–22 minutes. Remove from the oven and place the pan on a wire rack to cool. Serve warm or at room temperature.

Orange Blossom Buñuelos

This jelly doughnut recipe—*sufganyot* in Hebrew, *buñelo* in Spanish—is adapted from Gil Marks's *World of Jewish Desserts*, which traces the origins of these treats to the fifteenth century. This recipe comes from the Sephardic tradition of buñuelos, also spelled bimuelos, which are soaked in syrup. While this variety of doughnut is drenched in orange blossom, other popular varieties include rosewater and lemon.

Buñuelos may come from Spain, but they are featured in the cuisine of many Latin American countries, including Argentina, Colombia, and Mexico. They are known to have been consumed first by the morisco population in the Iberian Peninsula, which explains their ubiquity in North Africa, Turkey, and elsewhere in the Mediterranean. They might be flavored with anise, thinly rolled, or cut or shaped into individual bites. We know that conversos included them in their cuisine. In Mexico in 1643, Margarita de Rivera's family talks of the consumption of "fritters and honey" during wedding ceremonies.

MAKES ABOUT 30 BUÑUELOS
Preparation time: 25 minutes,
  plus rising
Cooking time: 30 minutes

1 tablespoon active dry yeast

1 tablespoon granulated sugar

1½ cups warm water

3½–4 cups all-purpose flour

¾ teaspoon kosher salt

2 teaspoons orange blossom water, divided

1 packed teaspoon grated orange zest

2 tablespoons vegetable oil, plus more for frying

1 cup honey

1. In a large bowl, mix together the yeast, sugar, and warm water and let sit until foaming, about 5 minutes.

2. Meanwhile, whisk together 3½ cups of the flour and the salt in a medium-size bowl and set aside. Add 1 teaspoon of orange blossom water, the orange zest, and 2 tablespoons of oil to the yeast mixture and stir to combine. Add the flour mixture to the yeast mixture in 2 batches, stirring with a sturdy spoon until a shaggy dough forms.

3. Turn the dough out onto a work surface and knead, adding up to ½ cup more flour as needed, until the dough is elastic and smooth, 5–10 minutes. (You might not use all of the flour.) Put the dough back in the bowl, cover with a clean, slightly damp tea towel, and let rest until doubled in volume, 1–1½ hours.

4. Heat 2 inches of oil in a medium saucepan set over medium heat until it reaches 350°F on a digital thermometer, and line a large plate with paper towels.

5. Using lightly oiled hands to prevent sticking, pinch off rounded table-spoons of the dough and roll into balls. (The fritters will puff and swell in size in the oil. Resist making them too big, or they will not cook through the middle.) Working in batches of 4 or 5, gently drop the dough balls into the hot oil and fry, turning once, until golden brown, 3–4 minutes total. Remove with a slotted spoon and transfer to the paper-towel-lined plate to drain.

6. In a small bowl, stir together the honey and the remaining 1 teaspoon of orange blossom water and microwave in 20-second bursts until it pours easily. (You can also heat the mixture in a small saucepan set over medium heat for 2–3 minutes.) Drizzle the honey over the buñuelos and serve hot.

Coffee Honey Cake

Apparently, varieties of the honey cake have accompanied Jews throughout their diasporic journey. In Egypt, they were made with yeast dough, with mashed legumes in the ancient Near East, with barley loaves full of pomegranate seeds, raisins, and pine nuts during the Roman Empire, and in varieties closer to what we eat today in medieval Spain. The fact that, given its sweetness, honey is traditionally eaten on Rosh Hashanah, makes it possible to imagine a narrative across history in which various members of the same Jewish family, but in different periods, congregate around their honey cake as they look back and forward in time to understand their overall connection.

Our recipe comes from Ilan's grandmother, with the distinction that it is made of Mexican cocoa powder and autochthonous brewed coffee. Indeed, one finds it humbly on the table during afternoon breaks—Shabbat or siestas—along with strong black coffee, varieties of tea, and digestifs. What makes it particularly Jewish Mexican is that it shows up during festivities decorated with sliced kiwis and grapes on top or else with a glaze made of instant coffee powder and vanilla extract that is drizzled over the cooled cake. On top, you might also put crushed dulces cristalizados.

SERVES 8
Preparation time: 15 minutes
Baking time: 30 minutes

2¼ cups all-purpose flour

1 teaspoon baking powder

1 teaspoon baking soda

1 teaspoon ground cinnamon

¼ teaspoon ground cloves

¼ teaspoon ground anise

¼ teaspoon kosher salt

3 large eggs

1¼ cups granulated sugar

½ cup honey

½ cup cocoa powder, sifted

1 cup brewed coffee, cooled to room temperature

Confectioners' sugar, for dusting, optional

Sliced kiwis and grapes, vanilla-coffee glaze, and crushed dulces cristalizados, optional

1. Heat the oven to 350°F and lightly grease a 9 × 13-inch baking dish.

2. Whisk together the flour, baking powder, baking soda, cinnamon, cloves, anise, and salt in a medium-size bowl and set aside.

3. In a large bowl, beat together the eggs, sugar, honey, and cocoa powder until fully combined. Beat the flour mixture into the egg mixture in 2 batches, alternating with the coffee.

4. Pour the batter into the baking dish and smooth the top, then bake until the top springs back when pressed and a tester inserted into the center of the cake comes out clean, 25–30 minutes. Remove from the oven and let cool completely. Just before slicing and serving, dust the top of the cake with confectioners' sugar, sliced fruit, glaze, or crushed dulces cristalizados, if desired.

Malaga Raisin Wine

Bobe Miriam, Ilan's grandmother, lived in a first-floor colonial apartment in Colonia Hipódromo, a block away from Parque México, in Mexico City. She was known for making her own wine, dozens of bottles of it, every fall and for her grandchildren's Bar Mitzvahs. We found a nearly identical recipe for wine in Margaret's Baba Malka's collection. Raisin wine can refer to two beverages. The first, wine brewed from raisins instead of fresh grapes, is known for its intense, sweet flavor. The other, traditionally Jewish, raisin wine refers to the ritual drink prepared from soaking raisins in water over heat for a prolonged time. The result is a nonalcoholic beverage that is consumed by Jewish communities most commonly on Passover. Raisin wine grew to popularity within the Americas, likely as a result of a lack of kosher wine options, in the nineteenth and early twentieth centuries and is still enjoyed today for slow making and gifting.

SERVES 16
Preparation time: 30 minutes

4¼ cups dark raisins, ideally Malaga raisins

8 cups water

2 cups granulated sugar

1. Soak the raisins in 2 cups of warm water and, using a mixer, blend them to a thick paste, adding more water if needed. Pour the mixture into 12-ounce Mason jars (approximately 6), dividing it evenly among the containers.

2. Bring the remaining water to a boil, add the sugar, and stir until dissolved. Pour over the Mason jars and mix thoroughly.

3. Cover each jar and allow to sit for a week at room temperature, away from direct light, mixing at least once daily.

4. Strain the liquid to remove the remaining fruit skins after 1–2 weeks.

Mezcal de Eliyahu

Mezcal is a category of distilled spirit made from agave. The name originates from the word *mexcalli*, which describes cooked agave in Nahuatl. Although some describe mezcal as a working-class version of tequila, the truth is that, like pulque, mezcal has an older history that goes back to the colonial period in seventeenth-century Nueva España, which is how Mexico was known before its war of independence.

Unlike tequila, which is made with blue agave, mezcal can be made from more than thirty agave species, varieties, and subvarieties. It is handcrafted. About 90 percent of production takes place in the Mexican state of Oaxaca. Mezcal might be served in a *caballito*, a thumb-size glass (the Spanish word means "pony"), accompanied by slices of orange and by sal de gusano, a traditional Oaxacan spice made from sea salt, toasted and ground agave worms, and variety of dried chiles. Or it can be mixed with all kinds of juices and other ingredients.

La Comunidad consumes mezcal in multiple ways. Ilan likes to try different options. He drinks a small glass with friends on Rosh Hashanah, Purim, and Hanukkah. When Margaret's family would sing to Eliyahu during the Passover Seder, she misheard the Hebrew lyrics as "Alejandro Hanevi," and it continues to be a running joke in the family.

SERVES 4
Preparation time: 5 minutes

4 *caballitos* (small tequila glasses) mezcal

2 cups pineapple juice

1 small jalapeño chile, thinly sliced

½ cup minced fresh cilantro

1 lemon, halved

2 teaspoons sal de gusano

Sparkling mineral water and ice

1. In a cocktail shaker filled with ice, mix the mezcal with the pineapple juice, jalapeño, and cilantro. Shake well.

2. Using half a lemon, coat the glass rims with lemon juice and sal de gusano. Pour the mixed drink into each glass, topping off with mineral water and more ice to taste.

Paletas Manischewitz

Manischewitz, a popular American kosher foods manufacturer that originated in Ohio during the late nineteenth century, has somehow become a staple of La Comunidad. The company specialized in kosher wine and food, such as matzah, borscht, and gefilte fish. It became a corporation in 1923. For better or worse, its wine in particular has become an essential actor in Jewish popular culture. Some deem it too sweet and syrupy. Others argue that it is part of an old tradition connected with Jewish immigration to the United States in the late nineteenth century that has outlived its purposes. The palate, they say, requires a more subtle, lasting flavor.

Yet even though other kosher products have long been available, Mexican Jews, especially those belonging to the immigrant generation, have remained loyal to Manischewitz wines, either as part of their Shabbat or on other holiday meals. It is still served at circumcisions, Bar Mitzvahs, and weddings—so much so that a segment of the population feels nostalgia toward it, which isn't an impediment for all kinds of derogatory jokes. *Un copa de Manischewitz fortalece el camino—al panteón.* A glass of Manischewitz gives you strength on the road—to the cemetery.

This recipe takes Manischewitz out of its comfort zone by turning it to paletas. Who else but Mexican Jews would come up with such a sharp idea? The thick quality of the wine is put to good use. The key is to throw in orange peel and mix it with cinnamon and cloves. After trying it, you will never think of Manischewitz the same way again. In fact, you will realize how much the Yiddish-speaking immigrants settling in Calle Jesús María—or, for that matter, in New York's Lower East Side—in the 1920s truly missed.

. . . .

MAKES 6 PALETAS
Preparation time: 40 minutes
Freezing time: 5 hours

1 (750-milliliter) bottle Manischewitz
  sweet red wine

3 wide strips orange peel

4 whole cloves

1 cinnamon stick

2 cups water

Thinly sliced limes and tangerines,
  optional

1. Add the wine, orange peel, cloves, and cinnamon stick to a medium saucepan set over medium-high heat. Bring the mixture to a boil, then lower the heat to medium and cook, stirring occasionally, until the liquid reduces to 1 cup, 30–35 minutes. Remove from the heat and let cool, then strain out and discard the spices and orange peel.

2. Stir the water into the strained wine syrup, then divide the mixture evenly among 6 paleta or flat popsicle molds. If desired, add a slice of lime or tangerine into each mold. Freeze until solid, at least 5 hours.

Shabat

Across the world, Shabbat (in Spanish, Shabat), the day of rest, brings in the opportunity for peace and reflection. It is a reminder of the cyclical nature of time and a reminder to pause. In Jewish mysticism, it is also the day in which the Shechinah, the female aspect of the divine, returns to earth to accompany its children, the people of Israel. Aware of its symbolism, observant Mexican Jews prepare for this weekly holiday by making special arrangements for the Friday table, such as baking challah, preparing wine, and cooking a family dinner. Some change how they dress, either in more elegant or extra-comfortable clothes, while others prepare for breaks with technology or other routines of the workweek.

Shabbat table settings among Mexican Jews often rely on the colorful textiles and folk art from the region, featuring plenty of contrasting colors, embroidered flowers, or other natural elements in Mayan or Otomi design. Mexican Jewish photographer Ruth Lechuga captured vibrant examples of this craftwork through her collecting and photographs, many now on display at the Franz Mayer Museum in Mexico City. At the center of the Shabbat table are a pair of candles, a Kiddush cup for blessing wine, and a challah. Many of these ritual objects have their own migration histories, crossing by ship from eastern Europe to Mexico to the United States and moving from generation to generation. In her home today, Margaret, for example, uses candlesticks her great-grandmother carried from Poland to Mexico. It is common for families and synagogues to gift Kiddush cups and candlesticks to children when they reach the age of thirteen, the recognition of their adulthood and obligation to the Jewish community through minyan and meals inextricably linked.

Shabbat meals are described in detail through Mexican Jewish literature. Margo Glantz's book *The Family Tree* includes details about her family eating brisket, kasha, noodles, fruit salads, cakes, strudels, and, later, tea with more strudel. She describes her mother's hectic preparations: "Mamá serves noodle soup, we eat, rest, then she serves cold beef with beet, finally a dessert, a type of strudel that goes well with hot tea." At one point, Glantz states, "Sin cocina no hay pueblo. Sin pan nuestro de cada día tampoco," meaning that food is the expression not only of a people's character but of its spiritual life as well. (The sentences, incorporating a reference to Matthew 6:11, are difficult to translate. A loose rendition: "Food nurtures body and soul.")

The challah is often the initiation into the Shabbat meal, with the preparation of dough, braiding, and baking beginning before sundown. Our collection includes notable Jewish Mexican varieties, one sweet and inflected with spices from churros, the other savory with spiced jalapeño and cheese—as well as a recipe for Challah French Toast with Cajeta to bring Shabbat into late in the weekend or early in the workweek. Even in Ottoman families this Ashkenazi bread has become a feature. Other names for it are kitke, barches, koylatch, and shtritsl. A special offering, it is made of fine white flour, egg, water, yeast, salt, and sugar.

During the colonial period, Shabbat meals often served fish dishes as a way of avoiding unkosher meat. In the spectrum of observance, today Mexican Jews prepare Shabbat meals featuring endless possibilities. They might start with an appetizer with cheese, move into soups, concentrate on a principal dish accompanied with rice, vegetables, and salad, and conclude with an assortment of desserts, coffee and tea, pastries, and liquors.

Although Shabbat officially starts at sunset—following the lunar calendar, wherein the day begins at dusk—conviviality makes Friday night dinners last until midnight and beyond. Late-night conversation, political debate, board games, and other collective activities are commonplace.

. . . .

FRIDAY DINNER

Cheesy Jalapeño Challah (page 216)

Borscht con Crema (page 221)

Pollo Luis de Santángel (page 104)

Plantain Chile Kugel (page 228)

Cactus Tomato Salad (page 56)

Miriam's Cinnamon Sugar
Beer Cookies (page 172)

Café de Olla con Licor (page 196)

SATURDAY BREAKFAST

Pineapple Beet Juice (page 40)

Queso Yiddish (page 21) served
with assorted fresh fruit

Challah French Toast
con Cajeta (page 16)

Huevos con Machaca and
Refried Beans (page 29)

SATURDAY LUNCH

Wish on a Star Soup (page 71)

Niddo Vegetable Lasagna (page 113)

Abraham's Lentil Salad (page 55)

Malka's Mexican Chocolate
Babka (page 173)

Purim

Another festival commemorating a rebellion against an oppressive regime, Purim is a narrative-driven occasion built around the book of Esther, which describes the struggle against Haman in ancient Persia. Two women characters take the lead in this story, the named heroine, Queen Esther, who saved the Jewish people, and the more recently reclaimed and celebrated Queen Vashti, whose refusal to degrade herself is also highlighted. Talmudic scholars describe the start of this festival, at the beginning of the month of Adar, as the month of movement from grief to joy. In retelling the Purim story through reading of the spiel or the whole megillah, listeners are encouraged to participate through collective boos and cheers for heroes and villains, with costumes and song. Alcohol is often served at these readings, with the mitzvah of being drunk with sincere happiness.

The holiday centers around children, with costumes encouraged from the biblical story but room to find all kinds of favorite characters. It is an occasion to embrace humor as a tool against violence. It is therefore not a surprise that Purim is a favorite among Mexican Jews, known in Latin America for their propensity to tell jokes of all kinds as a response strategy against anxious situations.

In those jokes, the name of Haman is frequently substituted with villains in Mexican history: King Maximilian I, an Austrian archduke who reigned as the only emperor of the so-called Mexican Empire, between 1864 and when he was executed in 1867; dictator Porfirio Díaz, who ruled the country with an iron fist for more than thirty years, from 1876 until 1911, when revolutionaries finally deposed him; and President José López Portillo, whose mandate, between 1976 and 1982, ranks as one of the most corrupt in Mexican history. Every time one of these figures is mentioned, people make loud noises with *matracas*, rattles.

Hamantaschen are ubiquitous in Purim. These triangular pastries can be filled with the traditional poppy seeds, fruits, or chocolate, but innovations abound: rainbow-colored pastry, savory fillings for main course varieties, and sweet fillings of dulce de leche candies or spiced fruits. While the possibilities for fillings are infinite, the triangle shape is a constant, designed to resemble the hat worn by the evil minister Haman. In Ilan's childhood home, hamantaschen were made to look like sombreros.

Activities involve theatrical representations known as Purim shpiels. With roots in medieval Europe, these performances are one of the only instances in which Jews, defined by the prohibition against images, embraced the stage as an artistic form. In Jewish schools in Mexico, Purim shpiels conclude with refreshments, including an assortment of dulces.

In some homes, synagogues, or cultural centers, and even across college campuses, one activity during Purim is a mock public debate in which two contenders contrast the merits of a latke, which is part of the Hanukkah menu, and the hamantaschen of Purim. These debates resemble Talmudic disputes in which two opposing sides, the schools of Rabbi Eliezer ben Hyrcanus, a prominent sage in Judea in the first and second centuries, a disciple of Rabban Yohanan ben Zakkai, and the school of Rabbi Yehoshua. Rabbi Eliezer and Rabbi Yehoshua are, respectively, the sixth and seventh most frequently quoted Talmudist figures in the Mishnah.

Debaters in these games build their argument in deliberately implausible ways, attempting to prove that latkes are more important than hamantaschen and vice versa. Margaret and her husband debated on the merits of these foods for Bowdoin College Hillel, Margaret making the feminist case for hamantaschen. The debates are filled with humorous ancient and contemporary references connecting Jewish, Mexican, and world histories.

PURIM DINNER

Stuffed Artichoke Hearts (page 82)

Cumin Rose Kibbe (page 84)

Baba Ganoush Jerusalén con Chile
(page 120)

Israeli Salad con Queso Oaxaca
(page 124)

Orange Fig Hamantaschen (page 229)

Tequila with Basil "El Pogrom"
(page 170)

Rosh Hashaná

The holidays of Rosh Hashanah (in Spanish, Rosh Hashaná) and Yom Kippur frame the ten days—known as the Days of Awe—that inaugurate the Jewish calendar year. After the Shabbat, these are the most sacred days of the Jewish calendar. The rhythms of life shift during this window. Interactions with others are relaxed and meditative. Adults chant the liturgy while children play among themselves. The highlight of the ritual is the blowing of the shofar, which signifies the opening of the gates of heaven during the Days of Awe. This means that Rosh Hashanah starts festively but ends more somberly, as parishioners enter a meditative state in which they reflect on their individual activities of the prior year.

Rosh Hashanah ("head of the year" in Hebrew) takes place at the end of the summer and beginning of the fall. Significantly, the holiday does not mark the conclusion of the communal reading of the biblical narrative (that is the holiday of Simchat Torah). As a result, the Torah portion read during Rosh Hashanah and Yom Kippur actually have little connection with the content of these holidays themselves.

Among observant Mexican Jews, the start of the new Jewish year is a reminder that La Comunidad lives according to two calendars—that is, at the crossroad of two different traditions. People find a place for reflection, whether in synagogues, at community centers, or at home. They might begin reflecting on the past year and attend to hopes for the future. It is an opportunity to recalibrate, to think about one's future expectations. The Tashlich ceremony entails going to a body of water—a pool, a river, a lake, the ocean—and symbolically casting away one's sins. The custom includes literally throwing things (bread or stones, for instance) into the water while saying a prayer. It might also involve shaking the corners of one's clothes.

Ilan remembers a Tashlich ceremony at sunset in Xochimilco, one of the five big lakes on top of which the Aztecs built Mexico City. In one of the canals, and atop a *trajinera* (the Mexican word for "gondola"), friends and family would recite liturgy while depositing crumbs on the greenish water. All those participating in the festivity then told stories about what they felt had just concluded the previous year and what they were looking forward to in the year to come. The ceremony concluded with the breaking of a loaf of challah.

The Rosh Hashanah dinner is an occasion for extended families to gather together around food. A look at menus since the beginning of the twentieth century is evidence of how Mexican Jews have increasingly incorporated local tastes into their meals. Immigrants, Ashkenazic and Ottoman, cooked meals that resembled those from their places of origin.

ROSH HASHANÁ DINNER

Mango Jicama Salad (page 53)

Mushroom Huaraches con Pepitas (page 152)

Chelmelquitengo Lamb Tacos with Raisins and Pomegranate (page 132)

Pomegranate Margarita (page 203)

Coffee Honey Cake (page 236)

Orange Blossom Buñuelos (page 233)

Yom Kippur

La Comunidad dresses up for the High Holidays. Flavorwise, even with the fundamental twenty-four-hour fasting connected with them, Rosh Hashanah and Yom Kippur, and the ten Days of Awe in between, mark a crucial section of the Jewish calendar. Just like everywhere else in the diaspora, Mexican Jews wait for them with enthusiasm all year long.

The Yomim Noraim, the Days of Awe, in between Rosh Hashanah and Yom Kippur, are devoted to inner reflection. Approaching the divine with absolute humility, Mexican Jews make a personal balance of their behavior the previous year. This is a mystical period that coincides with the opening of the gates of heaven for *tshuvah*, repentance, to take place. The Israeli writer Shmuel Yosef Agnon, who won the Nobel Prize in Literature in 1966, in his book *Days of Awe* reflects on the importance of accompanying every meal with a prayer, as if they were a bride and groom: sound and taste go hand in hand to bring about a balance between the different dimensions of the universe. Agnon stresses the concepts of mercy and forgiveness during these days.

Observant Mexican Jews focus on the past year's events, reflecting on ways to correct wrongdoings and setting intentions for the year ahead. It is an alluring period of introspection. Looking inward rather than outward, reckoning with one's own ghosts, is a cleansing experience that refurbishes the spirit.

Throughout synagogues in Mexico, Jews attend the service of Kol Nidre, an evening service led through somber song—often one of the best-attended services across the calendar year. Cantors across denominations sing in absolute reverence, many individuals finding meaning in the familiarity of songs and prayers repeated from year to year.

Yom Kippur concludes this period of reckoning by fasting during the day of atonement. During the colonial period, conversos in Mexico would hide in order to engage in ritual without fear. They passed on the values of their Judaism in secret. In many ways, the fear of persecution made them believe that endurance and rebellion were the sine qua non of their existence.

La Comunidad prepares for the fast by gathering around 4:00 p.m. before Yom Kippur to eat a light meal, perhaps starting with a warming soup: Caldo Verde with Corn and Matzah Balls. Then, for twenty-four hours no connection with food is made. The breaking of the Yom Kippur fast is a joyful occasion, thirst quenched with Agua de Jamaica con Fresa and a casual array of dips and spreads to be shared in community: Avocado Egg Salad, Spiced Pickled Herring. By then Jews have prayed for forgiveness and to be inscribed by the divine in the Book of Life. In that sense, this is a holiday that emphasizes both determinism and individual responsibility.

Ironically, the fasting in Yom Kippur is a time for La Comunidad to tell jokes. For instance, the following one was conveyed to us by a correspondent in *Diario Judío*:

A Mexican Jewish patriarch dies just before Yom Kippur. He goes to heaven, where Rabbi Akiva greets him. "Shimele, we were hoping you would make it to the other end," Rabbi Akiva tells him. "There were all sorts of delicacies waiting for you!" "I know," the old Mexican Jew responds. "Eighty-five years are too many. Except on those fasts, I ate like the magnate Carlos Slim. My whole life was guided by the motto *Esn, fresn, un fargesn*—Eat, enjoy, and forget. But enough already. You have to be a masochist to forgo such delicacies on Yom Kippur in Mexico. Let others do the penitence. Tell me, Rabbi Akiva, up here—what's on the menu?"

EREV YOM KIPPUR

Caldo Verde with Corn and Matzah Balls (page 127)

Citrus Parsley Sea Bass (page 99)

Mediterranean Couscous with Chipotle Salsa (page 125)

Cilantro and Mint Salad (page 61)

Paletas de Jamaica con Limón (page 194)

BREAKING THE FAST

Agua de Jamaica con Fresa (page 46)

Avocado Egg Salad (page 212)

Spiced Pickled Herring (page 39)

Mango Noodle Kugel (page 215)

Cinnamon Churro Babka (page 176)

Pésaj

Conversos in Mexico felt a singular connection with the holiday of Passover (in Spanish, Pésaj). It reminded them of their expulsion from Spain in 1492. They saw obvious connections between the exodus from Egypt and their plight in alien lands. They called matzah pan censeño, meaning "unleavened bread." A few Judaizing conversos openly bought their pan censeño from bakers, risking being recognized by the inquisitors. But scores of others would prepare it by themselves. It was simply a plain dough of flour and water, mixed without salt or yeast.

In their book *A Drizzle of Honey*, David M. Gitlitz and Linda Davidson mention that in 1642, one conversa in Mexico, Beatríz Enríquez, described to the inquisitors how she baked matzah with her mother. They quote Beatríz's testimony:

> Three days before Easter . . . having sent the house slaves to see the processions, her mother laid on the table new tablecloths or towels, and then the new knife, and in the new bowl put the [white] flour, and from the new pitcher poured some cold water, and mixed and kneaded the flour with both hands, with a fire already kindled in the new brazier; and after having blessed each separate thing, and having kneaded the flour, she broke three small pieces off of the dough, reciting certain prayers over each one . . . of which she only remembers the following: "Blessed art Thou, Adonai, who gave us your laws, holy and blessed, blessed and holy." Then she kneaded the three pieces together and threw them into the fire, reciting the same prayers, and if the dough popped when she threw it in, her mother said that that was a sign that the God of Israel had approved the festival. . . . And she made three flat cakes, or she could make five or six or as many as she wanted. (286)

To recall the escape from bondage in Egypt, many Mexican Jews juxtapose the symbolism of Mexican history. In some families, the image of pharaoh is replaced by a favorite iconography of a Mexican president known for corruption, such as José López Portillo, Carlos Salinas de Gortari, or Andrés Manuel López Obrador. There are also reproductions of El Chupacabra, a mythical animal with prominent human teeth known for devouring goats in the middle of the night. Likewise, the reading of the Haggadah is seasoned with direct references to Jewish immigration from the Pale of Settlement and the Ottoman Empire; for Mexican Jews in the United States, it is an opportunity to reflect on immigration across borders and crisis and suffering of our own times.

Since only unleavened bread—that is, matzah—is eaten during Passover, before the holiday a thorough cleanup of Mexican Jewish homes collects any traces of leaven in the kitchen. Bread, tortillas, and other similar foods are thrown away. Converso Jews gathered on riverbanks to throw away the last portions. In Mexico City, those ceremonies might take place on Lake Xochimilco, in the southern part of the metropolis.

In the traditional Passover plate, the bitter herbs can include a variety of chiles. A *cascarón*, a hollowed and dyed egg filled with colorful confetti, is often on the Seder plate and is later broken in celebration at the meal's end. Readings during the Seder feature poetry about the expulsion from Spain in 1492, verses by conversos such as Manuel Levi de Barrios and by Latin American poets Pablo Neruda and Juan Gelman, whose work championed the struggle of oppressed peoples. Among Mexican Jews in the United States, there are references to "The New Colossus" by Emma Lazarus, the sonnet engraved on a plaque in the pedestal of the Statue of Liberty, while feminists include an orange on the Seder plate to include marginalized voices in Jewish leadership.

. . . .

SEDER FAVORITES

Borscht con Crema (page 221)

Huevos Haminados (page 34)

Snapper Ceviche con Maror (page 145)

Tamarind Street Corn Cups (page 121)

Gefilte Fish en Salsa Roja (page 209)

Chipotle Chicken Noodle and Matzah Ball Soup (page 207)

Mezcal de Eliyahu (page 239)

Lime Macaroons (page 178)

Apricot Almond Charoset Truffles (page 231)

Paletas Manischewitz (page 240)

Tahini Brownies (page 232)

Matzah Chilaquiles (page 27)

Shavuot

Shavuot in Hebrew means "weeks." This is the name of the harvest festival, providing Jews with time to connect with the outdoors, to experience the cycles of the seasons. Shavuot was the season for harvesting wheat, which in biblical times lasted seven weeks. Although the Torah doesn't explicitly state it, it marks the occasion in which the Israelites, through Moses, received the Torah on Mount Sinai, which, if placed in historical context, would have occurred around 1314 BCE. Traditionally the book of Ruth, about a Moabite woman who becomes part of the Israelites in part by accepting Yahweh as her god, is read during this holiday.

The celebration includes devoting a night to studying the Torah, known in Hebrew as Tiqqun Leyl Shavuot and in English as Rectification for Shavuot Night. One might do it alone or in group. The theme might be any part of the Bible, the Mishnah, or the Talmud, as well as kabbalistic texts.

Shavuot is centered on dairy, especially cheeses, although the reasoning behind this tradition isn't entirely clear: some believe that after traveling through the desert the Jewish people were too exhausted to prepare meat, so they relied on dairy; others hypothesize that dairy became a staple of Shavuot because it is during this season that grass grows in Israel, supporting cattle populations. Ashkenazim eat blintzes and kreplach. Syrian Jews eat cheese ravioli (kelsonnes) and cheese-filled pancakes (atayef). Rose, and its associated flavoring agent rose water, plays a prominent role in Sephardic Jewish households during this holiday. Eating cumin-rose kibbe is part of the ritual among certain families with roots in medieval Spain. Other converso families also consume various types of aged cheeses, yogurt, and milk.

Mexican Jews of different heritages embrace Shavuot in different ways: some enjoy blintzes or quesadillas, and others have incorporated a Moroccan cake made of seven layers called siete cielos ("seven heavens"). The architectural design of the cake is meant to resemble Mount Sinai, with seven ropes of dough meant to reflect the seven configurations of clouds that surrounded the mountain when Moses ascended it in order to receive the word of God.

In his book *The Seventh Heaven: Travels through Jewish Latin America*, Ilan explores the concept of seven heavens from myriad perspectives. It is connected not with the mystical sefirot but with kabbalistic imagery of ascendance, derived from Platonic philosophy. In various parts of the Spanish-speaking world, Ilan discusses with rabbis, activists, poets, mystics, and Talmudist scholars the meaning of seeking a union with the divine, among them using food to commune with spiritual aspects of ourselves and those around us.

SHAVUOT DINNER

Myriam's Tarator (page 62)

Squash Blossom Quesadillas
(page 162)

Cilantro Mousse (page 161)

Cold Pumpkin Salad (page 59)

Ofelia's Dulce de Leche Churros
(page 189)

SHAVUOT BREAKFAST

Pineapple Beet Juice (page 40)

Poached Eggs in Tomato
Chile Sauce (page 19)

Queso Yiddish Blintzes (page 24)

Sucot

The festival of Sukkot (in Spanish, Sucot) commemorates a seven-day journey in which Israelites in biblical times made pilgrimage to Jerusalem (one of three such journeys, known as Shalosh Regalim). In the diaspora, it lasts eight days. It originated as a holiday connected with the harvest. Over time, it has become an occasion to reject materialism and embrace the natural environment. Mexican Jews, like others around the world, build a sukkah, the Hebrew word for "booth" or "tabernacle." These are temporary structures, covered with overgrown palm leaves and other plants. Sukkot (plural of "sukkah") are a way to remember the agricultural dimension that provides us with food all year long. And they recall the transient life Israelites experienced after their departure from Egypt and during their forty-year odyssey in the desert, chronicled in the book of Exodus.

In Mexico, sukkot are typically simple three-walled structures, with a roof made of branches or other natural materials. Through the branches, you can gaze into the night sky and view the stars. They show up on rooftops and backyards and are decorated and used according to traditions of religious and cultural observance and invention. They can be decorated with biblical and Mexican motifs, fresh flowers, and bright lights and can include *altares*, with *veladoras* and iconography such as family pictures. There is a mitzvah tied to the holiday involving bringing together four different plants: *lulav* (palm frond), *hadass* (myrtle), *aravah* (willow branch), and *etrog* (citron). Since several of these items aren't available locally, many observant Mexican Jews order them from Israel. Others prefer to improvise with local plants and fruits.

People dance around the sukkah. As they recite the prayers, they hold the four species that become partners in the holiday, each one carrying a unique symbolism. Etrog, the fruit of the citron tree, is said to symbolize the heart, with a good taste and a good smell. Lulav, a frond from the date palm tree, is said to symbolize the spine, taste but no smell. Hadass, from the myrtle tree, is said to symbolize the eyes. And aravah, the willow branch, is said to symbolize the mouth and does not have a taste or smell. Through this attention to sensory experience, rabbinic tradition invites deeper engagement with Torah to cultivate the union of heart, spine, eyes, and mouth.

With the growth of drug cartels, spending time in the outdoors has become difficult in some parts of Mexico, not only in the nation's capital but throughout the country. For that reason, nowadays the festival of Sukkot feels more isolating. People have lost their freedom; instead, they celebrate the holiday on the roof or in the backyard. Jewish schools build sukkot in the schoolyard. Synagogues do the same. And there are of course sukkot at CDI, the Jewish community center. In recent decades, young Mexican Jews, in part because of these restrictions, have emigrated to other parts of Mexico as well as other places in the world.

Among young activists, Sukkot is an opportunity to connect with Indigenous communities. They have been an integral part of Mexican history, yet their proper place in the country's culture is still contested. Spending time under a fragile, natural roof makes us humble in that it allows us to experience the transient life. It is a custom, among some families, to reserve one of the nights of Sukkot to chant both Jewish and Indigenous prayers.

. . . .

VEGETARIAN SUKKOT

Jaco's Tartines de Aguacate con Jalapeño (page 38)

Cream of Zucchini with Cilantro Soup (page 68)

Saucy Cheese Stuffed Eggplant (page 87)

Cheesecake con Guayaba (page 191)

Ilan's Arroz con Leche (page 188)

SUKKOT LUNCH

Pati's Mushroom Jalapeño Matzah Ball Soup (page 66)

Grilled Corn Salad (page 54)

Brisket Tacos in Three-Chiles Salsa with Phyllis's Rhubarb (page 89)

Mexican Alfajores: Morir sin Sufrir (page 179)

Janucá

With Mexican Jews having roots in numerous places, Hanukkah (in Spanish, Janucá) is frequently an occasion to emphasize one's ancestry. This happens with songs. People will bring lyrics from Ashkenazi, Ottoman, and Mizrahi traditions, from places such as Hungary, Poland, Syria, Algeria, Germany, Israel, and other Latin American countries including Argentina, Cuba, and Brazil—and, of course, Mexico. A version of the Hebrew "Mi Yimalel?" (Who Can Retell?) might show up next to the Ladino "Ocho Kandelikas" (Eight Little Candles), followed by the huapango-style song "Cucurrucucú Paloma."

Or someone might combine the Yiddish tune "Kleyne Likhtelekh," written by Morris Rosenfeld, delivered in a ranchera rhythm, with the Turkish lyrics of "Dak il tas" (Strike the tray). The lyrics—a mix of Hebrew, Ladino, Spanish, and Yiddish—are:

> Dak il tas, toma'l tas
> Las muchachas meten bas
> En Shabat de Janucá
> Ajt teg de Janucá
> Lehadlik ner shel Janucá.
> El vino de la serada
> Que a mi muncho m'agrada
> A beber en Janucá
> Ocho dias . . .
> Mete la carne al tandur
> Taneremos un buen santur
> En Shabat de Janucá
> Ocho dias . . .

The Festival of Light commemorates the rebellion of the Maccabees against Seleucid occupation, particularly the miracle of the Temple in Jerusalem where a limited amount of oil was able to last for eight days. Typically, the menu includes latkes with Mexican crema and applesauce as well as sufganiyot or other fritters. In some households of La Comunidad, latkes plates are accompanied with mole, which is poured over the latkes and dusted with sesame seeds. In some Jewish families in the United States, the Festival of Lights offers an opportunity to incorporate ingredients from Día de los Muertos, the traditional Day of the Dead celebration that takes place at the beginning of November.

Día de los Muertos is an invitation to commune with beloved ones who are no longer with us. In Catholicism, there is a fluid connection between this world and the next, with a sense that the souls of those already departed are in communication with the living. In contrast, Judaism stresses the importance of *zakhor*, memory, as a bridge between the here-and-now and the hereafter. In what could be described as Jewish mythology, dybbuks, goblins, and other supernatural beings travel back and forth. During Hanukkah, some families make *altares*, offerings featuring numerous lights. They incorporate sugar skulls (*calaveras*) with Hebrew letters on their forehead, dreidels, and chocolate gelt and feature such fruits as apples, oranges, and pumpkins, along with candy and sufganiyot.

Our correspondents in *Diario Judío* regaled us with countless Janucá anecdotes. Parties might include piñatas. After playing with dreidels, children take turns trying to break the piñata. When its contents spill across the floor, children run to collect their prizes. The seven nights of Hanukkah allow for all sorts of improvisations.

FESTIVE JANUCÁ DINNER

Agua de Horchata (page 47)

Latkes con Mole (page 204)

Leek Fritters (page 130)

Falafel Taquitos (page 140)

Cactus Tomato Salad (page 56)

Sor Juana's Ricotta Buñuelos (page 184)

Kamish Bread con Cajeta (page 186)

L'dor v'dor

~~~~~~

THE HEBREW EXPRESSION *l'dor v'dor* means "from generation to generation." It is part of a prayerful song that involves swaying, arms wrapped around one's family and friends. The words are sung as part of weekly religious services, and for many Mexican Jews it is a centerpiece of their cultural values. How did we learn the tradition from our elders? What are the obligations and joys of passing tradition on to the next generation? And what are the stories that fuel these connections? The collection of recipes in this book is emblematic of l'dor v'dor, reminding us of how food connects us with the loved ones that are no longer with us while helping us to create memories with the ones around our dinner tables.

As could be expected, traditional values are passed along not only as part of sacred occasions—Shabbat, the High Holidays, and so on—but in the fabric of each day. No matter how frantic modern life might be, Mexican Jews take pride in ceasing every activity they are in, no matter how important, to bring family and friends around the same table, food and care bound together.

Archival photographs depict Ashkenazi and Ottoman immigrants in Mexico, and their descendants, congregating around food on various occasions. These black-and-white images are a reminder of the speed with which, at the beginning of the twentieth century, the newly arrived organized themselves. Community building through food was instrumental in the continuity of l'dor v'dor. As time went by, each generation incorporated new elements according to their own customs. Still, as the chant reminds us with a kind of weightiness, we are connected backward and forward to our predecessors and descendants in *n'tzachim*, eternity.

Food unquestionably is the central tool for the survival of Jewish Mexican identity across generations. The collective tasting, making, observing, and enjoying these foods attests to the malleability and endurance of La Comunidad. •

Top: Xochimilco *simchas*, unnamed group, photo courtesy of Manuel Taifeld. Bottom: The Poplawsky and Sod families, shabbat, Mexico City, photo in author's possession.

ZAFTIG

××××××××××××××××× ×××××××××××××××××

The Yiddish word *zaftig* means "healthy, plump, and vigorous." It's a wish for Jewish parents for their growing children. The term is equally applied to food: "May you have a zaftig meal and may your dreams be zaftig, too!"

The artistic team behind this volume coalesced around common interests. The photographs are by Ilan Rabchinskey, a Jewish Mexican artist, photographer, creative director, and writer born in 1980 whose grandparents, looking for freedom from persecution, migrated to Latin America from places including Ukraine, Russia, Austria, Germany, and Poland. His award-winning photography, distinctly informed by his travel, curiosity, and a multitude of diverse cultural sensitivities, can be seen in numerous places, from magazines to books to films such as Alfonso Cuarón's *Roma*. He loves falafel and borscht (particularly the one his Russian grandmother Emma used to make when he was a boy) just as much as ceviche, suadero tacos, and squash blossom quesadillas.

Food stylist Ricardo Rafael Treves is of Sephardic ancestry. He is half Turkish—from Aleppo, which at the time was part of Turkey—on his mother's side, half Greek on his father's side. His forebears reached these destinations after the expulsion from Spain in 1492. The family originated in Seville, Spain. On the patrilineal side, his great-grandfather immigrated to Mexico, through the port of Veracruz, before the First World War.

The principal dish in the cuisine Ricardo grew up with were bourekas, tapa de espinaca (spinach soufflé made with egg and feta), shakshuka, and tortitas de pollo con poro (chicken tortas with leeks). His mother became a food stylist because she wanted to tell stories. After her death, Ricardo followed in her footsteps. "We are made of complex stories," he believes. "Our duty is to pass them along in distilled ways. I'm a Mexican Jew because of my heritage and because of the family stories that shaped me. I grew up in the southern part of Mexico City, away from the cultural centers where Mexican Jews always moved around. In that sense, I felt like a black sheep."

What makes a Jewish Mexican meal? The adaptation of the two sides, the dialogue, overt or hidden. To wrap up the effort and joy that went into *Sabor Judío: The Jewish Mexican Cookbook*, Irma Appel cooked *una comilona*, a feast beginning with plated salads of baby lettuce, hearts of palm, and honey mustard dressing. Warm savory dishes quickly followed: stewed beef in wine, mushroom farfel, green beans, corn, and for dessert a plum beet cake, strudel, and assorted fruit. Everyone in the team was present. Ilan Rabchinskey photographed the meal with an overhead camera that took snapshots at successive moments. The event served as a metaphor of the journey we had all shared together.

And now *you* are part of our table. *¡Adio! Zait Gezunt! ¡Hasta pronto!* •

Acknowledgments

We have benefited from the accumulated wisdom of generations of Mexican Jewish people—Sephardic, Ashkenazi, and Mizrahi—who handed down their traditions to subsequent generations. Over a decade, we have corresponded with their descendants, dispersed all over the world, and listened to the stories of why these recipes were first made, how they have been adapted, and the memories they carry. We are grateful to every one of them for their generosity. We especially want to mention Vilma Alvarez; Irma Appel; Alice Gojman Backal; Hinde Becker; Jorge Bercovich; Licha Bessudo; Gina Poplawski Boyle and Don Boyle; Tammy Buchwald; Ginde and Benny Burak; Josefina "Vicky" López Caballero; Enriqueta Castro; Carolina Chaimovich; Martin A. Cohen; Lina Croisette; Mari De Leon; Karen Drijanski; Hilda Edelman; Maia and Daniel Eisen; Hilda Etterman; Tamar Fasja; Anita Feinsod; Helen Forgach; Margo Glantz; Samy Goldzweig; Elizabeth Lugo Hernández and Juan Gabriel Rincón Hernández; Deborah Holz; Sandra Kleinburg; Yudi Kravzov; Deborah Largman; Claudio Lomnitz; Elena and Enrique Lorberfeld; Myriam Moscona; Angelina Muñiz-Huberman and Alberto Huberman; Eliezer Nowodworski; Anat and Soli Nurko; Samuel Nurko; Ishai z'l and Sara Podgaetz; Eddie and Kim Poplawski; Evelyn Poplawski; Phyllis Poplawski; Silvia Poplawsky; Becky Rubinstein; Esther, Fay, and Dan Schuller; Jacobo Sefamí; Dafna Shveid; Edith Singer; Ada Smoller; Estela Sod; Teddy Sod; Alejandro Springall; Frida Staropolsky-Shwartz; Joshua and Isaiah Stavchansky; Liora Stavchansky; Manuel Taifeld; Gina Tavel; and Elena Vasquez Felgueres.

The public first asked for a cookbook following a public conversation between Ilan Stavans and Pati Jinich sponsored by the Jewish Food Society. It became a reality as a result of the enthusiasm of Elaine Maisner. Our editor at University of North Carolina Press, Cate Hodorowicz, masterfully shepherded the manuscript through the editorial process. Gracias to Erin Granville for shepherding the book through the editorial process and to Laura Jones Dooley for her expert copyediting. We appreciate the support we received from Alane Mason and Melanie Tortoroli at W. W. Norton, as

Margaret Boyle and Ilan Stavans at Claustro de Sor Juana, Mexico City, January 2023.

well as the passion for food and truth-telling from Arielle Eckstut and David Henry Sterry. Marnie Lamb did exceptional work creating the index, and Dwight Ramsey's proofreading was superb.

Thank you to our two readers for their unqualified enthusiasm and invaluable suggestions for this book.

Enrique Chmelnik at the Centro de Documentación e Investigación Judío de Mexico (CDIJUM) serves as the memory archive for the Mexican Jewish community. Likewise, Samy Goldzweig, president of the Jebrá Kadishá of the Mexican Kehilá, is an invaluable—and beloved—resource about the community's past.

The extraordinary stylist Ricardo Rafael Treves did wonders in his Mexico City studio, bringing in his own Sephardic heritage to the table. His team included José Ángel Elizondo Calvillo, Sonnja Cabrera Galina, Lorena Gutiérrez Albarrán, Teresa Mendoza Barajas, and Selene Olmos.

Photographer Ilan Rabchinskey brought out the flavors of Jewish Mexican cuisine with his versatile camera. He masterfully directed, lit, and composed each stylized recipe image in the studio and also traveled the crowded streets of the Mexican capital together with us, eating along the way, savoring colorful paletas, walking through serpentine popular markets, and visiting old synagogues and cemeteries. He was supported by Jair Franco and Ximena Hernández.

Alison Sparks has been cooking Mexican Jewish food for over thirty years. Her latkes with mole and brisket tortas are legendary. Andrew Lardie is the extraordinary partner of the kitchen and daily life, and Nora and Beatrice are our consummate sous-chefs, and the joyful soul of our family histories and future.

We are grateful to our respective colleges, Amherst and Bowdoin, for supporting our research for this book. We extend special gratitude to our students and their love and curiosity about diaspora food and stories, with special thanks to Izzy Miller and Ella Rose.

For Further Reading

Today the keeper of the collective memory of La Comunidad is sociologist Mónica Unikel-Fasja. In charge of the research wing of Sinagoga Histórica Justo Sierra 71, leading engaging tours across what she calls "la judería," what once was the Jewish neighborhood for early twentieth-century immigrants. "In time, around the synagogue on Calle Jesús María no. 3 sprung grocery stores, bakeries, and other spaces that function as 'cultural transmitters,'" she tells us. "You could buy challah nearby just before Shabbat dinner, as well as matzah for the Passover Seder."

Unikel-Fasja's grandparents came from Ukraine and Lithuania in the 1920s. They opened a sweater store on Calle Argentina. Her idea to lead Jewish tours of downtown Mexico City came about in the early 1990s, after Unikel-Fasja herself was in one of Jewish London. The tour guide she got was an inspiring speaker. It crossed her mind that Mexican Jews deserved the same kind of historical Virgil. Since the first tours ended up at the synagogue on Justo Sierra, she was given the key. In time, she became comfortable in the place and the Jewish community asked her to lead a research organization. Over the decades, Unikel-Fasja has helped foster a revival of interest in Jewish history in Mexico.

Alice Gojman Backal is the first historian to focus her scholarly endeavors in La Comunidad. Her work focuses on the Inquisition in Nueva España and on Nazism in Mexico. Martin A. Cohen's books focus on the plight of the conversos. Other important historians are Claudio Lomnitz, whose memoir, *Nuestra América: My Family in the Vestige of Translation,* chronicles the peripatetic journey of his grandparents across numerous diasporas.

Aside from being a poet, novelist, and memoirist, Angelina Muñiz-Huberman has done substantial research of Jewish mysticism. Writers Jacobo Sefamí and Myriam Moscona have published important contributions on the Sephardic community, including the role of Ladino.

Mexico City's first Jewish and second woman mayor Claudia Sheinbaum Pardo, elected in 2018, comes from the marriage of Ashkenazi and Sephardic immigrant grandparents who arrived in Mexico in the 1920s and 1940s.

Her left-leaning politics—she belongs to Morena (the Spanish word means "dark-skinned"), a party created by Andrés Manuel López Obrador, who was the nation's president from 2018 to 2024—fits squarely with Bundist and other ideologically driven movements among the Yiddish-speaking population of eastern Europe from the nineteenth century onward. Sheinbaum's vigorous presence in Mexican politics showcases the degree to which Mexican Jews have become a normal part of the cultural landscape.

This list comprises an introduction to some of our essential readings about Jewish food, Mexican food, and the Jewish Mexican community. It includes cookbooks, poetry, novels, memoirs, biographies, historical accounts, and select essays.

. . . .

Arellano, Gustavo. *Taco USA: How Mexican Food Conquered America*. New York: Scribner, 2013.

Bayless, Rick, with Deann Groen Bayless. *Authentic Mexican: Regional Cooking from the Heart of Mexico*. New York: William Morrow, 1987.

Benarroch de Bensadon, Ana. *Dulce lo vivas: La repostería sefardí*. Madrid: Ediciones Martínez Roca, 2006.

Berliner, Isaac. *Shtot fun palatsn: Lider un poemes*. Drawings by Diego Rivera. Farlag "DerVeg," 1936.

Boyle, Margaret E., and Sarah E. Owens. *Health and Healing in the Early Modern Iberian World: A Gendered Perspective*. Toronto: University of Toronto Press, 2021.

Cimet, Adina. *Ashkenazi Jews in Mexico: Ideologies in the Structuring of a Community*. Albany: State University of New York Press, 1997.

Cohen, Adèle Rivka. *Los placeres de mi cocina judía en la tradición sefardí*. Madrid: Parsifal Ediciones, 2003.

Cohen, Jake. *Jew-ish: Reinvented Recipes from a Modern Mensch*. Boston: Houghton Mifflin Harcourt, 2021.

Cohen, Martin A. *The Martyr Luis de Carvajal: A Secret Jew in Sixteenth-Century Mexico*. Introduction by Ilan Stavans. Albuquerque: University of New Mexico Press, 2001.

Cohen, Sandro. "Los intelectuales judíos en México." *Memoranda-ISSSTE* 3, no. 17 (March–April 1992): 12–14.

Covarrubias, Sebastián de. *Tesoro de la lengua española o castellana* (1611). Madrid: Turner, 1977.

Cung Sulkin, Paloma. *Judios por herencia, mexicanos por florecer: Una mirada infantil al proceso de integración*. Mexico City: La Kehile / Asociación Yad Vashem de México, 2012.

Del Águila, Rocío, and Vanesa Miseres. *Food Studies in Latin American Literature: Perspectives on the Gastronarrative*. Fayetteville: University of Arkansas Press, 2021.

Field, Kendra T. "The Privilege of Family History." *American Historical Review* 127, no. 2 (2022): 600–633.

Finkelman de Sommer, Maty. "Instruye a tus hijos." In *Generaciones judías en México: Kehila Ashkenazi (1922–1992)*, edited by Alice G. Backal. Mexico City: Comunidad Ashkenazí de México, 1993.

Gervitz, Gloria. *Migrations: Poems, 1976–2020*. Translated by Mark Schafer. New York: New York Review of Books, 2021.

Gitlitz, David M., and Linda Kay Davidson. *A Drizzle of Honey: The Lives and Recipes of Spain's Secret Jews*. New York: St. Martin's Press, 2000.

Glantz, Margo. *The Family Tree: An Illustrated Novel* (1984). Translated by Susan Basnett. London: Serpent's Tail, 1991.

Godsmit, Shulamit, and Natalia Gurvich, eds. *Sobre el judaísmo mexicano: Diversas expresiones de activismo comunitario*. Mexico City: Universidad Iberoamericana, 2009.

Goodman, Matthew. *Jewish Food: The World at Table*. New York: Harper-Collins, 2005.

Halabe, Liz Hamui de. *Los judíos de Alepo en México*. [Mexico City]: Maguén David, 1989.

Herrera, Hayden. *Frida: A Biography of Frida Kahlo* (1983). New York: Harper Perennial, 2022.

Jinich, Pati. *Pati's Mexican Table: The Secrets of Real Mexican Home Cooking*. Boston: Houghton Mifflin Harcourt, 2013.

———. *Treasures of the Mexican Table: Classic Recipes, Local Secrets*. Boston: Houghton Mifflin Harcourt, 2021.

Kaufman, Rachel Bernstein. *Many to Remember*. Loveland, OH: Dos Madres Press, 2021.

Kennedy, Diana. *The Essential Cuisines of Mexico*. New York: Clarkson Potter, 2009.

Koen Sarano, Matilda. *Kuentos del folklor de la famiya djudeo-espanyola*. Ankara: Gözlem Yayincilik, 2021.

Koenig, Leah. *The Jewish Cookbook*. New York: Phaidon Press, 2019.

———. *Little Book of Jewish Feasts*. San Francisco: Chronicle Books, 2018.

———. *Modern Jewish Cooking: Recipes and Customs for Today's Kitchen*. San Francisco: Chronicle Books, 2015.

Krauze, Ethel. *De cuerpo entero: Entre la cruz y la estrella*. Mexico City: Universidad Nacional Autónoma de México, 1990.

La Cruz, Sor Juana Inés. *Poems, Protest, and a Dream: Selected Writings*. Translated by Margaret Sayers Peden. Introduction by Ilan Stavans. New York: Penguin Books, 1998.

Lavin, Mónica, and Ana Benítez Muro. *Sor Juana en la cocina*. Mexico City: Planeta, 2021.

Lomnitz, Claudio. *Nuestra America: My Family in the Vertigo of Translation*. New York: Other Press, 2021.

Martínez, Mely. *The Mexican Home Kitchen: Traditional Home-Style Recipes That Capture the Flavors and Memories of Mexico*. New York: Rock Point, 2020.

Martínez Montiño, Francisco. *The Art of Cooking, Pie Making, Pastry Making, and Preserving*. Edited and translated by Carolyn A. Nadeau. Toronto: University of Toronto Pres, 2023.

Moscona, Myriam. *Ansina*. Madrid: Vaso Roto Ediciones, 2016.

———. *León de lidia*. Tusquets, 2022.

———. *Tela de sevoya / Onioncloth*. Translated by Jen Hofer with John Pluecker. Los Angeles: Les Figues Press, 2017.

Moscona, Myriam, and Jacobo Sefamí, eds. *Por mi boka: Textos de la diaspora sefardi en ladino*. Mexico City: Lumen, 2013.

Muñiz-Huberman, Angelina. *Rompeolas: Poesía reunida*. Mexico City: Fondo de Cultura Económica, 2012.

———. *La sal en el rostro*. Mexico City: Universidad Autónoma Metropolitana, 1998.

———. *El sefardí romántico*. Mexico City: Conaculta, 2014.

Muñiz-Huberman, Angelina, ed. *La lengua florida: Antologia sefardi*. Mexico City: Fondo de Cultura Económica, 1989.

Nabut, Hanady. *Mediterranea: A Vibrant Culinary Journey through Southern Europe, North Africa, and the Eastern Mediterranean*. Salem, MA: Page Street, 2022.

Nissán, Rosa. *Like a Bride, Like a Mother*. Translated by Dick Gerdes. Introduction by Ilan Stavans. Albuquerque: University of New Mexico Press, 2002.

Ottolenghi, Yotam, with Sami Tamimi. *Jerusalem: A Cookbook*. Berkeley, CA: Ten Speed Press, 2012.

Piñer, Hélène Jawhara. *Sephardi: Cooking the History, Recipes of the Jews of Spain and the Diaspora, from the 13th Century to Today*. Boston: Cherry Orchard Books, 2021.

Presilla, Maricel E. *Gran Cocina Latina: The Food of Latin America*. New York: W. W. Norton, 2012.

Rivera, Guadalupe, and Marie-Pierre Colle. *Frida's Fiestas: Recipes and Reminiscences of Life with Frida Kahlo*. New York: Clarkson Potter, 1994.

Riveros, Gabriela. *Olvidarás el fuego*. Mexico City: Lumen, 2022.

Roden, Claudia. *The Book of Jewish Food: An Odyssey from Samarkand to New York*. New York: Alfred A. Knopf, 1996.

Romano de Salame, Amelia, with Bahie Buzali de Ambe, Estrella Daniel de Caín, and Millie Daniel de Chattaj. *Safra Dayme: Cien años de cocina judeo-damasquina en México*. Mexico City: AmbarDiseño, 2012.

Rubinstein, Becky. *De la cocina de la abuela (adivinanzas)*. Mexico City: Cuica, 1988.

———. *Hadas y ensal-hadas*. 2nd ed. Mexico City: Trillas, 2019.

Sadow, Stephen. *I Am of the Tribe of Judah: Jewish Poems from Latin America*. Albuquerque: University of New Mexico Press, 2024.

Seligson, Esther. *Negro es su rostro / Simiente*. Mexico City: Fondo de Cultura Económica, 2010.

Singer, Edith. *March to Freedom: A Memoir of the Holocaust* (1993). Santa Clarita, CA: Impact, 2008.

Stavans, Ilan. *The Disappearance: A Novella and Stories*. Evanston, IL: TriQuarterly, 2007.

——. *The New World Haggadah*. Santa Fe, NM: Gaon Books, 2015.

——. *On Borrowed Words: A Memoir of Language*. New York: Viking, 2001.

——. *The Return of Carvajal: A Mystery*. University Park: Pennsylvania State University Press, 2016.

——. *Return to Centro Histórico: A Mexican Jew Looks for His Roots*. New Brunswick, NJ: Rutgers University Press, 2011.

——. *The Seventh Heaven: Travels through Jewish Latin America*. Pittsburgh, PA: University of Pittsburgh Press, 2019.

Stavans, Ilan, and Steve Sheinkin. *El Iluminado: A Graphic Novel*. New York: Basic Books, 2012.

Sternberg, Robert. *The Sephardic Kitchen: The Healthful Food and Rich Culture of the Mediterranean Jews*. New York: HarperCollins, 1996.

Tausend, Marilyn, with Ricardo Muñoz Zurita. *La Cocina Mexicana: Many Cultures, One Cuisine*. Berkeley: University of California Press, 2012.

Trejo, Danny, with Hugh Garvey. *Trejo's Tacos: Recipes and Stories from L.A.* New York: Clarkson Potter, 2020.

Twitty, Michael W. *Koshersoul: The Faith and Food Journey of an African American Jew*. New York: Amistad, 2022.

Witt, Shifrah Devorah, and Zipporah Malka Heller. *The Best of Mexican Kosher Cooking*. Lakewood, NJ: Israel Bookshop Publications, 2011.

Woldenberg, José. *Las ausencias presentes*. Mexico City: Cal y Arena, 1992.

Zadoff, Efraim. "Un análisis comparativo de las redes educativas judías de México y Argentina, 1935–1955." In *Judaica Latinoamericana*. Jerusalem: Editorial Universitaria Magnes, 1988.

About the Authors

Ilan Stavans, one of today's preeminent essayists, cultural critics, and translators and a *New York Times* best-selling author, is the Lewis-Sebring Professor in the Humanities, Latin American, and Latino Culture at Amherst College, the publisher of Restless Books, and a consultant to the *Oxford English Dictionary.*

Margaret E. Boyle is director of Latin American, Caribbean and Latinx Studies (LACLaS) at Bowdoin College and associate professor in romance languages and literatures and LACLaS. A Mexican American from Los Angeles, she has published books and essays on early modern history, gender, health, food, and language practices. She directs Multilingual Mainers, which promotes intercultural conversations and the study of languages other than English.

Index

Page numbers in bold refer to photos.